FROM FEAR TO LIMITLESS LOVE

FROM FEAR TO LIMITLESS LOVE

YOUR PATH TO FINDING SELF-WORTH, HARMONY AND BLISS

Devadas T Chelvam

Cover Design by Mark Ihle
Cover image © Chun Guo | Dreamstime.com

Pictures re-printed with permission.
ISBN: 0997607440
ISBN 13: 9780997607444

Humbly dedicated to
All the Children of Divine Mother
Also called Heavenly Father, Jehovah, Allah,
Brahman, Tao, Nirvana or Ultimate Reality

"Like the Bee gathering honey
from different flowers,
the wise man accepts the
essence of different Scriptures
and sees only the good in
all religions."

(Srimad Bhagavatam)

GLORY OF ALL THINGS

Wake up, to all things wake
Nothing for granted take
See the miracle of everything
Life is amazing to the awake.

Big or small, pain or pleasure
To the awake it's all a wonder
Taste life in all its nuances
Watch in awe as Lord Siva dances

Frolic and play in creation
As God dreams this universe
And dances away in elation
One hidden in things diverse

Awaking from unknowing we find
We have entered God's own mind
As His children we joyfully play
When all falsehood we truly slay

Blind and steeped in darkness
Frantic to hide lonely emptiness
At passing phenomena we snatch
Onto beliefs and dogmas latch

While Truth pursues us from within
Why our hearts to face we fear!
Love for all things genuine
Opens our hearts the Truth to hear.

Vanity and pretension within
Ignorance and misery prime sin
Fear, anger, hatred follow
Leading one quite low

Life does Love bequeath
Alert and aware, breathe
Grateful for every breath
Peace and Joy, our wealth.

Everything is a miracle
Truly a glorious spectacle
Oh! Life is a merry laughter
Though we may cry or falter.

In God all things are one
She shines in everyone
Saints, Her love in action
Sages, His wise revelation.

CONTENTS

FOREWORD

This book is about those fortunate individuals who have been able to pass their lives in immediate and intimate conversation with God. To read of the blessed persons chronicled here is to realize a fact of the human condition we should never lose sight of – God gladly and openly communicates with His creatures.

For the vast majority of humankind, including those who are actively pursuing a religious path, God seems remote, transcendent, unavailable, even to His devout followers. In *Limitless Love,* Devadas Chelvam tells a different story. He recounts the lives of devotees from all parts of the world and all denominations whose lives have been blessed by the persistent, joyous, ever-loving presence of the Lord Himself.

These stories are told with a sympathy and immediacy that leave one with the feeling these saints and sages, far from being rare and exotic instances of the human condition, have lived their lives as God would have all of us live. The joy and love that pervades these individual narratives seems so natural and immediate that we can't help feeling that this is how our Creator would wish to deal with each and every one of us.

To read this book is to sense that God is offering us a "Romance with the Infinite." How can we resist the call of these words by Paramahansa Yogananda, one of the subjects of this book?

"The greatest romance is with the Infinite. You have no idea of how beautiful life can be. When suddenly you find that wherever you are, God comes and talks to you and guides you, the romance of divine love has started."

Dr. Quincy Howe
Former Professor of Classics and Religion
Scripps College, Claremont, California

PREFACE

Christ said: "Truth shall make you free." Like Christ all the spiritual Masters urge us to know the truth of our being that can free us to be limitless love and endless bliss. I did not think always in such terms. Coming from a deeply religious background as a Catholic priest, I shifted to the opposite pole of not believing in life beyond death or love.

Totally unexpected was the profound personal experience that made me feel intuitively the presence of my late father in my room and his love for me as much more real than my body or other sensory phenomena. It started me on a long journey of study and reflection.

Thinking about the philosophical issues that underlie religion, I gained certain insights which I share with the readers here. The sages presented in this book dazzle us with their amazing lives and inspire us to cultivate unconditional love for ourselves and others. The last chapter gives certain practices that enable us to be daily more peaceful and joyful.

"En Chellappillai" (my precious child) is the endearing Tamil phrase that Ammachi kept repeating softly into my ears, as I knelt enfolded in Her loving embrace. Well known as the "hugging saint," Ammachi or Amma[1] from South India travels around the world, with apparently inexhaustible energy, blessing millions of Her devotees personally by Her affec-

1 Ammachi and Amma mean 'Mother' in Malayalam, the language used in Kerala, India.

tionate gaze, smiles, tears, hugs and wise words. She is the embodiment of unconditional love and compassion, come on earth to heal suffering humanity and all creation.

Amma, I started writing with Your permission. Then I encountered a persistent block and could not proceed any further. When I told You about my difficulties, Your surprising response was a happy laughter and another affectionate hug. I was so dull as to imagine that You might not have understood me, and tried to state it a little more clearly. It was a wonder that You responded in the same manner again.

Immediately it dawned on me that Your exuberant laughter and loving hugs were a hidden blessing on the process of preparing and presenting this book to its readers. Mistakes or not, this book is all Yours. You must graciously bestow on the readers a delightful desire to live as limitless love.

A four-year old child in a car with her mother was crying. The mother asked her why she cried. The child pointed to the picture of Ammachi in the car, and observed that She was so beautiful. Her mother pressed the child further to find out why she would cry, while looking at Amma's image. The child's mother was utterly stunned to hear her daughter's response: "Is it not O.K. to cry for God?"

Two years later, the mother told this writer that she was still puzzled about her child feeling that she was crying for God, while looking at the picture of Amma, whom she had not yet seen. Many devotees report crying for a long time after meeting Amma for the first time. They said that they did not know why they cried, whereas the little girl in the car understood. Not only is it O.K. to cry for God; such holy tears or a deep yearning for Truth is the one thing necessary in life.

"If a man knows himself, he shall know God"

St. Clement of Alexandria

"Our self-knowledge is our beauty. In self-ignorance, we are ugly."

Plotinus

Limitless Love and Awareness

Everyone is looking for love, children in their parents and siblings, adults in their partners and friends. However, hardly anyone is satisfied with the love they experience. Actually we need not look outside ourselves for love, since limitless love is our very nature.

The sage who has captured the hearts of many millions in this age is Ammachi. She worships all the thousands gathered in various venues to see her, as "embodiments of pure love and supreme consciousness." It is truly marvelous to hear from a sage, that we are limitless love and pure awareness, playing temporarily in a bodily form.

We need to find the truth of our own being and experience genuine freedom. If we are sincere and earnest about finding the truth, we can realize that we are infinite awareness. That means, we are one with everyone and everything, and are essentially peace, love and joy.

We pretend that we know ourselves and others when actually we do not know. Forgetting the ever present beauty and wonder of life, we indulge in harsh and hard judgments about ourselves and others, as we are conditioned to do so from early childhood. To escape from the prison of past conditioning and see our innate innocence and beauty, we have to give up our false identifications.

True identity has to be present and permanent. Our body is constantly changing. Bodily cells die and disappear; new cells are formed continually.

Then essentially we are not the body, hence not young or old, male or female, sick or healthy. Those attributes belong to the body we are currently using, and not at all to our essential being. Our name, education and profession also mean merely looking at the surface, and not at our central reality.

Personality with its good and bad habits keeps changing. Past history and the story we tell ourselves when we want to know who we are, clearly miss the mark. Personality and personal history do not point to our essential nature. Race and religion have very little to do with our real identity.

We are not Americans, Africans, Asians or Europeans. None of us is exclusively Christian, Muslim, Hindu or Buddhist. We do not belong to any country. All the countries, religions and languages belong to us, since they are floating in our limitless awareness.

The process of finding the truth about ourselves or Self-realization requires much effort. But straining after it may mean more tension and greater ego that separates us from others. The ego has to be eliminated for the Spirit to shine in us. It happens when we realize that all our acts including our breathing belong to God. He alone is the Doer. Then the effort becomes effortless and peaceful.

Toward the end of his brilliant life, the great scientist Albert Einstein is said to have regretted that he had worked hard to understand the distant stars, while ignoring the closest star, namely himself. "What does it profit a man if he gains the whole world and suffers the loss of his own soul?" asked Christ (Mt. 16:26).

Very rare are the people who find their soul, or the true Self. Such are the sages of all the ages. Having cast their little ego, with its innumerable desires into oblivion, they exert complete control over their mind and body. Nature, in admiration, puts herself willingly under their control. All the worldly glory and power cannot give even a hint of the immense joy in which they constantly abide.

Materialists hardly know matter, whereas the spiritual masters know spirit and matter. They can manipulate matter in whatever way they want, far beyond the limits of ordinary human knowledge and imagination. What seems altogether impossible for a materialist is simple and easy for the sage.

Kerala, a state in South India, is known for its extremely high literacy rate. Intellectual life in that state was dominated by materialism and rationalism. Vallickavu is a small fishing village in Kerala. The villagers thought that Sudhamani, who is now known as Ammachi, was a "crazy girl" when she was growing up in Vallickavu. She studied only up to the fourth grade, and acted like a lowly but cheerful servant to family members and the poor people in the village.

In 1975, at 21 years of age, Sudhamani walked into a neighboring house, where the ceremonial reading of the life of Lord Krishna was going on. It was amazing to see her features and complexion being transformed to appear like Lord Krishna. According to Hindu scriptures, blue is the color of Krishna. Devotees of Lord Krishna started worshipping her, glad that the Lord had taken temporary possession of Sudhamani. Some rationalists who happened to be there were disturbed by this phenomenon. They demanded that she perform a miracle if she were Lord Krishna, though they did not believe in the possibility of miracles.[1]

Sudhamani replied that she came on earth to make them realize the greatest miracle, namely the presence of God in their hearts, and not to indulge in phenomena, which are ephemeral. Since the rationalists continued to insist, saying they would believe if she performed a miracle, she agreed to do so a week later at the same place.

Word passed around the neighboring villages about the promise of a miracle. More than a thousand people gathered around the house. Some unbelievers perched high on trees to get a better view, and expose what they deemed would be a fraud.

Sudhamani was again transformed to look like Lord Krishna. She asked one of the doubters to bring a pitcher of water. After sprinkling it on the people as holy water, she asked the man who had brought the water to look into the pitcher. The water had turned into pure milk! It was distributed to all the people around.

Then she called another skeptic, and instructed him to put his hand into the same pitcher. To his astonishment, the milk was transformed into a

1 See Ammachi by Swami Amritaswarupananda, M.A. Center, San Ramon, California, 1994, pp.84-87

fragrant pudding (normally made with bananas, raw sugar, raisins and rock candy boiled in milk). More than a thousand people enjoyed eating this delicious pudding, yet the pitcher remained full!

The skeptics were still not convinced. They declared that it was due to mesmerism; the taste and the smell of the pudding would vanish within a few seconds. To their disappointment, it lasted for days but hardly made a dent in their dogmatic unbelief. Miracles are not possible for them, even if they happen before their very eyes. Their impossibility is a fundamental postulate in their materialistic belief system.

Belief is different from direct experience or knowledge. Sages speak not out of belief, but from direct experience or intuitive knowledge that is much deeper than material experience and intellectual inference. If we want to attain the level of being and knowing of the sages, we need to believe in their words and live in their blessed company, at least mentally.

Many years of intense suffering can suddenly plunge certain individuals into the heart of truth to their utter amazement, as they realize that they are truly pure awareness, limitless love and perfect joy. Altogether unexpected was the enlightenment of Eckhart Tolle and Byron Katie.

As Seminary students in Sri Lanka, we were happily spending our vacation in Hatton with its beautiful hills, waterfalls and rivers. There I read the book 'Existence and Existent' by the French philosopher Etienne Gilson. It moved me deeply and I was feeling high for days.

One moonlit night, after dinner, I walked up a hill alone, thinking about what I had read. While I stood enjoying the beauty of the moon shining on the hills, it occurred to me that the hills, the moon and my thoughts were real due to existence which is the essence of God. It plunged me into such depths of ineffable happiness that I was jumping up and down for joy.

Somewhat similar was the experience of reading the amazingly powerful book by Eckhart Tolle titled 'The Power of Now.' The author writes about the wonderful process of his own awakening to the splendor of Reality. He stresses the importance of going beyond thoughts, being in the Now, and thus escape the prison of the past and the illusion of a future.

Eckhart Tolle was teaching at Cambridge University in England as a graduate student. He had suffered from severe suicidal depression from early childhood. One night he was in intense dread and despair, more than ever before. The thought: "I cannot live with myself any longer" kept repeating in his mind. Eckhart suddenly realized that there were two selves in him, and only one could be his true self.

It was such a shock that his mind stopped, all the thoughts disappeared and he was drawn into a vortex of energy. He felt an intense fear, and heard an inner voice tell him: "resist nothing." Then the fear too disappeared, as he plunged into a void inside him. He does not remember what happened afterwards.

He woke up to hear the sweet melody of a bird chirping outside, and opened his eyes to see the light of dawn filtering through the curtain. He felt that there was "infinitely more to light than we realize. That soft luminosity filtering through the curtain was love itself,"[2] he wrote.

Eckhart Tolle described his experience further: "Everything was fresh and pristine, as if it had just come into existence. I picked up things, a pencil, an empty bottle, marveling at the beauty and aliveness of it all. That day I walked around the city in utter amazement at the miracle of life on earth, as if I had just been born into this world."[3]

Eckhart Tolle's false and suffering self had vanished altogether. He spent almost two years sitting around in park benches in a "state of the most intense joy." People approached him wanting for themselves the palpable peace that he seemed to emanate. Answering their questions, he became eventually a spiritual teacher.

Strangely enough, Eckhart Tolle did not know about the possibility of Self-realization before his own enlightenment. It took some years before he came to know that there were, and are other Self-realized Masters.

'The Power of Now' provides some powerful techniques to find inner peace and realize our true Self. As our thoughts and feelings veil the peace and joy within us, witnessing them without any judgment (if judging

2 The Power of Now by Eckhart Tolle, New World Library, Novato, CA, 2004, p. 4

3 Ibid, pp. 4-5

happens, see it as another thought) allows us to see the silent space underneath the thoughts. As we continue to witness, which means, accepting and surrendering to what is, the silent space deepens, and we feel the peace and joy.

Another technique is to feel the life energy within our body. Stretch the right hand in front, feel the energy in your palm; then, feeling the energy, go up the arm to the shoulder, neck, and thus on to the left side. Continue to feel the energy in the face, head, chest, stomach, abdomen, thighs, knees, calves and the feet. As we continue to be aware of the life within the body, we can feel the same energy spreading around our body to connect with plants and other things near us.

Practice this technique as often as you can, especially as you wake up, and before you fall asleep. Once you get into the habit of practicing it, there would be no need to go part by part. You will feel the energy in your whole body and around you at once. This practice improves the quality of life. The body becomes more healthy, and the mind calm.

Byron Katie, a successful middle-aged business-woman, suffered from depression, paranoia, rage, and despair that steadily got worse for ten years, in spite of the medications and psychotherapy. She was in a half-way house attic, lying on the floor, since she felt unworthy to use the bed. One morning, she woke up to find that her self-centered personality with its stressful thoughts had vanished. Joy welled up from deep within, breaking out in long bouts of laughter.

When she returned home, the family members noted the profound change. Katie remained so peaceful and happy that people brought their troubles to her and were healed. I felt much love and acceptance from her, participating in her transformational workshops. She teaches us to stop blaming others or ourselves, but to be here and now, accepting and *loving what is* (the title of her book).

Byron Katie was with her daughter Roxanne in the labor room during the delivery of her granddaughter. Katie looked at her daughter and the grandchild with love, and was smiling, when suddenly the child stopped breathing, and the hospital staff were in a panic, as they worked hard to revive the child.

However Katie continued to smile cheerfully, while she looked at them. Eventually the child started to breathe again. Later Roxanne expressed her gratitude to the mother for her joyful presence during the ordeal.

Katie had some blood tests and saw a doctor who checked the test results, and announced with a long face that she had cancer. Katie laughed and the doctor was naturally confused. Later more tests were done, and the diagnosis was reversed. Katie laughed again. She was always in a state of joy, and totally surrendered to God's will. Hence Katie was able to smile when her grandchild stopped breathing, and laugh as the doctor diagnosed her to have cancer.

Once Katie was visiting at a hospital a friend, who had a cancerous tumor. The doctors had told the patient that she would live only for a few more days. The friend told Katie that she loved her. Katie replied that it was untrue; she could not love anyone until she loved her tumor. The friend acknowledged that what Katie said was true, and was grateful.

When we understand and accept that all our problems and pain are a blessing, and are happy with ourselves, only then can we love ourselves fully. Without loving ourselves we cannot love others.

Negative emotions such as fear, anxiety, sadness or anger cover up our real nature which is love. These emotions may be conscious or unconscious. Negative emotions leave our system, revealing the love within, only when they are brought into our awareness and felt fully. Unfelt emotions are trapped in the body like vortices of energy. Unfortunately we are conditioned to resist feeling our negative emotions fully.

Suppression and excessive expression of negative emotions separates us from others, and strengthens our ego. It does not allow the emotions to pass through us. Thus we get stuck in negativity, and are unable to see the Truth of our being. The only way to open our hearts to love is to feel our negative emotions thoroughly. It is done properly when we relax more and more into the energy of such emotions, and let them pass away.

Cultivate compassionate kindness towards yourself. It results in stable self-confidence that makes you accept and allow the negative emotions to flow through you in all their intensity. Then you can free yourself from all negativity and self-pity, and your heart will blossom forth to love all unconditionally.

It is a common human tendency to identify people with their acts, especially when the acts are seriously wrong. Such identification spells immaturity. There are sins, but no sinners. There are crimes, but no criminals. The Masters do not identify us with our evil acts, since they know that we are essentially perfect.

Dr. Hew Len is a psychotherapist who worked at a state mental hospital in Hawaii with criminally insane mental patients who had committed serious crimes like murder, rape and so on. Due to their violent behavior, they were heavily medicated; the patients were in shackles for hands and feet, when they had to be moved around.

The hospital staff was quite demoralized; the rate of employee absenteeism was rather high. The nurses and physicians walked around the wards with their backs to the walls. Dr. Hew Len did not see the patients individually or in groups for therapy. Alone in his room, he looked at the patients' charts and worked on cleaning or healing his own consciousness, as he was aware of being one with the patients.

Consequently there was a radical change in the patients. They were not violent any longer. The medications were gradually reduced; the patients did not need the shackles to walk around, and were taken outside for recreation and exercise. The staff was glad to come for work, but after three years of Dr. Len's therapy, the ward had to be closed, since the patients were being released as cured. Dr. Len used a healing method called Ho'oponopono. Ho'o means 'make' or 'cause', ponopono stands for 'perfection'.

Ho'oponopono is an ancient healing technique from Hawaii that cleans our memory or consciousness of any negativity such as fear, anger, hatred, shame and guilt. It is a matter of using four phrases: 1. I am sorry 2. Please forgive me 3. Thank you 4. I love you.

Think of any person you resent even slightly, and keep saying the phrases. The words may be addressed to the person concerned by name, while you remember that you are speaking to the true divine Self within us all. Then you know that you are forgiven and feel grateful as your heart is healing. The external results are secondary. Say the words again and again, until the healing or cleaning is complete.

All must take full responsibility for the state of their mind and heart. We attract all that happens to us. Not others, but we alone are 100% responsible for our thoughts and feelings. Genuine humility, courage and truthfulness will enable us to act with faith and confidence to heal ourselves here and now, and live in limitless love.

People are unwilling to tolerate garbage in their living room in order to keep it clean for unexpected visitors. God and the great Masters are always in our hearts. Hence the utmost importance of keeping our hearts clean now and always for their sake!

There are many reasons for anger. When we are angry, we feel superior. This sense of superiority is needed to compensate for the sense of inferiority that comes from our subconscious mind which carries the memory of the numerous ways we have been put down by others from early childhood.

Digging a little deep into ourselves, we can see that we do live with some sense of shame and guilt. Thus we cultivate the habit of being hard on ourselves. Then it becomes quite easy to be hard on others. Human life seems to be a constant struggle between inferiority and superiority complexes.

All of us are conditioned to act in particular ways due to our past history and the pressures of the present context. When we look at the context in which the people whom we criticize and condemn acted, we would realize that they had little option, and were conditioned to act as they did. They were not free to act differently.

Feeling hurt and angry as a consequence is also a conditioned reaction. When we are in any way threatened, our body and mind are programmed to defend and attack as a survival mechanism. Thus we are not free to react otherwise. Freedom comes in only when we cultivate the habit of understanding reality as it is. To move beyond our conditioning and have the freedom to understand reality, we need to look at our conditioning, and inquire as to the nature of our consciousness.

When children are born in this world and start to grow, they have no sense of separation, and feel one with everything. The sense of separation and proper boundaries are inculcated gradually into the children through the process of socialization. Responsible adults teach them to fear and look for danger in the environment, and thus learn to survive.

Christ was referring to the initial innocence, fearlessness and the sense of oneness of children, when He exhorted the disciples to be born again and become like little children in order to gain eternal life. What is eternal life? What is real about me? Who am I? My body is utterly impermanent. My personality with its good and bad habits is also always changing. The personality or ego emphasizes the sense of separation. If we look for the ego behind all the thoughts and feelings, it vanishes like an illusion.

As things around me and my body continually change, thoughts and feelings are also changing. The consciousness in me that witnesses the changing phenomena remains the same. As we calmly witness our thoughts and feelings, that witnessing consciousness can be seen as pure awareness.

Awareness knows no distinction or extinction. It seems to give reality to everything and everyone. No form is real apart from awareness, though awareness itself has no form. All this can be known intuitively, if we take the time to look deeply into ourselves.

The more we identify with our unchanging awareness, the more we would be able to accept ourselves and others as we are, with our strengths and weaknesses. Then we can be peaceful enough to feel unconditional love and compassionate kindness towards ourselves and others. There would be no need for apology or forgiveness. It would be a simple matter of right understanding.

Daily introspection is needed to see whether there is even a slight resentment against anyone in your heart. Be compassionately kind toward yourself and visualize yourself and the other person as covered by a golden light of limitless love, peace and joy. Then pray deeply for that person or do ho'oponopono. You may repeat these exercises several times a day until the negative feeling is completely gone.

Ammachi and Her devotees greet each other with the words: 'Namah Shivaya'. These Sanskrit words mean worshipping the other person as a manifestation of Supreme Consciousness and Limitless Love. Human contact is always a holy encounter, if we only know the truth about ourselves.

As we are essentially awareness, we have no beginning or end. The Masters say that we are eternal and one with everyone and everything. Thus we are truly limitless love and endless joy. We get superficial glimpses of our essential nature now and then, especially when we pray or meditate deeply, engage in selfless service, and are receptively in the presence of great Masters.

To dive deep enough into pure awareness and be established permanently in the state of limitless love, joy, power and wisdom is final liberation or enlightenment. That is the main purpose of our life, and requires continuous effort and alert mindfulness. Then life becomes altogether meaningful and we flow with ease and enthusiasm.

Though one may be enlightened without the help of any religion like Peace Pilgrim, Eckhart Tolle and Byron Katie for example, most Masters have come from various religious traditions. Hence we propose to examine religion and its underlying principles in the following chapter.

UNDERSTANDING RELIGION

This age of materialism and unbridled selfishness sees conflict everywhere. Social, economic, cultural and political interests are pulling people apart. Progress in technology, coupled with spiritual regression, has brought us to the brink of total destruction. If religions also continue in a conflict mode, there can be no hope for humanity.

Instead, one needs to adopt a scientific attitude towards religion. An open mind that accepts and appreciates all religions, scriptures, and spiritual practices is very much needed now. Spirituality must be weaned from religious dogmatism and fanaticism.

A dogmatic Hindu would say that only the Hindu scriptures teach the truth. For Christians and Jews, the Bible alone is the holy book. Hundreds of Christian denominations, each interpreting the Bible in their own unique way, believe that only they possess the truth. Muslims believe that the Koran is the final word on divine revelation.

Imagine a person who has tasted in all his life only one fruit, for example, an apple. Presented with a pineapple, he would recoil, saying it cannot be a fruit, since it looks so different from an apple. He would say the same about a sweet mango, since it does not have the shape of an apple.

Crazy as such a scenario sounds, dogmatic believers act in a similar manner. That has been my own personal experience, growing up as a fully convinced Catholic in Sri Lanka. I was raised by a very devout Christian family in a predominantly Hindu culture. The nuns at school taught us that the Hindu temples and religious services were demoniacal!

Even as a little six or seven year old child, my mind weaved dreams about saving sinners from Satan and the fires of hell. I wondered why all the other Catholic boys did not share my clear and firm determination to become a priest.

After High School, I entered the Catholic seminary to study philosophy for three years and theology for four years. Most of the students plunged into these subjects with much enthusiasm and energy.

Reading the books of Plato and Aristotle, and the works of Saints Augustine and Aquinas was intellectually exhilarating. All the biographies of the Catholic saints that I devoutly devoured thrilled me to the core.

The professors at the Seminary were erudite scholars, educated in Europe, with expertise in their respective fields. Unfortunately the Seminary taught us that among religions, only Catholicism possessed the complete truth, and others may approximate it a little here and there.

The awe-inspiring lives of the numerous non-Catholic saints and sages with their profound teachings were a closed book to us. We were hardly aware of the deep devotion and the simple faith of the Hindu, Buddhist, and Muslim villagers facing their daily hardships and toils with a serene countenance. In ignorance, we labored with the certainty that they needed the Catholic belief system to attain salvation.

I was ordained a priest in December 1960, and assigned to serve in the North of Sri Lanka. My eager attempts to convert non-Catholics did not succeed. I continued in my zeal to save the so-called sinners among Catholics from hell.

While conducting a weekend retreat at a convent-school, I preached such a terrifying sermon about sin and hell that the girls flocked in large numbers to the local priests for confession. One of the priests later asked me why I had frightened the children so much about hell, but his question did not trouble me, as I was content to be saving souls from the fires of hell.

When doubts started to arise in my mind as to how a loving, merciful God could allow souls to suffer eternally in hell, I suppressed them quickly.

The doctrine of eternal hell was a dogma of the Church that one had to accept. How could I doubt what was taught by such brilliant minds as Saints Augustine and Aquinas?

The turning point in my thinking came with the controversy in the Church about the morality of birth-control. Some erudite moral theologians were courageous enough to say that the Church had to change its traditional opposition to artificial methods of birth control.

The willingness of the Church to accept the rhythm method of birth-control as natural and moral, while condemning artificial methods as immoral, seemed to be arbitrary. Morality of any act is determined primarily by the personal motive behind the act, unless the act is intrinsically evil. Avoiding pregnancy is the purpose for adopting birth-control, whether the methods are natural or artificial.

No one can reasonably claim that the artificial methods are intrinsically evil. Moreover using artifacts is a natural human development. To be logically consistent, the Church should condemn chemical medication, and surgery using machine-made implements, which, of course, is absurd.

I was deeply disturbed to find that the Church had misled millions of people into believing that they were committing mortal sins, and were in danger of hell by using artificial methods of birth-control.

Then I wondered whether the Church could be wrong about the dogma of hell itself. Studying the subject in depth, I found that eternal damnation was a false conclusion, based on scriptural misinterpretation. The dogma of eternal hell was thrust on people for political reasons, as will be explained later.

Being fully convinced of my position, I detailed my findings in a lengthy paper, drawing on scripture and philosophy to bolster my argument that God cannot punish anyone for eternity. I distributed it to about a hundred priests, asking for their critique and comments. Not a single one raised any objection. A few said that they had no adverse comments, but warned me not to share my ideas with the lay people, since it could disturb their simple faith.

As more doctrines of the church continued to collapse in my mind, in order to save my faith in God and Christ, I accepted a scholarship to study at a prestigious inter-denominational institution, namely Union Theological

Seminary of New York City in 1970. Union Seminary could not prevent my downward spiral, since I hardly prayed, and sided with the scholars who doubted the divinity and historicity of Christ.

Intellectual problems about God continued to confuse and trouble me. The question arose whether God can be infinite and unlimited, with a creation that is clearly distinct and separate from Him, since creation by its very existence, limits God.

Grace of God is said to be necessary for salvation. Why does God give His grace to some, and not to others? Theologians say that everyone is given sufficient grace to succeed, but only those who receive efficient grace, do so. If the so-called sufficient grace is not truly sufficient to be actually effective, there is no point in getting such grace. All the evil and horrors in the world have puzzled many thinkers throughout history. Some concluded that, if there is a God, He is either very cruel or too weak.

Realizing that these problems were intellectually insoluble, I decided that questions that had no adequate answers should not be asked, and opted to be an agnostic. Quitting the Church, I was happy to serve children and families as an adoption worker at New York Foundling Hospital, and spent much time with friends.

Agnosticism and materialism seemed to be the only sane philosophical attitude to adopt. It was an immense relief to be finally free of all the questions that had perplexed my mind and heart for so many years. When some friends told me that I would eventually get back into religion, I merely laughed, being quite sure that it was impossible.

Incredibly the "impossible" became possible in 1977, when my materialistic framework started to break apart in an altogether unexpected manner. The experience with all its details is still vivid in my memory. I was living alone at a fifth floor walk-up apartment in mid-Manhattan. One Friday evening after dinner, I decided to explore my mind in depth. Foregoing the usual distractions of TV, telephone, books, snacks, drinks etc., I was intent in observing my thoughts and feelings, and stayed awake the whole night.

Flat on my back in the living room, I was unusually calm, yet quite alert, when around seven o'clock in the morning I became aware of my father's presence in the room. About ten years had elapsed since my father passed away. We called him Aiyah. As a materialistic unbeliever, I did not think that he continued to live after his death.

Suddenly I felt Aiyah to my left, a little behind me, about three or four feet up. I did not perceive him with my physical senses, yet clearly I felt his presence, and internally heard his words in English: "I love you."

Though Aiyah knew a little English, he had spoken to his children in Tamil only. He had been a good provider, but a strict disciplinarian, not given to external expressions of love. As he was humorous and friendly with other people, I resented the fact that he had been apparently cold towards me. Therefore this was a very pleasant surprise.

Aiyah kept repeating the words "I love you," and I felt the vibrations of love flowing over me, through my body and spreading around me. My immediate reaction was the thought: "So love is real! And this is love!" The sensation of love was not physical, but more subtle and spiritual. I felt as if I was floating in a sea of love. It was an absolutely astonishing experience for mc.

After the initial shock and delight, the materialistic mind intervened to say: "This must be a hallucination; what else can it be?" An immediate intuitive response sprang from the depths of my being, very clear and certain: "If this is hallucination, then my body and the walls around me are a greater hallucination, because Aiyah's presence and his love that I feel are much ***more real*** than my body or the walls and the furniture that I can see now."

Sensory perceptions can be deceptive. What I perceive may not be objectively valid, as seeing a mirage of water in a desert. Some stars that are already extinct are still seen by us, due to the distance of many light years for the image to reach our eyes. Hence there is always a possibility of error in an intellectual inference based on sense perception.

Intuition is different. I may not know who or what I am, but that I am cannot be doubted. It is known intuitively. Seeing my father and feeling his love was an intuitive experience. Hence in my inner awareness it was much more real and certain than our everyday sensory perceptions.

The experience lasted for about fifteen minutes and faded away slowly, leaving me happy in the knowledge that Aiyah is still alive with genuine love for me, and we would go on living even after death. The intuitive assurance that I received from deep inside myself, left no room for any doubt about life beyond death.

The question whether God could be real, arose in my mind. I put a stop to that thought immediately, being afraid to face the apparent contradictions that would appear in the intellect, and to feel the anguish of mind and heart endured years earlier, if I delved into the subject of God again.

I did not go in search of God. He came lovingly seeking me out, like the "Hound of Heaven" of the poet Francis Thompson. A literary critic described this poem as the most beautiful piece of English literature of all times:

> I fled Him, down the nights and down the days;
> I fled Him, down the arches of the years;
> I fled Him, down the labyrinthine ways
> Of my own mind; and in the mist of tears
> I hid from Him, and under running laughter.
> Up vistaed hopes I sped;
> And shot, precipitated,
> Adown Titanic glooms of chasme'd fears,
> From those strong Feet that followed, followed after
> But with unhurrying chase,
> And unperturbed pace,
> Deliberate speed, Majestic instancy,
> They beat-and a Voice beat
> More instant than the Feet-
> "All things betray thee, who betrayest Me"

What woke me from the six-year-long slumber of agnosticism, and brought me back to God, was the amazing book: *Autobiography of a Yogi* by Paramahansa Yogananda.[1] A few months after the marvelous encounter with Aiyah and his overflowing love, I attended a Silva Mind Control weekend seminar led by Paul Grivas, whose dynamism and intelligence I

1 Published by Self Realization Fellowship, Los Angeles, Ca., 1946

greatly admired. When he found out that I was an agnostic, but had been a priest earlier, he insisted consecutively for three days that I should read the *Autobiography*.

Buying it reluctantly, I took the book home, wondering why I was wasting my time with such nonsense. I expected to glance through a few pages, and put the book away quickly. Instead, it turned out to be an awesome, explosively exhilarating experience. Reading just a few pages, tears started flowing freely, while I laughed heartily.

Crying and laughing alternately, I was glued to the book that whole night. A deeply intuitive intimation that I could trust the saintly author completely, made me gratefully receptive, as he was introducing me to Christ-like Masters of the modern era.

All the philosophical questions about God with which I had struggled earlier lost their relevance. Masters are aware of God as the only Reality or Noumenon behind the phenomena of human experience. They live in the light of Truth, and are genuinely free. I can walk with them towards the full freedom of finding the Truth or God here on earth.

Great spiritual Masters have appeared in India even recently. Then I had to change my mind about Christ. He does not have to be a mere legend; He must be true. My early devotion to Lord Jesus Christ started bubbling up in my heart again.

A neighboring Catholic church pulled me like a powerful magnet. I started going for daily mass, and participated in the services fervently. In addition, I went for Catholic Charismatic meetings where the soulful singing and passionate prayers uplifted and soothed my heart.

Unfortunately my discussions with the members of the Charismatic community later were a stark contrast. Their dogmatic parochialism and abysmal ignorance of other religions convinced me that I had to turn away from such intellectual intolerance, and breathe the free air of truth, while pursuing the spiritual goal of salvation or liberation.

It is fear that holds people in the bondage of falsehood. Some religious leaders who are themselves fear-ridden, saddle their followers with blind beliefs, warning them about dire punishments from God, if they question or try to clarify their beliefs. Believing that God loves us unconditionally removes fear from our hearts, and makes us realize that we are innately wired for truth.

Paramahansa Yogananda was dictating to his secretary Tara Mata, and once used an unusual word. Tara Mata, quite proficient in the English language, told him that there was no such word in English. Yogananda advised her to check in a dictionary, as Divine Mother had given him that word. (Indian Masters talk about God as Divine Mother, whereas Christ referred to God as Heavenly Father.) She looked at two dictionaries, but did not find the word. Since Yogananda insisted, she checked another dictionary, and was surprised to find it there.

Yogananda continued to dictate, and asked Tara to edit it. Later he found a grammatical error in the edited version, and asked Tara Mata why she had not corrected it. She replied that she thought Divine Mother had given him the particular sentence. Yogananda roared with laughter, wondering how she could be so stupid.

Any human being, however great, can be mistaken. No one is infallible, neither the Church nor the Bible. It is our duty to look for the truth everywhere. As the ancient Tamil poet Valluvar said:

> *Epporul yar yar vay kedpinum*
> *Apporul meyporul kanpatharivu*
> Whatever you may hear from whomsoever
> To find its true meaning is wisdom.

In the Bible, there are stringent laws about the observance of Sabbath, prescribing immediate death to anyone who breaks them. These laws ignore human sensibility, and the primary duty of man to take care of his family and the sick. Christ cut to their roots, and let the laws fall with His words: "Sabbath was made for man, and not man for Sabbath." Anyone could have come to the same conclusion, by inquiring into the meaning and purpose of Sabbath.

A few more examples of horrendous commands from the Bible: children who verbally abuse their parents should be killed according to Exodus and Leviticus. Homosexuality is punishable by death. Fortune-tellers and mediums (those who facilitate communication between the living and the dead) must be stoned until they die.

Thus the scriptures understood always literally and interpreted indiscriminately are a serious obstacle to spiritual progress. The biblical passages that advocate aggression, cruelty and violence to the extent of killing innocent infants and animals belonging to the so-called enemies, can be taken to represent man's inner struggle between good and evil habits.

Scriptures

Scriptures of all religions are revered by their adherents, rightly so, as they embody divinely inspired and inspiring words. Bible, Koran, Vedas and all the scriptures were composed and compiled by many writers and editors, over a long period of time, from various traditions, sometimes with interpolations, alterations and mistranslations.

Words were often attributed to Masters to validate later traditions. Legends tend to accrue around sages. It is difficult to distinguish between history and legends in the scripture. Such distinction need not be a matter of much concern, as the stories in general, whether historical, legendary or mythical are valuable for spiritual growth.

To consider one holy book alone as the word of God is to forget that God communicates through the whole of creation His majesty, beauty, love, joy and wisdom. He expresses Himself through everything. Then, what is not God's word?

It is easy to pretend that we understand the scriptures. Better to accept humbly that we do not grasp them properly. The help of spiritual Masters is required for it. Moreover, the exemplary life and the inspiring words of an authentic Master are the scripture that we need to study attentively, and ponder with reverence for our spiritual growth.

Most modern scholars of the Bible are agreed that it is composed from divergent traditions of various groups, reflecting their opposing views and historical changes. It is also heavily influenced by the ancient myths of the Egyptians, and the other neighboring nations.

Six days of creation narrated in the Bible is a story that should not be understood literally. This is clear from the fact that God is said to have created the sun and the moon on the fourth day. Time and space are created by God; yet creation over a sequence of days means it is a time consuming process. Gradual evolution, taking millions and millions of years for the present status of nature, is not opposed to the concept of creation.

Problems arise due to the confusion of Divine creation with human creation. Our acts of creation are bound by time, whereas God, as the cause of creation, is beyond time. Being pure consciousness that is eternal or ever **now** (past and future being included in the eternal "now"), God is actually creating at the present moment, giving reality to each and every phenomenon or external manifestation. To relegate God merely to the origin of the universe in historical time is a philosophical error, since He is the author of space and time.

Scientists now believe that the physical universe started at a definite time, though billions of years ago. To think that this scientific theory gives room to the concept of a Divine Creator is a misunderstanding of creation. As the eminent philosopher St. Thomas Aquinas pointed out, the universe could have been without a definite beginning in time. Hindu sages affirmed this many ages ago.

God is not needed to explain the origin of things in time. Uncaused Cause, Unmoved Mover, Universal Intelligence, Ground of being, Infinite Consciousness, True Self, Silence, Tao, and Nirvana are words used for God, intuitively reflected in our consciousness, here and now, as the Noumenon behind all the phenomena, the changeless Reality behind changing matter.

The story of Adam and Eve in the garden, with the tree of good and evil and the tree of life, the talking serpent, and God walking in the garden is obviously a myth. Gary Greenberg, the president of the Biblical Archaeology Society of New York shows a clear connection between this story, and the other ancient myths from the Middle-East in his book: *101 Myths of the Bible.*

The stories about Eternal Hell with fire and brimstone, and the Day of Judgment are also ancient myths that the Hebrews brought into their tradition quite late. These myths are mentioned in the New Testament, which also has numerous other passages that affirm universal salvation both explicitly and implicitly.

Universal Salvation

The belief in universal salvation and reincarnation was widespread in early Christianity. It was taught by Origen, the famous father of the Church in the third century. He was known to be a very holy man. My professor of New Testament at the seminary said that Origen was the most brilliant biblical scholar that the Church ever had. This gifted genius mused, with poetic imagination inspired by faith, that Christ will be stretched out on the cross until the last demon in hell is saved and brought into heaven.

These beliefs were overturned centuries later due to manipulative politics. The drama enacting the change was mainly staged by Emperor Justinian. He reasoned that his subjects could be more easily controlled, if they lived in the fear of eternal hell. Hence he convened an ecumenical council where the majority of the bishops were forced to condemn Origen's teachings. All his books were burnt. Pope Vigilius. who headed the Church at that time, did not attend the Council nor did he approve officially the condemnations.

Denial of universal salvation amounts to the negation of the infinitely joyful, loving and powerful God. He cannot be blissful and loving, while allowing His children to suffer eternally in hell. God would be rather weak due to his incapacity to conquer evil and convert it into good.

My nephew was only five years old when he said to his mother "Certain boys hurt me at times and I get angry with them. Later I forgive and we are friends again. Then how can God send people to hell and make them suffer forever? Does not God love us much more?"

Paramahansa Yogananda was once conversing with a farmer in Seattle, Washington. The farmer claimed that most people are sinners and are bound to burn in the fires of hell forever. Yogananda tried to reason with him, but failed to convince him otherwise.

Then Master changed the subject, referring to the farmer's wicked son being the cause of constant sorrow to the father. The farmer was wondering how the Master knew about his son, and said he would be ever grateful for Master's help to resolve his problem.

Yogananda asked him in a serious tone whether he had a large oven, two trustworthy friends and a strong rope. The farmer answered that he had them, while feeling some misgiving. He also stated that his son was a heavy sleeper, coming home having consumed much liquor.

The Master seemed to be enthusiastic as he said: "Tonight, heat your oven as hot as possible; call your friends asking them to be quiet until your son is fast asleep. Then let them tie your son securely with the rope and shove him into the hot oven."

The farmer was furious as he shouted: "Fiend! Murderer! This is outrageous! Whoever heard of a father burning his own son? I wouldn't do such a thing, even if my son were ten times more wicked."

Yogananda gently and calmly asked him, if he could not bear the thought of burning his wicked son alive, how can the eternally loving Heavenly Father make his children burn forever in hellfire and brimstone? Master told him that his love for his son was a reflection of God's infinite love. The farmer realized that the God of love cannot punish us forever, and we punish ourselves for our sins.

God, out of His love and wisdom designed that sin should be followed by pain sooner or later. It is a cause-effect relationship with mathematical precision. Pain is proportionate to the evil act. Hence it is well defined and limited. The way of suffering seems to be the only means by which man can be motivated to free himself from the bondage of his ignorant, sinful self and find God or his true Self.

It may appear that there is an everlasting hell. One who suffers intensely may feel for the moment that there is no end to it, seeing no possible escape. When he humbly surrenders himself to the pain and sorrow as flowing from God's love and wisdom to purify him, he begins to feel peace which later changes into joy.

Through meditation, prayers and compassionate acts we can expand our consciousness to feel peace, love and joy within ourselves. That is a glimpse of God's Presence for the start. Perseverance on the spiritual path with determination, concentration and the guidance of a true Master leads to cosmic consciousness and the glorious realization of our utter oneness with God and His whole creation.

Reincarnation

The famous English philosopher, David Hume declared that reincarnation is the "only system of this kind that philosophy can hearken to."[2] No other theory can explain the great inequality of man at birth.

Unless understood from the perspective of *karma*, or the consequence of actions and habits of past lives, we cannot make sense of some children being born healthy into wealthy, virtuous families, as opposed to those born sick or handicapped, to poor, criminal parents. Apart from the hypothesis of reincarnation, there is no possible way to escape from concluding that God must be unjust, unfair and arbitrary.

The concept of original sin does not explain why certain children grow up with evil tendencies, whereas others are exceptionally holy and innocent from early childhood. Only in reincarnation can we find an explanation for child prodigies like Mozart, or for even normal children being able to speak a language fluently, without having the time or experience necessary to make the numerous linguistic connections required to speak a language fluently.

Some people do remember their past lives with detailed information about previous relatives, in far-away places which they had not visited in the present life, and their memory was later confirmed by others. There are many such well documented and properly verified cases from different parts of the globe that cannot be explained except through reincarnation.

I was showing some pictures of spiritual Masters to my three year old grandniece Thevika. When we came to the image of Paramahansa Yogananda, she was excited and said: "He is the one! He is the one who showed me Appa and Amma (parents). I was in this place with very beautiful lights. Oh they were so beautiful! He came to me and showed Appa and Amma in this house. Then he said: "you are going to them; they will take care of you."

Now Thevika is twenty years old and does not remember telling me this story. A similar incident was narrated by a Yogananda's monk during a service that I attended at New York City Center.

A young couple who are devotees of Yogananda told him this story. They had a three-year old daughter. The mother gave birth to another child recently

---

2 David Hume, Essays: Moral, Political and Literary, London, 1875, p.409

and brought the infant home. Their daughter asked her parents to leave the baby's room, as she wanted to be alone with the baby and speak to her.

They were puzzled and turned on the amplifying system before they left the room. From the outside they were amazed to hear their daughter say: "Baby, like you I too came from God; but now I am beginning to forget Him. Please speak to me about Him. Please talk."

Such incidents confirm the inspiration of the poet William Wordsworth in his ode: Intimations of Immortality from Recollections of Early Childhood,

"......But trailing clouds do we come
From God, who is our home
Heaven lies about us in our infancy."

Most of us do not remember our past lives, as otherwise we cannot cope with the problems of our present life. The memory of past lives can be also a hindrance to spiritual progress.

As a scientific theory may be verified through experiments, Yogananda said that yoga meditation is an internal experiment that validates reincarnation. An advanced yogi can clearly see into his past lives.

Brother Anandamoy, a direct disciple of Yogananda, said that in meditation he discovered the technique to see into his previous lives, and was about to do so, when another monk interrupted him to say that Master was calling him. Immediately he went to see the Master, who advised him against what he had been on the verge of doing, since looking into past lives could be an obstacle on the spiritual path.

Removing our attachment, interest and energy from externality, and going within in meditation, is the way to find God. It means being silent enough to be free of imagination and the memory of present life. Then it is all the more reason not to be concerned about the past or future lives. Once we realize that finding God is the only way to escape from misery, how can we be interested in other lives, instead of working out our liberation here and now?

Rebirth is the result of *karma*, which is the law of cause and effect extended to morality. Some object to the theory of *karma*, saying it is a harsh, retributive law that does not take into account the love and mercy of God.

On the contrary, in Lord Buddha's words, "the heart of it is Love, the end of it is Peace and Consummation sweet."[3] Sylvia Cranston offers a striking example to explain *karma* in this context:[4] "A violinist learns from dissonant, spine-chilling sounds what movements of bow and fingers to avoid, and discovers at last how to play beautiful, soulful music. How long this will take depends on his effort and talent. According to *karmic* doctrine, the same is true in mastering the human instrument."

Karma is mistakenly confused with fatalism, which is merely an excuse for moral laziness. Man is always free to change his *karma* around, since he was the cause of *karma* in the first place. Moreover, realizing his perfect unity with God, he can rise totally above *karma* at any moment.

Reincarnation is the result of ignorance or illusion. Only the illusory ego tied to an astral body can reincarnate. Spirit is beyond reincarnation. It ever remains the same, without beginning or end. Liberation consists not in attaining perfection, but in realizing the perfect nature of the soul.

In the great Indian epic, *Mahabharata*, Lord Krishna explains to Arjuna that it was his duty as a warrior prince to fight in a righteous war. He goes on to enlighten him about the essential truth that though Arjuna may kill his enemies, the sword cannot touch their soul. "No weapon can pierce the soul; no fire can burn it; no water can moisten it; nor can any wind wither it. The soul is not cleavable; it cannot be burnt or wetted or dried. The soul is immutable, all-permeating, ever calm, and eternally the same." (*Bhagavad Gita*, 2:23-24)[5]

When man loses his physical body, his inner light body or the astral body continues to function in astral worlds, until he is ready to come back to earth for further purification. Final liberation happens when man finds his Soul or true Self, which is supreme Consciousness or Awareness.

Awareness is not many, but one, though there may be many with awareness. The knowledge of people may be more or less, but their awareness ever remains the same, transcending time and space.

---

3 Quoted in Reincarnation, Compiled and Edited by Sylvia Cranston, Theosophical University Press, Passadena, California, 1998, p.12

4 ibid, pp.12-13

5 Translated by Paramahansa Yogananda, SRF, Los Angeles, 1995

The concept "two" is not the same as the word "two." The words, whether written, spoken or merely in the mind, are material images; as images, they are conditioned by time and space, and can change, but the meaning of certain concepts like "two" never changes. Even the concept of time is not time-bound, nor the concept of space spatial. Matter itself, as a concept, is immaterial.

Since we are used to identifying ourselves with our bodies, we forget that certain concepts are not bound by time or space. Human intelligence of concepts, unlike their images and words reflected in man's brain, is beyond time and space. Identifying the intelligence with the brain, or body-identification is ignorance.

Ignorance is mere pretension, according to the great sage Ramana Maharshi. Since it is all too common, it seems to be quite normal and non-pretentious. But deep within ourselves, we know that we are aware, and awareness as such is pure. Awareness in and by itself, being not composed of matter, cannot decompose or have an end. That which cannot end, can have no beginning either.

Pure awareness or the true Self knows no change, has no birth or death, hence does not reincarnate. That is the reason why knowing one's soul or the realization of the true Self means liberation from ignorance or the state of delusion. "The Self is never born nor does it ever perish; nor having come into existence will it again cease to be. It is birthless, eternal, changeless, ever-same [unaffected by the usual processes of time]. It is not slain when the body is killed." (Bhagavad Gita, 2:20)

A great yogi like Paramahansa Yogananda could consciously stop all bodily motion, including the heart's movement in deep meditation or *samadhi. Samadhi* is temporary death. When yogis bring their consciousness back into the body, movement and life start again.

Death is under the conscious control of spiritual Masters. Hence their death is called *mahasamadhi* or great ecstasy. This is possible only for fully enlightened sages, who are constantly in a state of *samadhi*, while experiencing the world as well. Their awareness is expanded to be one with Divine consciousness, thus omnipresent and omniscient.

Yogananda said that even in deep sleep, he was aware that he was sleeping. His close disciples often experienced the omnipresence and omniscience of their Master, who demonstrated that he knew their thoughts, wherever they were.

God Found Within

"So God created man in His own image" (Gen.1:27). Created in His image, we truly reflect God. Going deep within ourselves, we can find Him. But it is not easy to go within, since we are bound to externality and sensations, due to our habitual attachments and aversions. Selfless service, prayers and meditation are the means that enable us to go within, and find God.

St. Teresa of Avilla was a great Spanish mystic of the sixteenth century, and a reformer and founder of many convents. She used to advise her sisters in the convent about the importance of going within. Theresa communed with God deeply and went into ecstasy often, so that at times the sisters saw her levitating high up even in the refectory.

Levitation is not a mere fantasy. Mr. Oliver Black was married with children, a multimillionaire supplying car parts to Ford Motor Company, when he met Paramahansa Yogananda. I was privileged to stay with Mr. Black for a month in Michigan. He told us about his levitation once.

He had been meditating with Yogananda for three days, and went to the airport to get back to Detroit. Since he had more than an hour to wait, he sat in a secluded area to meditate. When he got up to leave, he found that he was not only full of joy, but in midair, about two feet above the floor. Fearing that others seeing him might faint, he managed to force himself down to the floor with some effort.

Such phenomena are not needed, and should not be sought on the spiritual path. Visions, supernatural phenomena, and even the power to perform miracles do not indicate spiritual progress. Ever increasing peace is a sure sign, but even craving for peace can be egoistic and an obstacle on the spiritual path.

"The kingdom of God is within you," said Christ (Lk.17:21). By going within, we can find God in silence. "Be still, and know that I am God" (Ps. 46). When you find God, you will discover that there is no within or without, since God is center everywhere and circumference nowhere.

Mother Theresa was a modern saint, capable of going deep within herself and communing with God in silence. Once a reporter asked her how she prayed, and what she said to God. She answered that she did not say anything to God, but merely listened to Him.

The reporter wanted to know what God told her. She replied that God also did not talk, but just listened to her. As the reporter seemed to be rather puzzled by this response, Mother Theresa said that if he could not understand it, she could not explain further. Silent communion with God is an intuitive inner experience, beyond words and thoughts.

The Virtue of Image-Worship

Many religions including Judaism, Islam, non-Catholic Christianity and reformed Hinduism decry idolatry as an abomination. The Ten Commandments from the Bible start with a clear injunction against idolatry and making images: "You shall not make for yourself a carved image, any likeness of anything that is in heaven above, or that is in the earth beneath, or that is in the water under the earth, you shall not bow down to them or serve them." (Exodus 20:4-5)

However, making images is essential to man as much as breathing or eating. Words are images. We cannot think or talk without using images and symbols. Every word that we utter is an image that refers to something else. The word God is not God. It is a symbol for God. Brahma, Yahweh, Jehowah and Allah are all words first, and as such, are images or symbols that refer to the ultimate Reality.

Moses and the prophets were using images to prohibit the use of images. Why? They were teaching a fundamental truth, namely, that God is invisible Spirit, and cannot be confined to any material thing. When Moses came down from the mountain with the tablets of Ten Commandments, he found the Israelites worshipping a golden calf, drunk and unruly, caught in the heat of lust. In rage, Moses threw the tablets at them. Idol worship, in this instance, was a mere pretension and not genuine worship.

One who honestly worships an idol is humble, feeling a sense of awe and gratitude to the Divine Presence in the image. The attitude of the Israelites showed that they confined their God to the golden calf and ignored His presence in their bodies and hearts, as they indulged in alcoholism and sexual promiscuity.

When we kiss the photos of loved ones, it is an act of communion with the beloved that does not merely end in the image. God and His saints are omnipresent, and are aware of our desire to worship them, even as we go near the holy images and idols. God is present in every little thing completely, though He transcends all things. Hence anything can reveal His Divine Presence.

Idolatry can be a virtue or a sin, depending on the attitude of the idolater. Limiting God to any particular thing is the sin of idolatry. Condemning idolatry indiscriminately and arrogantly, while limiting God to a particular religious sect, set of doctrines and one holy book is paradoxically an act of sinful idolatry. On the other hand, those who humbly worship idols with pure devotion and love, begin to feel the presence of God first in the idol, and then everywhere, in everyone and everything. Hence they are not guilty of confining God to any particular thing, and are practicing the virtue of image-worship.

In the Broadway play "Equus," the main character was a young man who worshipped his horse as God. He was brought to a psychiatrist to be rid of his delusion. The psychiatrist knew that he could help the boy to be freed of his delusion, but was concerned that in the process, the patient would be deprived of his passionate enthusiasm and joy.

Perhaps, instead of ceasing to worship the horse, he could have been helped to see even more the divinity in the horse, and cultivate one-pointed devotion. It would have enabled him to see divinity in himself and everywhere else. To see God in the horse was not delusion; not to see God anywhere is the real delusion. We all suffer from it. Not a psychiatrist, but only a saintly sage can facilitate freeing us from our common delusion.

The sages know God more directly and clearly than this world. Their senses are not dull, but sharper than that of ordinary people; they see the world even more clearly, yet find God to be the sole Reality behind this world.

Naren Datta came from an aristocratic family in Calcutta. A well-educated, brilliant youth, he was keen on finding the real truth behind words and traditions. Searching for God, he had the habit of asking spiritual people whether they had seen God. He did not receive a satisfactory answer, until he met Ramakrishna Paramahansa.

Ramakrishna told him then and there that he sees God more clearly than Naren with whom he was talking. Immediately Naren realized that Ramakrishna knew God intimately, and would help him toward his long sought goal of realizing the divine Presence. Later, Naren, well known around the world as Swami Vivekananda, became a luminous sage, inspiring thousands of people in India and abroad to cultivate genuine devotion to God, and compassion for the poor and the suffering masses.

The primary path to God for Ramakrishna Paramahansa was image-worship, as for millions of Hindus before and after him. From a young age, he worshipped the idol of Mother Kali following the prescribed rites meticulously, washing and wiping the idol, dressing it in beautiful clothes, waving incense and lamps and feeding the idol, while chanting the relevant mantras in Sanskrit.

For Ramakrishna, God in the aspect of Divine Mother Kali was truly present in the idol, though hiding Herself there. Daily he shed tears, intensely imploring Her to reveal Herself. The intensity of yearning for God had reached such a peak, that he felt he could not live any longer without seeing his Beloved. At that point, Divine Mother revealed Herself to Ramakrishna in Her glorious beauty and love.

Later Ramakrishna attained final liberation, realizing total oneness with the infinite Absolute. Yet he preferred to remain a devotee, lovingly conducting the daily worship in the temple to the idol of Mother Kali. He knew through experience that God is transcendent and immanent, personal and impersonal, formless, yet assuming forms to please His devotees.

The belief of many Hindus in the real Presence of God in the idols is quite similar to the belief among Catholics of the real Presence of Christ in the Holy Eucharist. Deeply devotional idol-worship and intense devotion to the Holy Eucharist have produced a great many saints in both religions.

Omnipresent Spirit can take numerous forms, and enthrall the devotees with the many aspects of the one Godhead. Practice of polytheism by Hindus is much misunderstood. It is not at all a denial of monotheism. Instead, one can go even deeper into monotheism through polytheism, perceiving the magnificent manifestations of one God in multiple forms and aspects. Hindu practice, prayers, scripture and philosophy emphasize the essential unity of all the Gods and Goddesses.

Unity is absolutely fundamental to Hindu philosophy. Its dominant system is called Monism. Enunciated by an extraordinary genius and a saintly sage, Sankara, who wrote beautiful devotional poetry extolling Gods and Goddesses, monism insists on the essential oneness of ultimate Reality or God. Anything apart from God is unreal or illusion for Sankara. Yet, as a devotee, he kept a distinction between himself and God. He sang: "O God, I belong to you, whereas you do not belong to me, as the wave belongs to the ocean and not the ocean to the wave."

St. Catherine of Siena, in her mystical communion with God, heard these words: "Catherine, always remember this most fundamental truth: I am; you are not." Though we can affirm with Sankara and Catherine that everything apart from God is unreal, it is also true and heart-warming to view all things as real, imbued with the reality of God's Presence in them.

Incarnation

God seems to be pursuing man now, more than ever before. Materialism is leading him blindly towards self-destruction. Materialistic dogmatism arose as a reaction to religious dogmatism, superstition and exploitation. Feeling the despair of this age, God has taken human forms to be with us, and show the way to genuine peace.

More than a hundred years ago, the great sage Vivekananda predicted that this age will see many incarnations of God, especially coming out of India. Idolatry is man using images and forms to go towards God. Incarnation is God using forms to come towards man.

The concept of incarnation is rather abhorrent to some religionists. It would seem like limiting God who is unlimited, which is a blasphemy. Yet God can continue to be unlimited while taking on some limitations of a particular form to manifest Himself. Incarnation as a logical possibility flows from the concept of creation.

God is not limited by His creation. Creation, though limited, is nothing but a manifestation or expression of God. He would be limited by His creation, if there were any dualistic opposition between God and creation. God and creation are not two, but one. He is the sole Reality behind the phenomena of creation.

Only God is. Everything else is a mere dream of God. Time, space, and all the universes moving around in them are a play of His infinite Consciousness. Our very being is a participation in His Being. To think that we can be ever separate from God or the rest of creation is an illusion. God adopts a human form to free us from such an illusion, which is riddled with confusion and misery.

To think that incarnation is impossible for God is to limit Him. The main motive for affirming that incarnation is not only a possibility but an actuality, that it happened not once but many times, is the testimony of saints and sages. If they are able to see the fullness of God's Supreme Consciousness present in a human being, and adore him or her as an incarnation of God on earth, then we have no alternative but to accept it as true.

Long before Christ, Indian sages who were contemporaries of Rama and Sita adored them as incarnations of God. Later, Lord Krishna and His spouse Rukmini were acclaimed as incarnations by the sages who lived at the same time.

When Christ came to Palestine, there was no tradition of acknowledging an incarnation in that area. St. Peter was inspired to accept Him as Lord, and adore Him. But he could not continue consistently with that understanding. Christ's disciples seemed to have come to the realization of His divinity gradually, and mainly after His death and resurrection.

The disciples of Christ were fully convinced that Jesus alone was God incarnate, hence the only begotten Son of God They did not know about other great incarnations of different eras.

Usually we think that we are separate from God, and from each other. Actually no one can be separate from God and apart from the whole of creation. God is our essence, our very being.

In that sense we too are incarnations of God, though unlike Lord Jesus, we are ignorant and unaware of our true Self or God. Christ came on earth to make us become aware of our innate divinity. If we realize the truth of our being, we too can do all that Christ did, and more.(John 14:12)

To think that we are real in our separate identities is an illusion, which is the work of Satan according to Paramahansa Yogananda. Apart from God, we are nothing. In God we are one with everyone and everything.

"Be nothing in order to be everything," said St. John of the Cross. The sense of being utterly nothing, or genuine humility enables us to sincerely seek for truth in everything. "Truth shall make you free," said Christ.

From joy I came, for joy I live

From joy I came, for joy I live
and in Thy sacred joy I shall melt again.
Teach me to find my joy not in the world but in Thee. Discovering Thy presence
in the joy born of meditation and good actions, I shall feel no need for pleasures born of the misguided senses.
O Father Thou art ever new Joy; Thou art the lasting Joy of the soul; Thou art the Joy that I seek. [6]

6 Paramahansa Yogananda, Whispers from Eternity, (Self-Realization Fellowship, Los Angeles) p.50

"Worship God, as if you see Him;
And remember that if you do not see God,
God still sees you."

"The best people are those who are most useful to others."

"Protect and honor the earth, for the earth is your mother."

Prophet Muhammad

CHRIST, KRISHNA AND BUDDHA

Some Christian scholars believe that Christ is spiritually significant for man, though He did not live as a historical figure on this earth. The story of Christ is said to be a legend and not proper history. The same view is held by a few Hindu scholars with regard to Lord Krishna, and by some Buddhists about Lord Buddha.

In 1920, Paramahansa Yogananda gave a talk in Boston about yoga and mentioned Lord Jesus as a great Yogi who lived on this earth two thousand years ago. A man in the audience later wrote to him anonymously: "I was quite inspired by your speech on yoga, but you should not have mentioned Christ, as He is a mere legend."[1] Yogananda prayed to be led to this man.

One day, he walked into the Boston Public Library, approached a man who was seated reading a book, and asked him: "Sir, excuse me. Why did you write the letter stating that Christ is just a legend?" The man was stunned. "I am sorry, but how did you know that I wrote the letter? I did not mention it to anyone." "Sir, please know that the Spirit that led me to you today tells me that Christ is not a mere legend. He lived on this earth as described in the gospels," replied Yogananda.

Saints, both ancient and modern testify that Krishna, Christ and Buddha lived in this world, mingling and interacting with people, preaching the way of salvation as described in the scriptures. Their testimony should be enough for us.

1 Quotes remembered from a Self Realization Fellowship Service Reading

Paramahansa Yogananda founded an organization called Self- Realization Fellowship to carry on his teachings. Some years ago I spent two months in their Hidden Valley Ashram in Escondido, California. The monk in charge then was Brother Achalananda, a humble intellectual, with a smiling face.

Once I approached him with a problem: "Brother, for the few years I have been meditating, I have tried to cultivate devotion to Paramahansa Yogananda, but I have no special feelings towards him, I feel close only to Lord Jesus."

He chuckled a little, saying: "Is that a problem? Does it matter? When you die, not Lord Jesus or Yogananda, but Lord Buddha may come to usher you into heaven. All the great Masters are absolutely one; they share the same supreme consciousness. It does not matter to what divine form you feel close, as long as you have genuine devotion."

Christ, Krishna and Buddha are great incarnations who have come on earth as saviors of the world during different periods of history. Their statements and the convictions of their followers may appear to indicate that each one is the "sole Redeemer" of the universe.

Lord Jesus:

> "I am the Way, the Truth and the life. No one comes to the Father except through Me" (Jn.14:6). He referred to God as Father. The chief apostle Peter acknowledged His divinity with the words: "You are the Christ, the Son of the Living God." (Mt.16:16).

Lord Krishna:

> "Of this world I am the Father, the Mother, the Ancestor, the Preserver, the Sanctifier, the all-inclusive object of knowledge, the Cosmic Aum, and also the Vedic lore.
>
> (Bhagavad Gita, 9:17)

Prince Arjuna to whom Lord Krishna unveiled Himself responded:

"The Primal God art Thou! The Pristine spirit, the Final Refuge of the Worlds, the Knower and the Known, the Supreme Fulfillment! Thine Omnipresence shines in the universe, O Thou of Inexhaustible Form!

(Bhagavad Gita, 1l: 38)

Lord Buddha:

"I now desire to found the kingdom of Truth upon earth, to give light to those who are enshrouded in darkness, and to open the gate of deathlessness." (The Gospel of Buddha: XV: 4)[2]

Kondanna, the first disciple to grasp fully the doctrine of the Holy One, uttered these words:

"To the Buddha, the doctrine of the
Holy one will I look in faith.
He is the Lord of the world, who yoketh
Men like oxen, the Teacher of Gods
and men, the Exalted Buddha."

(The Gospel of Buddha: XV11:10)

There is an apparent contradiction in this. Christ, Krishna and Buddha are three different persons, yet they claim to be the one undivided Truth. How can it be?

The difficulty arises from our perception, because when we say "I," we refer to our individual ego or self, limited to a particular body, mind, and

2 The Gospel of Buddha by Paul Carus, National Book Trust, New Delhi, 1975

personality separate from other bodies, minds and personalities. The illusion of ego is our central reality.

The goal of spirituality is the loss of the illusory ego and finding one's true Self, which is the Self of all. Enlightenment or liberation is the full realization of the true Self or God Who is eternal Truth and inexhaustible, ever new Bliss.

Those who know God become one with His infinite consciousness or Truth itself. When they come back to earth as incarnations, they may assume the illusory ego slightly in order to function in this world and set an example to others. Deep inside, they are aware of their true Self.

Krishna, Buddha, and Christ spoke from their full awareness of the true Self, when they referred to themselves as the Supreme Truth. They were not speaking as individual egos, separate from others.

Problems arise when we identify the great Masters with their individual bodies or forms, and think of them as separate from others. Ammachi said: "Those devotees who think of me as merely this body only are committing a sin." Approaching an image, we see the person pictured in the image. Similarly the bodily form of an incarnation must be seen as a manifestation of infinite consciousness and energy.

We must accept humbly that we know nothing about a Master, since we operate from the illusion of an ego. We can grow in understanding little by little, as we drop the ego more and more through meditation, prayer and selfless service. Faith in a Master and surrender to Him or Her are necessary in this process.

Mere belief in a Master or confessing that Jesus is your Lord and Savior is not enough for final liberation. One must live sincerely and steadfastly according to the guidance given by the Master. Only then does belief turn into faith which alone can save us. Christ was emphatic about this when He said: "Not everyone who says to me "Lord, Lord" shall enter the kingdom of heaven, but he who does the will of my Father in heaven" [Lk.7:21].

Faith is an inner experience of peace and joy, or God's holy Presence. Our sinful habits need to be destroyed first before Truth may be experienced in the core of one's being. "Blessed are the pure of heart, for they shall see God"

[Mt.5:8]. Praying to Christ, Krishna, Buddha or other Masters for the grace of repentance and faith is a good start.

This does not mean that we have to indulge in a sense of guilt, condemning ourselves as sinners. Our attitude must be quite the contrary. Our essential nature as children of God is ever pure. We are utterly precious in the sight of God Who sees our soul as His eternally perfect image and loves us unconditionally.

Sins are superficial to us; identifying ourselves with our sinful habits reinforces them, and gives undue importance to the changing ego. Instead, we can start confidently affirming the Presence of God within us, here and now, again and again, until we begin to feel the loving Presence.

Jesus Christ

A heavenly angel announced the birth of Jesus to His mother, telling Mary that she would conceive without union with a man, and give birth to the Savior. Joseph, betrothed to her, was troubled by Mary's untimely pregnancy. An angel appeared to him in a dream to explain that Mary's pregnancy was due to the Spirit of God.

Lord Jesus was born at Bethlehem in Palestine about two thousand years ago, as an expression of the infinite love of God. An angel announced His birth to some shepherds guarding their sheep at night, advising them to go the stable and worship the holy Infant.

The birth of Jesus was celebrated by His parents, angels, shepherds and the three wise men from the East. It is still honored everywhere as Christmas with much jubilation. The hymn 'Joy to the world' aptly describes the feelings of many people during this holy season.

At age twelve His parents took Him to the great temple in Jerusalem. There was such a big crowd that the parents lost sight of Him while coming back from the temple. Going back to look for Him, they were surprised to find Him engaged in a lively discussion with some learned elders, who were amazed by the knowledge and wisdom of the child.

Jesus started His public ministry at age thirty. Unlike other preachers of that time, He spoke with the authority born of His inner experience and the consciousness of God as our loving Father. He stressed the importance of forgiving one's enemies, and loving them as well, simplifying life, living joyfully surrendered to God, and being actively compassionate towards the poor and suffering.

The power of performing miracles issued easily from Lord Jesus. He changed water into wine at the request of His Mother during a wedding reception. A few loaves of bread and fish were multiplied to feed four or five thousand people. A man born blind was given sight. The dead were raised to life. There are many more marvels mentioned in the four gospels that describe the life of Jesus so vividly.

As bees gather around a flower, disciples, both men and women, were often near the Lord, drinking the nectar of His words, and basking joyfully in His loving Presence. Twelve disciples were specially chosen by Him to spread His message. They were called apostles. Peter was their chief.

The disciples misunderstood the mission of Jesus. Being Jews, they thought that He was the promised Messiah, sent by God to free the Jews from political oppression, and establish a peaceful and righteous kingdom on this earth. Hence, when Jesus predicted that he would be persecuted and killed in Jerusalem, it shocked Peter and the other apostles.

The words and acts of Jesus antagonized the Jewish religious leaders because He ignored tradition, presenting a radically different concept of God to the people, and claiming to be one with God, which seemed to be a blasphemy to them.

When the leaders tried to stone Him for the blasphemy, His response was to say that they too were divine, quoting the scripture: 'Is it not written in your Law, "I have said, "ye are gods"'? (John 10:34) But their minds and hearts were completely closed. Therefore they plotted to kill Him with the cooperation of the Roman authorities.

The disciples scattered and hid themselves in fear when the Lord was tortured and killed on the cross. They were quite disheartened and in distress after His death. Their sadness changed to ineffable wonder and pure joy, when they realized that He had really risen from His death. He appeared to them again and again, proving that death had no power over Him.

Only then did the apostles understand that Jesus is truly one with God, and that the divine life was available to them as well, if they had genuine faith in God and sensed the presence of Christ in their hearts. Thereby they gained the courage and wisdom necessary to preach the gospel or the good news of salvation publicly.

"Father, forgive them; for they know not what they do" [Lk. 23:34], thus prayed Lord Jesus for His cruel tormentors, in the midst of His agony on the cross. It is a fundamental law that sin is followed proportionately by pain sooner or later.

Sin proceeds from inner misery which deepens further through sin. Christ was acutely conscious of the present and future misery of His enemies. Hence His prayer was a spontaneous expression of His deep compassion and love.

Christ did not focus on the evil done to Him. There was no room in His heart for self-pity, and consequent hatred. Christ did not judge, blame or condemn His tormentors. He knew that they did not understand themselves or Him.

1. They were not aware that it was their own misery that had turned into anger, hatred, and wanting to inflict pain on Christ.
2. Nor were they conscious of the karmic law that their acts of torture would eventually result in much more pain and misery for themselves.
3. The immense love that Christ had for them was beyond their ken.

Mothers love their infants dearly, as flesh of their own flesh. A million times more is Christ's love for us, because we belong to Him essentially. He is our True Self, the Heart of our hearts. The love of Christ is eternal and unchanging, hence unconditional. He can have no enemies. His love for all, whether they are saints or sinners, remains the same forever.

Christ-like Masters and their genuine disciples keep the world in equilibrium, through the power of love expressed in deep meditation, prayers, and selfless acts of service. Christ's prayer: "Father, forgive them, for they know not what they do" must be etched in our hearts as a shining light to guide our practical life, if we are keen about peace in this world.

God is not only transcendent and unchanging joy; He is also immanent, thus experiencing the pain of all creation. Perfect Masters, being one with God, experience the same pain also. It is impossible for us to imagine the amount of pain involved.

When a monk affectionately offered to share some of the pain that Ammachi was taking on Herself to relieve the burden of Her devotees, She was pleased with his intent, but told him that if She were to give him even an infinitesimal part of Her pain, he would be shattered to pieces!

Therefore the external sufferings that Lord Jesus endured are little compared to being in the heart of the pain of all creation. Masters accept such pain due to their unlimited joy and love.

Pure Consciousness is
Unlimited, pure Bliss
Creation, a bubble floating
In the vast Consciousness-ocean
Creation in immense pain
God and Masters take it in
Superficial to them, it is
Compared to the infinite Bliss
Of Supreme Consciousness.

Many Christians believe that the resurrection of Christ was a unique event. To understand the death and resurrection of Lord Jesus Christ, and place them in proper perspective, a comparison with other Masters' last moments on earth may be helpful.

Yogananda's Guru was Sri Yukteswar, who, as a young disciple had surrendered himself to the great Guru Lahiri Mahasaya. When Lahiri Mahasaya wanted to leave his body, he gathered all his devotees around him, had a banquet with them, gave them an inspiring talk, sat in a lotus posture, and consciously exited the body in meditation.[3]

His body was cremated by the disciples later in the evening. On the following day, He appeared to three of his devotees at different places, at the same time, namely ten o'clock in the morning, and talked with them, as described in the *Autobiography of a Yogi.*

Paramahansa Yogananda was meditating at his Los Angeles headquarters, when he heard the voice of his Guru Sri Yukteswar: "Return to India. Soon I shall swim out of the body and on to the shining abode. Yogananda come." Gladly heeding the request of his Master, Yogananda reached Bombay by ship in August 1935.

Sri Yuketeswar was perfectly healthy when he met with Yogananda. Though he was quite well on March 9, 1936, Sri Yukteswar, after intimating to his disciples that he was leaving the body, sat in a lotus posture in meditation, and passed away peacefully.

On June 19, 1936, at the Regent Hotel in Bombay, Yogananda saw the fleshly form of Sri Yukteswar, and embraced him tightly in an excess of joy. They conversed together for many hours; Sri Yukteswar explained about life in different astral worlds, good and evil spirits, and how he was helping advanced souls towards full liberation in an astral world called Hiranyaloka. He instructed Yogananda to tell others about his resurrection.[4]

Great Masters like Lahiri Mahasaya and Sri Yukteswar were perfectly one with God in their consciousness. Hence they were not bound to any material form. They could manifest themselves to earthly beings through one or more forms, and were free to abandon such forms as needed or to adopt new forms after death.

Lord Jesus also had the same divine consciousness, and consequent control over His death and resurrection. After His death, only His body was confined to the grave, but He Himself was free, and ever alive. "Today, thou shalt be with me in paradise," He told the repentant robber on the cross.

---

3 Autobiography of a Yogi, pp. 395-398

4 ibid, pp.475-496

Christ was always in paradise, being consciously one with God. Transfiguration, when he appeared to Peter, James and John, gloriously conversing with Moses and Elias, was merely an external manifestation of His constant consciousness.

Manifestation of His Presence to the disciples after His death was entirely under His control. Christ was not identified with any particular body, and could create body or bodies to manifest Himself according to the needs of His devotees.

Mary Magdalene was a close disciple who did not recognize the Lord, and mistook Him for a gardener until He called her by name. It means she saw a different body initially. The disciples on the road to Emmaus encountered the same problem. They did not know Him while He walked with them and explained the Scriptures to them. They came to understand that He was the Lord, only when He broke bread with them later.

The great sacrifice for Christ was not death, but being confined to the body in conception, birth and earthly life. He accepted the limitations of a human body for thirty three years, out of His immense love for us. Freeing Himself from the body through death, the Lord revealed Himself to receptive people, choosing His own time and form of manifestation. He appeared as glorious and bright light to St. Paul, and ever since, has manifested Himself to thousands of devotees numerous times.

Over many centuries, not only great saints but simple devotees of Lord Krishna, in thousands, have testified to seeing Him as a playful child, youth and adult, hearing the sweet music of His flute, and conversing with overflowing love.

Lord Jesus praised the faith of the centurion, because he acknowledged the omnipresence and omnipotence of Christ, with the words, "Lord, I am not worthy that You should come under my roof; but, say the word and my servant shall be healed." [Mt.8:8] Christ did heal the servant without going to his house. His omnipresence did not cease with His death.

Therefore His rising on the third day, and ascending to heaven after forty days, are merely external and symbolic expressions of spiritual truths. Death, resurrection, and ascension of Christ signify our death to sin, rising to a new, divine life, which is the same as ascending to a life with our Divine Father/Mother in heaven. This symbolism has value to all human beings, and not merely to Christians.

Saints, including Christian saints like Padre Pio for example are known to have appeared in two different places at the same time. It is called bilocation. Yogananda has written about his experience as a youth with a saint who manifested bilocation.[5]

This phenomenon shows that the saints are conscious of being pure spirits that can assume or manifest through one or more bodies as they want. When the gopis who were madly in love with Lord Krishna yearned that He be near them personally, He manifested Himself in many bodies, dancing with each gopi at the same time.

The resurrection of Christ means that He continues to live, and manifested Himself to others on this earth after His death. These facts are not unique to Christ. Some Christians believe that the bodily resurrection of Christ is so central to Christian faith that it would collapse without the facts of empty tomb and so on. They forget that Christ is far beyond birth, death and resurrection, which were mere phenomena.

St. Paul gave much importance to Christ's resurrection, responding to people who did not accept life after death. The focus of faith should be Christ Himself and His consciousness, which is infinite and eternal, transcending time and space. "Before Abraham was, I am," He said. With these words He affirmed His eternal presence. What are death and resurrection to such a One?

Christ as God is omnipresent. He shines as peace, love and joy in all human beings, animals, plants and the whole universe. The main obstacle to experiencing the omnipresence of Christ is the habit of negative judgments.

This habit arose as a result of negative conditioning from early childhood. When we learn to let go of judgments, and accept the eternal, unconditional love of Christ for us, the consequent sense of peace and joy will enable us to love ourselves as well as others. Pure love is union with everyone and everything in Christ.

---

5 ibid, pp.26-33

Lord Krishna

Five thousand years ago, Mathura in India was ruled by a tyrant, King Kamsa who had close contact with evil spirits, and was informed that he would be killed by his nephew. When his sister Devaki gave birth to a beautiful male baby, the child's father, Vasudeva, knowing that Kamsa was intent on killing the infant, brought him immediately to the village Gokula.

The village chieftan, Nanda, and his wife Yasoda, were the blessed foster parents of the divine child. The baby radiated such beauty and bliss that milkmaids (*gopis*) and cowherds (*gopalas*) from the village were drawn to the house of Yasoda, to fondle and play with the baby, or just watch him with love. Yasoda was beside herself with happiness as she nursed the baby, keeping the child on her lap.

The child was only three months old, when Yasoda was looking tenderly at his cherubic face. He opened his mouth as if to yawn, and Yasoda was amazed to see the whole universe – sky, earth, stars, planets, sun, moon, oceans, and rivers – inside his mouth. Then she realized that her baby was indeed the Supreme Ruler of the universe.

Vasudeva sent the sage Varga to Gokula so that he could name the baby. Realizing how the child had captured the hearts of all the people in the village, Varga called him Krishna, meaning "the stealer of hearts".

King Kamsa, intent on finding the whereabouts of Devaki's child in order to eliminate him, called on demons to assist him in this venture. Three demons went to Gokula in different guises at various times to kill the child. Instead, they were destroyed miraculously.

Once the child started walking, he ran into so much mischief that Yasoda had to run behind him constantly to protect him. The gopis could not stay away from Krishna; with Yasoda's consent, they would bring him to their homes, and feed him the milk, butter, and curd that he seemed to enjoy very much.

There were days when the Gopis saw the child Krishna stealing butter and curd, sometimes making holes in the pots, to feed the other boys, cats and monkeys that followed him everywhere. He would run away when the gopis tried to catch him, with a guilty look on his face.

The gopis went to Yasoda to complain about the theft, and wondered how he could be there at her home playing innocently, giving them occasionally a knowing look. Yasoda could not fathom their complaints, since Krishna had not left her during this time. Yet she compensated the gopis for the damage they had suffered.

The villagers were concerned that King Kamsa had come to know that Krishna was in Gokula. An elder suggested that the whole village should move to the nearby forest. Soon the forest was converted into a fertile garden called Vrindavan, not unlike the Garden of Eden.

Vrindavan was truly a paradise for the villagers, as they enjoyed the delightful company of child Krishna, herding their cows with other boys, playing exquisite music on his flute, and dancing with the young and the old.

Several miracles were performed by Krishna to protect the villagers. Once there was a large forest fire that threatened to engulf Vrindavan, but Krishna ran towards the fire, and made it disappear by swallowing it.

Many days of torrential rain were about to wash away Vrindavan in a huge flood. The villagers' prayers to all the gods were of no avail. In desperation they went to Krishna, who lifted the nearby mountain Gowardhan and held it aloft, to protect the villagers until the rains abated.

The *gopis* (milkmaids) had poured their heart out to Krishna from his infancy. As He grew to be a charming, playful boy and later into a powerful young man at age twelve, the maidens' love for Him increased exponentially to become a passionate romance, yearning intensely that He become their spouse and lover. "In whatsoever way people approach me, in that same guise I will go to them, for people approach me in many ways," Lord Krishna said to Arjuna in the Bhagavad-Gita.

Hearing the magical sound of His flute, the gopis ran to Him, leaving the tasks they were involved in. In order to test their love for Him, the Lord advised them to go back to their husbands and homes. "To have an illicit relationship with a lover is a bar to heaven and a stain on one's reputation on earth. By thinking of Me and meditating on Me, you will attain a high state of spiritual love, which is far better than physical love.

Go back to the security of your own homes therefore, or else be forever branded as abandoned women, crazy with love for Krishna."[6]

Only a soul that is constant in its love for God in spite of the darkness of trials, tribulations, and a sense of abandonment, can attain perfect union. This has been true in the lives of all the saints. The gopis were sad and confused. "Hearing the enthralling melody of Your flute, who is the woman who will not be charmed, and drawn away from the path of duty? Therefore, O Manamohana, charmer of winds, please place Your cool, fragrant, lotus like palms on our fevered heads and assuage the heat within our hearts."[7]

With these words, they sank to the ground in a state of despair. The Lord lifted them, wiping away their tears with the tip of His yellow garment, and brought them to the banks of river Yamuna, where they could play the game of love. They sat around Him, stroking His limbs, hair and face, kissing Him softly, as He gazed on them with love.

Then in their minds occurred the proud thought that they were so clever and charming, as to attract the Lord Himself. Immediately He disappeared from their midst, and the forest became dark and menacing, with wild beasts howling at night.

The gopis' pain of separation from Krishna was intense and unbearable again. They roamed the forest, looking for Him in earnest. Suddenly they realized that Radha, the greatest lover among them, was missing, and realized that she had gone away with Krishna.

As the gopis continued their search, singing and crying in agony, the Lord reappeared among them. "How could you think that I had left you?" tenderly He asked. "At every step you took, I took one beside you. Every time you faltered I held you up. How else do you think you have remained safe in this jungle, infested with wild creatures at this time of night?"[8]

He brought them again to the banks of Yamuna; as they caressed Him, He explained to them the nature of perfect love. Then He led them in a mystical dance known as "Rasalila," where Krishna took many forms to dance with each

6 The Play of God by Vanamali, Blue Dove Press, San Diego, California, 1998 p.70. Lord Krishna comes alive with a divine beauty in this deeply spiritual book.

7 ibid, p.71

8 ibid, p.75

gopi at the same time, while He stood in the center playing the flute. Each gopi felt that she was alone with the Lord, so perfect was their concentration. In the perfection of their selfless love, they were not two but one; He alone existed.

Soon Krishna had to depart from Vrindavan to Mathura. His parents, Devaki and Vasudeva, were held as prisoners in a dungeon. Kamsa kept his own father, Krishna's grandfather, Ugrasena too as a prisoner. Krishna killed Kamsa and released them all.

His parents, who had been unable to express their love for Krishna for the past twelve years, embraced Him with tears. So did His grandfather Ugrasena who was installed as the King of Mathura. Kamsa had been thinking of Krishna day and night with fear and hatred, though he had an unquenchable thirst for final freedom. Hence the Lord granted him liberation due to his intense concentration.

Lord Krishna did not go back to His beloved gopis, foster parents, cowherd companions, and all the people of Gokula. Their days were spent reminiscing about Krishna with songs, plays and acts of worship.

Many princesses from various kingdoms in India were the ardent devotees of Lord Krishna. Rukmini was a princess who pined constantly for Lord Krishna. As a king, Lord Krishna could take many wives. He married them all, including princess Rukmini.

While speaking to His wives, He extolled the greatness and purity of the gopis, especially Radha as examples of perfect love, and invited the gopis to spend a day and night at the palace. Rukmini and the other queens saw that the humble gopis had no interest in worldly riches or beauty, but were intent only on hearing about Krishna or talking about Him. Then they humbly realized that the gopis were indeed the greatest devotees of the Lord.

According to Srimad Bhagavatam, the Hindu scripture of devotion, "those who meditate on the divine love of Krishna, and upon the sweet relationship between Him and the gopis, become free from lust and sensuality."[9]

Reading and reflecting about the gopis' love for Lord Krishna, one can easily start crying for God. Ammachi often stresses the crucial importance

9 Srimad Bhagavatam, Translated by Swami Prabhavananda, Capricorn Books, New York,1968, p.200

of crying for God, as five minutes of such crying is equivalent to an hour of meditation.

Krishna's love for the gopis and His many wives was expressed with total detachment. They realized that He was a perfect celibate and a true ascetic, in spite of engaging in love-play.

Similarly the Lord was involved in many battles where He killed His "enemies." But there was no fear, anger, or hatred in His heart. His eyes never stopped twinkling with a serene smile that lingered around His lips as well. How could the Lord stop loving everyone, as He is their true Self?

Lord Buddha

Twenty-five hundred years ago, King Sudhodana and Queen Mayadevi of Kapilavastu in Nepal, were blessed with a son named Siddhartha. Angels from heaven attended on the mother during childbirth, informing her that the child would be a great Master and Redeemer of mankind.

The king summoned the sage, Asita, who told him that his son was destined to become a savior to the whole world. Mayadevi knowing that she would soon depart from this world, asked her sister, Pajapati, to take care of the future Buddha, and her husband. Shedding copious tears, Pajapati agreed. Later she married the King, and was a loving stepmother to Siddhartha.

He was handsome and brilliant, yet pensive and quiet, spending much time meditating under a jambu tree. The king's kinsfolk feared that if they gave their daughters in marriage to Siddhartha, he would not be able to protect his wife or the kingdom. Siddhartha resolved this problem by asking his father the king to organize a competition, where he proved that the whole of India had none equal to him in bodily strength, fighting skills, mental acumen and knowledge.

His cousin, Yasohdhara, loved him deeply. They were happily married, and had a son named Rahula. King Sudhodana thought that his son's love for his wife and child would keep him bound to the family and the kingdom. He built a beautiful, luxurious palace to let them live in comfort amidst worldly pleasures, cut off from the normal hardships and sorrows of the world.

But the prince wanted to see the world. The king arranged for the city to be decorated, as the prince rode through its streets with his charioteer Channa. By the roadside they met an old man with wrinkled face and sorrowful mien. The prince asked Channa the reason for such an appearance. Reluctantly Channa explained that the man had been a child and a healthy youth once, but had become old, and was showing the normal symptoms of an advanced age. Siddhartha was moved deeply by the phenomenon of old age.

Then they moved through many beautiful scenes, but on the way-side saw a sick man, body disfigured, gasping for breath, and groaning in pain. Channa explained to Siddhartha that sickness was not uncommon among people. This fact disturbed the prince even more.

As they continued on through various streets, they were stopped by a funeral procession carrying a corpse. The prince shuddered at the sight of a lifeless body. Channa told him that death was the inevitable end to all human life. The phenomenon of death affected Siddhartha's mind and heart to the core. Seeing that Siddhartha was so disturbed, Channa turned the chariot around to go back to the palace.

His wife pleaded with the prince to explain the reasons for his profound distress. He said that everywhere he saw the impression of change, and his heart was heavy to see that people grow old, sicken and die. It was enough to take away his zest of life.

That night the prince sat under the jambu tree to meditate, and had a vision in which he was told that he was born to deliver mankind from the wheel of sorrow, by becoming the Buddha, and finding the life that knows no beginning or end.

He walked back to his bedroom, determined to cut clean all his ties to the family and the world. Looking at his sleeping wife and child, whom he loved deeply, tears flowed freely as he wrenched himself away from them. He never looked back while he walked out of the palace. He cut his long hair and cast off his royal garment for a rough gray cloth.

First he went to two famous Brahmin teachers who taught from the Hindu Scriptures. He could not accept their doctrines and explanations. He found the animal sacrifices in the temples offensive, wondering how a new wrong could expiate old wrongs. Certainly the slaughter of an innocent animal cannot blot out the evil deeds of mankind.

Determined to find the true path towards enlightenment, he wandered until he came to a jungle where he found five ascetics, given to rigorous discipline and severe austerities. He joined them, and practiced meditation and mortification of the body with such zeal, that they considered him their master, though he was junior in age.

After six years of torturing himself, he found his body to be quite weak and his mind nowhere near the goal. Deciding to give up this mode of life, he was walking away when he fainted due to weakness and hunger. The five ascetics left him, thinking that he was dead. A herdsman's daughter called Nanda offered him rice-milk, and he revived; he started taking more food from Nanda. The five ascetics saw the change in their Master's behavior, and left him thinking that he had lost his purpose.

Siddhartha chose the middle path, renouncing both extremes of asceticism and worldly indulgence. He seated himself under a Bo tree, determined to find the truth through meditation. Under the Bo tree Siddhartha's consciousness expanded, and he was enlightened as to the true nature of reality. He found the ego, the sense of being separate from others and subject to numerous desires and vanity, to be altogether illusory, and awareness to be changeless, with no beginning or end. Thus he became Lord Buddha, his face shining with an unearthly light and pure joy.

He sought out the five austere ascetics who had renounced him, and did not care for him when he appeared to be dead. He went to Benares in search of them. They were astonished to see the lustrous body and the luminous face of their former Master, and bowed to Him in awe.

He explained to them the importance of following a middle path between worldliness and extreme asceticism. "Sensuality is enervating; the self-indulgent man is a slave to his passions, and pleasure seeking is degrading and vulgar.

"But to satisfy the necessities of life is not evil. To keep the body in good health is a duty, for otherwise we shall not be able to trim the lamp of wisdom, and keep our mind strong and clear.

"He who recognizes the existence of suffering, its cause, its remedy and its cessation has fathomed the four noble truths.

By the practice of loving kindness I have attained liberation of heart...I have even now attained Nirvana."[10]

These five disciples became the nucleus of a spiritual community that expanded quickly. Thousands wanted to gain liberation by following the teachings and example of Lord Buddha, who stressed right moral behavior, right thinking and mindfulness as the way towards liberation. According to Ammachi, spirituality can be summed up in one word: mindfulness. When we are deeply mindful, we become aware of the connection between inordinate desires, base thoughts and consequent misery. Evil habits then become weaker and drop off gradually.

Back in Kapilavastu, King Sudhodana heard that his son was now the famous Lord Buddha, compassionate, and caring about the ills of mankind. He sent a messenger requesting the Lord to come and see His father and teach the true doctrine to His relatives. The Blessed One agreed.

Suddhodana went out with his ministers and relatives to receive his son. He rejoiced to see the great change in Siddhartha, who appeared to be full of peace, joy, beauty and dignity. Yet the father was also sad at losing his son and the heir to the throne.

Lord Buddha consoled his father, acknowledging the great love the royal parent had for the renouncing son, and the consequent sorrow. He explained how the king could open his heart equally to others, and find the joy of Nirvana.

Profoundly affected by the Buddha's words, the King shed tears of joy. His heart had endured years of sorrow after his son resolutely renounced family and worldly life. Now that the father experienced the wonderful fruits of the son's renunciation, he was content to let the Buddha wander around the country preaching the way of salvation to others.

The king returned to the palace, Buddha stayed in a grove outside the city. On the following morning, he went to the city with a bowl in hand begging for alms. Hearing about it, the king hastened to remonstrate to his son

10 The Gospel of Buddha by Paul Carus, pp.42-45

for disgracing him. Surely He knew that the king could supply Him and His disciples with all the food they needed. The enlightened prince told the king that the sacred tradition of begging for food, and living on alms, belonged to the ancient line of Buddhas, from which he had descended.

The father brought the Lord to the palace to be greeted by the members of the royal family; Siddharta's wife, Yasodhara, was not among them. The king sent for her, but she refused to come. Then Buddha went to her apartment with two disciples, and saw that she was still in deep grief after seven years. She had shaved her head like her husband, given up all luxury, and was living like a recluse. When she saw Buddha, unable to contain herself, Yasodhara held His feet, and wept bitterly.

The Blessed One spoke to her kindly, telling her how she had assisted Him in former lives when He was a Bodhisattva, and that her present noble attitude would change her sorrows into heavenly joy. Not only Sudhodana and Yasodhara, but also Buddha's half-brother, Nanda, and cousins, Ananda and Devadatta, accepted the Lord as their Master.

A few days later, Yasodhara dressed her seven-year old son, Rahula, in splendor, and sent him to Buddha to claim the spiritual heritage from his father. After blessing the child, Buddha left the palace; but Rahula followed Him, insisting on receiving his inheritance. Realizing that the child was determined to endure all the difficulties of the spiritual path, Buddha accepted him as a monk.

Yasodhara, too, wanted to join the Sangha [Buddha's spiritual community] and be a nun, but Buddha refused her request three times as there were no women in the Sangha yet. When His stepmother, Pajapati, and several other women went with Yasodhara to request admission, He started a nunnery for them.

Lord Buddha walked throughout India preaching his gospel of peace and compassion to thousands. Many found the noble path of liberation by listening to his enlightening words and being inspired by the power of his divine example. Once, during His travel, He came to a temple where some people were enthusiastically attending to a religious ceremony. The local prince was presiding over it, and a lamb was about to be sacrificed as part of the ceremony.

Buddha's heart wept at the plight of the lamb. He pleaded with the prince to release the lamb, and to sacrifice him instead. The prince and his subjects were so moved by Lord Buddha's compassion, they not only spared the lamb, but sacrificed their own minds and hearts to the Enlightened One. They became his ardent followers.

Lord Buddha taught that self is an illusion. Realizing this truth one can attain liberation, as there would be nothing to hold the desires and attachments. "Anatta," meaning non-self, or no-soul is central to Buddhism.

Christ said: "What does it profit a man if he gains the whole world, and suffers the loss of his own soul?" [Mk.8:36] Finding the soul is salvation for Christ, whereas loss of the soul is liberation for Buddha. How can there be such a contradiction between the essential teachings of Masters?

Lord Krishna in Bhagavad Gita, Chapter VI, verse 7 says "The tranquil sage, victorious over the self (ego), is ever fully established in the Supreme Self (Spirit), whether he encounters cold or heat, pleasure or pain, praise or blame."[11]

The problem here is not due to some philosophical differences among the Masters. It is a matter of semantics. The word 'Self' is used with varied, or almost opposite meaning. Loss or negation of the lower self (false and illusory) is necessary to attain the higher Self or the Soul. Desires that bind man, manifesting as pride and self-hatred, flow from the lower self or the ego. The lower self separates itself from others through superiority or inferiority complexes. The higher self or the soul, on the other hand, being a reflection of the Supreme Self or God, is a realization of the fundamental unity of everyone and everything.

"Soul is in a sense everything," said Aristotle. To be everything, we have to be nothing, as the mystical poet St. John of the Cross would say. That means "anatta" (no-self). While understanding the meaning of anatta in its proper context, it is important not to be rigidly dogmatic, and deny the different meanings and values possible for the same word as used by other Masters. We

11 Translated by Paramahansa Yogananda in his book, God Talks with Arjuna, SRF, LA, 1995, p.599

will explore the concept of Self further in the chapter on Ramana Maharshi, a modern sage.

Anatta (no-self, non-identity) is a gloriously liberating concept. Identification with a country, language, religion, race, profession, or even a body is a matter of social convention, and not a permanent reality. Fortunately with the process of globalization, an increasing number of people are not giving importance to such identifications. If I am nothing, I am free to be everything.

There is a grave misunderstanding about Lord Buddha among some people. They say that He refused to answer questions about God, hence His teachings are supposed to be atheistic. Hindu scriptures teach that God is Satchidananda, meaning Truth-Awareness-Bliss.

Being an embodiment of Truth-Awareness-Bliss, Lord Buddha emphasized discrimination, detachment, moderation, meditation, mindfulness, devotion, faith, love, compassion, and peace, as necessary for liberation. Can there be any better way to find God, Who is ineffable joy and wisdom? "Be still and know that I am God" (Psalm 46:10). Silence or Nirvana is another name for God.

Lord Buddha continues to transform the minds and hearts of people all over the world, through many renowned Buddhist teachers in the modern era. The most influential among them are the Dalai Lama, and Thich Nhat Hanh, who valiantly espoused non-violence in Vietnam, during its horrendous war.

Christ, Krishna, Buddha and all the Masters share the same Supreme Consciousness of which we also are a part, though not aware of it. Their only intent is to extend that awareness to us all, and make us realize our oneness with them, in love and joy.

> *"He reviled me; he injured me; he defeated me; he robbed me." In those who harbor such thoughts, hatred never ceases.*
>
> *"He reviled me; he injured me; he defeated me; he robbed me." In those who do not harbor such thoughts, hatred ceases.*

Hatred is never appeased by hatred in this world; it is appeased by love. This is an eternal law.

One should not pry into the faults of others, into things done and left undone by others. One should rather consider what by oneself is done and left undone.

Dhammapada
(Words of Lord Buddha)

Mata Amritanandamayi

AMMACHI

Ammachi, also known as Mata Amritanandamayi, is an amazing manifestation of utterly pure and selfless love, comforting and consoling those who come to Her in the thousands, wiping their tears and Her own tears. She pours Her heart out so much, that to stay in Her presence is to witness a continuous miracle. Even strangers are moved to tears of joy, as they see Her ministering to the sick and the old, small children and the teens.

She was born on September 27, 1953 at Vallikavu, a fishing village located on the South-Western coast of India.[1] Her parents named her Sudhamani. She did not cry at birth like other children. Instead, she had a bright smile and a penetrating gaze at her mother. Her complexion was dark blue. That is the color of Lord Krishna and Mother Kali, according to Hindu Scriptures. Sudhamani's parents were not aware of the sacred significance of the color blue. They thought that the child was sick, and brought her to many doctors, who could not find any other symptom to indicate an illness.

After a few months the blue color faded away, and Sudhamani remained dark in complexion. At the age of six months, she surprised the people around her, by walking and running easily. Then she started talking clearly in her native tongue Malayalam.

As she grew up, she chanted beautiful songs that she herself composed spontaneously to Lord Krishna. She would sit in deep meditation or ecstasy, totally lost to this world. Occasionally she had what appeared to be fainting

1 The basic facts about her life are taken from the official biography titled AMMACHI by Swami Amritaswarupananda, M.A. Center, San Ramon, California, 1994.

fits, falling to the ground unconscious, rolling around crying and laughing, due to divine ecstasy.

The parents could not make any sense of her behavior, and considered her insane. They had never seen anyone behave like this, nor did they have much understanding of spirituality, in spite of being very religious. Neither the parents nor the villagers were aware that Sudhamani was steeped in divine bliss.

Sudhamani was treated like a crazy servant at home. She woke up very early to clean the pots and pans, sweep the house and the compound, prepare meals, feed her siblings, and get them ready to go to school. Though a bright student, she stopped going to school in fourth grade, since her mother fell sick, and was unable to do the household tasks. Sudhamani's chores were endless. She took care of the cows and other domestic animals, finding food for them and keeping them clean. She also cared for the sick and the elderly from neighboring houses, bathing and feeding them.

Her heart bled for the poor even when she was a child. She would take food from her house to feed them. Once she gave the golden bangle of her mother to a poor man, to sell and relieve his dire poverty. Though beaten severely for this act and similar deeds, Sudhamani continued to behave in the same manner.

She was in the habit of chanting the divine names of Lord Krishna, and visualizing Him everywhere, while she was busy with her chores. Her nights were spent mostly in soulful songs to the Lord, and ecstatic meditation in communion with Him. Children from the neighborhood were fond of Sudhamani, as she would lead them in singing devotional songs to the Lord, and acting out various scenes from the life of Lord Krishna.

Responding to the demands of relatives, Sudhamani, now a teenager was sent to work as a servant in their homes. Though extremely hard working, she continued her spiritual practices, and also taking food items to feed the poor, in spite of severe punishment by the relatives. Her family was humiliated by the bad name she brought upon them, being branded as a "crazy thief."

When she returned home, the cruel treatment by her mother and elder brother, Subhagan, increased even more. He was an angry young man, bent on controlling others, especially women. Sudhamani's singing and dancing in divine ecstasy infuriated him. Though he heaped abusive words on her, and often beat her up, Sudhamani showed no fear or change in her behavior.

She never allowed her pain to turn into resentment even slightly. Instead, she would bring her sorrows to Lord Krishna, telling Him about the cruelty of the people around her. As the intensity of her devotion to the Lord increased, He favored her with many visions, playing and dancing with her at nights. Eventually she realized her complete identity with the Lord.

The bliss of her divine union was hidden from others, until she revealed it partially in September 1975 during her first "Krishna Bava," which means manifesting the appearance and the mood of Lord Krishna in her own body. As Sudhamani assumed Krishna Bava regularly near a small banyan tree outside her house, devotees of the Lord went in ever greater numbers to this place, not only to see the Lord, but also to talk about their problems and sorrows, and ask for relief. After Sudhamani listened to them, and occasionally gave specific instructions, their distress would often vanish immediately, or a few days later.

During this period, there was a cobra that used to move around the area freely and terrify the villagers. One day, this cobra approached the spot where Sudhamani was giving Krishna Bava. People moved aside in fear. To their horror, Sudhamani caught the cobra, touched its flicking tongue with her own tongue, and released it. The venomous snake crawled away quickly, and never troubled the people again.

As the number of devotees attending the Bava increased, it provoked strong opposition from the people who wanted to stop this religious fervor at any cost. They gathered about a thousand youths from neighboring villages, and organized themselves as "The Committee to Remove Blind Beliefs." These people not only employed nefarious tactics to harass and abuse Sudhamani, but also tried to kill her several times.

The miraculous failure of their attempts to destroy her, and Sudhamani's courageous and peaceful acceptance of the prolonged persecution, eventually convinced the opponents that she was divinely protected. Some of the inimical leaders were transformed to become her ardent devotees later.

Sudhamani could not continue with her devotional exercises, as she felt not merely united, but identified with the Lord. One day, she had a vision that changed her profoundly. She saw the enchanting form of Divine Mother in a radiant light. From that time on, her longing to see the Mother again and merge into Her was so intense, that she could not eat or sleep, let alone do the normal chores, though she was able to conduct the Krishna Bava regularly.

As Sudhamani later recalled, "while walking I would repeat the Divine Name with each and every step. Always the next step was made only after chanting the mantra. If ever I forgot to chant the mantra while taking a step, immediately I would step backwards. Having withdrawn the step I would repeat the mantra. Only then would I proceed. The mantra which I used to chant was Amma, Amma." [Meaning Mother, Mother][2]

Since Sudhamani had perceived everything as pervaded by Lord Krishna, when she used to yearn for Him, and could think of nothing else, so too now, she felt the presence of Devi (Goddess) everywhere, though hiding Herself in all things. Once, in that mood, she crawled like a baby towards a coconut tree, and sat there pleading with tears, "Mother, my Mother! Why are you hiding from my sight? I know that you are hiding in this tree. You are in these plants, you are residing in these animals, these birds! The earth is nothing but you. O Mother, how You conceal Yourself in the ocean waves, and in the cooling breeze! O Mother, my elusive Mother!"[3]

In moods of extreme fervor and ecstatic flights of the soul, she would be found unconscious, covered with mud, on the ocean beach or in backwaters, and was nursed back to normal consciousness by a few friendly villagers.

Sudhamani could not eat the food from her house during the days of intense yearning for Divine Mother. One day she came out after meditation, thirsty and hungry. Lying in front was a cow from her house. It had its rear legs in a position, as if inviting her to drink the milk from its udders. Accepting it as God's arrangement, Sudhamani did exactly that to quench her thirst and hunger. From then on, the cow made sure to feed Sudhamani daily, before grazing or giving milk to its own calf. Family members tried hard to chase the cow away, but were not successful.

---

2 AMMACHI, pp.113 - 114

3 ibid, p.113

When Sudhamani sat outdoors and was immersed in meditation, snakes were seen to coil around her body. She loved parrots. One day a devotee presented a parrot to her. This parrot and two pigeons sat in front of her, and when Sudhamani sang to Divine Mother, the birds were seen to dance to the tune of the songs. Many animals were strongly attached to Amma, and served Her during these days of intense sadhana (spiritual exercises).

Later She recalled: "Strangely enough these animals could understand my feelings and act accordingly. If I cried, they also would join me in crying. If I sang, they would dance in front of me. When I lost my external consciousness, they would crawl over my body. When one gets rid of all attachment and aversion and attains equal vision, then even hostile animals will become friendly in one's presence."[4]

Sudhamani's unspeakable agony in yearning for Divine Mother reached its zenith when her voice choked and breathing stopped. She fell unconscious. That was the moment chosen by the Divine Enchantress to reveal Herself. She appeared to her, dazzling like a million suns, as Sudhamani's heart overflowed with love and bliss. Sudhamani described her experience in Her composition: "The Path of Bliss."

> The Divine Mother, with bright, gentle hands,
> Caressed my head. With bowed head, I told
> Mother that my life is dedicated to Her.
> Smiling, She became a Divine Effulgence
> And merged in me...
> Mother told me to ask the people
> To fulfill their human birth.
> Therefore I proclaim to the whole world
> The sublime truth that She uttered,
> "Oh, man, merge in your Self."[5]

---

4 ibid, p.135

5 ibid, p 141

After a few days spent in joyful seclusion, Sudhamani heard an inner voice say: "My child, I dwell in the hearts of all beings and have no fixed abode. Your birth is not for merely enjoying the unalloyed Bliss of the Self, but for comforting suffering humanity. Henceforth worship Me in the hearts of all beings, and relieve them of the sufferings of worldly existence."[6]

Then in addition to Krishna Bava, She started manifesting Devi Bava, expressing the feminine or motherly aspect of God. In the mood of Divine Mother, Sudhamani was equally affectionate and comforting to all the devotees that flocked to see Her. She would embrace them all, men and women alike, and speak lovingly with them. This was a huge shock to the villagers; they thought She was insane. In Kerala, a young woman was not supposed to talk with men, let alone touch them. Family members were ashamed of Her unconventional behavior.

So enraged was Her brother, Subhagan, that he arranged with his cousins to kill Her. When they confronted her, brandishing a sharp knife, Sudhamani calmly offered to die if they gave Her a few minutes to meditate. This angered them even more. One cousin jumped forward with the knife, bringing it to Her chest, as if to stab Her, but he could not move further, and fell back in agony, with acute pain on the same spot in his body.

He was taken to a hospital where his condition deteriorated in spite of the best medical treatment. Sudhamani visited him at the hospital to comfort him, and fed him with her own hands. He burst into tears, remorseful for his criminal act, and deeply aware of the love and compassion of his cousin. Later, he died.

The power and beauty of divine romance is far greater than worldly romance. Strong, handsome, educated young men from wealthy families, who could easily have found rich, beautiful women as romantic partners, instead, suddenly found themselves madly in love with a poor, illiterate young woman, so that separation from Her was unbearable anguish.

They could not understand what had happened to them or why, but there was no way to resist the purity, innocence, humility and the overflowing love of the Divine Mother, manifested in Sudhamani. Feeling blissful in Her holy Presence, they were miserable when forced to be away from Her.

---

6 ibid, pp.142 - 143

Balu, Rao, Ramakrishnan, an American named Neal, and two young women from Australia were among the renunciants who initially formed the nucleus of an ashram around Amma. Living conditions were rather austere. No comfortable place to sit or sleep, hardly any food to eat. Amma instructed them to spend eight hours in daily meditation, chant for long hours, and toil hard in manual work to build up the ashram.

Now it has expanded to house about a thousand monks and nuns, besides the thousands of householder devotees, who spend weeks or months staying at Amritapuri Ashram. It is scenically situated: a beautiful temple sits in front of a huge hall near a few high-rise buildings, surrounded by many coconut palms. The Indian Ocean is on one side, the bay waters on the other.

Miracles abound around Amma, the most significant miracle being the profound transformation of Her sincere devotees. Shayma was a small child with whom Amma used to play. One day Shayma suffered from a severe asthmatic attack; her grandmother immediately rushed the child to a hospital, but it was too late. Grandmother could not bear to hear the doctors say that the child was dead. Overwhelmed with grief, she brought the child to the ashram, and laid the body on Mother's sacred seat in the temple, since Amma was away in a villager's house.

Amma suddenly stopped Her devotional chanting, and hurried back to the temple. Grandmother cried pleading that Amma should save the child. Mother took the child, and then sat down, keeping the child on her lap. She meditated for a long time. The little girl revived slowly, and opened her eyes. Tears of joy flowed profusely from the grandmother, as she embraced Amma lovingly.

The most moving and inspiring of all Mother's miracles was her treatment and cure of Dattan the leper. His leprosy was so advanced, with putrid-smelling wounds all over his body oozing blood and pus, that even other leprous beggars avoided him. With mere slits for eyes and a hole for the nose, he could hardly see, or find food for himself; he felt that everybody despised him.

Miserable and desperate, Dattan wandered around, and came one day to the ashram, hearing of Amma. People tried to chase him away, but Mother directed that he should wait outside, until the end of the program. Sending most of the devotees out, Amma received Dattan lovingly, and embraced him as Her own dear child.

Afterwards She started licking his wounds, sucking the blood and pus, and spitting it out. Then She gave him a bath, pouring pots of water on his head. Smearing sacred ash all over his body, Amma's love and compassion towards Dattan was boundless.

The reaction of the few who witnessed Amma with Dattan was varied. Some fainted at the chilling sight, others vomited due to disgust, whereas Her close disciples wept with love and devotion at the extraordinary manifestation of Divine Mother's unbounded compassion towards Her child.

This treatment continued for three days a week at the end of the Bava program. After a month, Dattan was completely cured and appeared to be a new man, acceptable to society. Amma could have cured him instantly with a mere thought, but then we would have missed an opportunity to realize that Amma took Her present form mainly to manifest the unlimited love and compassion of God for suffering humanity.

In 1987, Amma started on her world tour to bless Her thousands of devotees in Europe, America, Japan and Australia. It is a blessed sight to observe Her sitting at a stretch, for long hours night and day, receiving Her children with love, and hugging each person who comes to Her affectionately.

Healings from serious illnesses like cancer when there was no hope from medical treatment, miraculous escapes from disasters that should have been fatal, such are the many amazing stories that one hears from Amma's followers.

My sister-in-law, Soruba, lives with her two daughters and husband Sri Rangan in Paris. Soruba laughs while she talks about Rangan becoming a happy little child in the presence of Amma, as She plays with him and assures him of Her protection.

He told me that he experienced an extraordinary manifestation of Amma's protection recently. Rangan was driving to work; as he approached a cross road, the steering wheel disappeared. In its place was Amma with Her loving smile. Then the car slowed down without his intervention, and stopped at the intersection, touching another car which suddenly came from the side-road, crossing the red light. Thus a fatal accident was avoided without injury to anyone.

Rangan was so moved by this experience that he could not go to work, but returned home. He was unable to speak about it with anyone, including his wife, until a few days later.

More than these stories are the heart warming narratives of devotees who were brought to Her holy feet in a miraculous manner. With tears in her eyes, Ila Campbell spoke about her coming to Amma for the first time. She is an Indian woman married to an American, and worked in Brookhaven National Laboratory as a scientist, intent only on making money and living comfortably, and was not at all religious, she said. She was raised with secular values and to look down on Hindu culture, scriptures, religious ceremonies, and Gurus. Reading J. Krishnamurti during her college years confirmed her skeptical attitude.

While on a vacation at her father's house in Mumbai, she saw on TV for a few seconds Amma conducting a religious ceremony at Her ashram temple in Nerul, about three hours away by car from Mumbai. It was announced that Amma would be there giving a program on the following day as well. The image of Amma with the question: "Who is she?" dominated Ila's mind throughout the day. She could not understand her sudden and urgent need to see Amma that she felt deeply, though she did not know anything about Her.

Moreover Ila was in bed with a severe cold and fever, and could hardly sit up. Her father was unwilling to drive her since he had a business appointment next day. Then she prayed fervently to be well enough, and have transportation to attend the program, if Amma wanted to see her. On the following morning she was amazed to find herself completely well, and her father offering to take her, since his appointment had been postponed.

When Ila got near Amma to be hugged, her hair stood up and mind went blank. All that she could do was to shed profuse tears, feeling finally "at home." Now, she finds that all her problems with the family or at work are easily solved, due to the grace of Amma, and her only goal in life is to cultivate the compassion and selfless love of Amma.

An ardent devotee of Amma, Ara Bagdassarian is a chiropractor in New York City. When he went to see Amma at Her ashram in India, he had a peculiar desire to massage Her shoulders and back. This holy task was given only to female devotees. Innocently he asked Amma for this special privilege. She laughed, but told him that he could do so, if he shaved his beard off and wore a saree like a woman.

Ara decided to fulfill Amma's conditions. As he joined the line of women waiting to see Amma, face clean-shaven and head covered with the tip of the saree, the women around him did not realize that he was a man. Amma saw Ara at a distance and burst out laughing. People around Amma could not understand why She was laughing so much.

Amma rolled with laughter as Ara approached Her slowly, and started massaging Her shoulders. She could not continue hugging the devotees with Ara around, hence She asked him to leave after two minutes. He was so full of joy, it seemed like two seconds to him.

The beauty of saints is that they are often full of laughter, like small children. Amma is especially known for it. The people who have been with Amma for a long time told Ara, that Amma had never before laughed like that, while receiving Her devotees.

How Ara became a devotee of Amma is itself a wonderful story. While being trained as a chiropractor, he had a spiritual mentor who told him that he would soon meet with Amma, and She would take him higher on the spiritual path. He knew nothing about Amma then. A few months later, he saw Amma in dreams, blessing and encouraging him in his healing work. Then he saw the picture of Amma at a friend's house, and recognized Her as the Mother of his dreams. Learning more about Her, he became a fervent devotee even before meeting Her in the body.

Michael Morelli, a large, friendly young man from New Jersey, sheds tears of devotion in the presence of Ammachi. He spoke about experiencing intense pain and bliss simultaneously for a few days. Michael had gone with Amma on the North Indian tour. Afterwards, with three friends, he proceeded to the towns in the Himalayan foothills.

He was walking along a road in Singlegory when he slipped and fell down, sustaining a deep cut on his thigh which bled profusely. The hotel manager brought him to a doctor, his wound was bandaged and he was given an antibiotic. The doctor told him that he was fit enough to travel to the ashram in Kerala, which could take about four or five days.

As he traveled by train and car, the pain from the wound was so unbearable, he felt that he was about to die. But he was not scared since he felt the presence of Amma throughout the ordeal. In Kerala, he went straight to the famous AIMS hospital of Amma.

At the hospital, the doctors told him that his condition was quite serious; the wound was badly infected, the infection had spread to the colon, and he needed immediate surgery. As the hospital staff got him ready for a colostomy, he was in excruciating pain. Then he felt his heart expand to experience an indescribable divine bliss that stayed with him for few days.

Now, Michael is back again in America working as a chef at a restaurant. He is grateful to Amma for making him endure the pain which opened his heart to divine bliss. He said that he continues to experience this bliss, on and off, for no apparent reason.

The four year old child crying for God, mentioned in the preface is now sixteen years old. Named Amritavarshini by Amma, she lives with her mother Madhurima and stepfather Terry in Eugene, Oregon. The child met Amma for the first time in November 2003 at San Ramon Ashram in California. Madhurima notes that the meeting was marked by an eloquent silence, as Amma gazed deeply into the child's eyes, and the child's gaze seemed to say that she was an old soul returning to her true Mother.

During the following year when Amma left the hall late at night after the program, Amritavarshini cried for a long time due to the pain of separation. Many devotees were involved in calming the child, assuring her that Amma would be back in the morning.

Madhurima finds herself often amazed and inspired by her daughter's extraordinary concentration and devotion during prayers. Then the child acts and plays around like the other children of her age. Amritavarshini was only three years old when she began to compose and sing songs spontaneously about God and love.

In May 2006, Madhurima was coming home from outside when she heard Amritavarshini crying rather loudly, and saw the child on Terry's lap as he was trying to console her. The mother was alarmed about what could have possibly happened to cause such pain to the child.

Amritavarshini and her stepfather had been talking about poverty and slavery. The child said she was glad that slavery had ended in the world. Terry referred to a National Geographic Magazine article which stated that slavery was still practiced in certain parts of Africa. It also had pictures of starving children. Amritavarshini immediately burst into heart-rending sobs. As the mother joined her husband in his effort to comfort her, the child wanted to contact Amma then and there, since she felt that only Amma could change such conditions, and she planned to give Amma all her savings for this purpose.

With some difficultly, Madhurima managed to persuade her that she could instead create a card for Amma, expressing her concerns and give it to Amma when She comes to Seattle during the following week. Madhurima wrote down word for word a letter for Amma as dictated by her daughter. A week later they joined the line of people waiting to see Amma, and again Amritavarshini started to cry. When Amma heard from Madhurima why her daughter was crying, Amma's heart melted. Embracing the child lovingly, She said that the world will be saved by children like Amritavarshini, and we all should bow down to them.

Born and raised in a rather religious Latin American Catholic home, Luis Gil de Madrid was quite attached to his mother and fond of the siblings. He was deeply devoted to Blessed Mary the Mother of Jesus, and recited the holy Rosary daily.

Making much money in New York City, he lived comfortably indulging in alcohol, cigarettes, and many parties. At the same time, he was also seriously seeking God, reading spiritual books like the Autobiography of a Yogi, biographies of Ramakrishna Paramahansa, Muktananda and so on.

Luis Gil de Madrid is known as Gil to his friends. Gil took lessons from Self-Realization Fellowship and was meditating regularly, yet yearned for a living Master. He visited many ashrams, bringing his friends there. Some of them committed themselves to the gurus of these ashrams, but Gil did not feel any connection to them.

He was praying to Mother Mary and crying daily to find a living Master. After he had cried much and gone to sleep on a certain night, he saw a person in a dream who said: "Stop crying. She has heard you." On the following day, he saw a flyer with a picture of Amma, announcing a meeting at a Yoga Center in Scranton, PA.

Instantly he recognized Amma as his Guru and was overwhelmed with joy. This happened in the fall of 1996. He went to the Yoga Center, chanted few hymns and listened to the talk given by a monk sent by Amma. Gil was thrilled to learn that Amma would visit New York City in July 97.

He had been smoking two and half packets of cigarettes per day when he went to see Amma at the Universalist Church in New York. The desire to smoke disappeared. His mind went blank, and he was full of peace and high energy.

A few months after Gil saw Amma in New York, his mother living in Puerto Rico passed away suddenly due to a stroke. He was heart-broken and cried profusely. To console him Amma appeared in a dream. In the dream Amma was bathing him in a pool of water, took him out of the pool and said, "why do you cry for your departed mother, when your Mother is always with you?"

Gil was intuitively aware that Amma was referring to Herself as the Divine Mother who cannot ever leave him. Now he prefers to serve others or spend time in solitude doing spiritual exercises. My wife and I came to know Gil from Amma's Satsangs (Spiritual fellowship) in Eastern Pennsylvania.

We were at Sheraton Hotel in Detroit for the retreat with Amma in November 2011. Gil saw two young African –American men wanting to enter the hall where Amma was embracing the devotees. The person at the entrance to the hall was a little annoyed that the young men were not registered for the retreat.

Gil called them to a side and explained to them that they could come back on the following evening, see Amma and receive a hug, since it would be a public program that did not require prior registration. They were visibly relieved, and were even happier to hear that they could bring their families as well.

Gil asked them how they had heard about Amma. It was an amazing story. They had not heard about Amma at all, and were coming to the hotel for another program, but changed direction and walked towards Amma's Hall without knowing why. They felt that they were guided in this process by some intelligent force.

On the following night the young men with their families met Gil after their dharshan (seeing a holy person). Their faces beamed with joy and they were in tears as they talked about their dharshan with Amma. One of the men said that he felt a strong sense of God's presence for the first time in his life, when he was with Amma.

Gill cries easily while he talks or hears about Amma. He was happy that Amma had guided him to help out the young men. I saw Gil talking to the young men on both days, and was grateful to hear this inspiring story about Amma's amazing grace.

Carl Fisher and I are in a group of Amma's devotees that meets regularly in New Jersey. At 2015 January meeting Carl spoke about his wonderful experience during Amma's retreat in Detroit two months earlier.

As Carl was going up to receive Amma's loving hug, his dominant thought was: "Amma, make me come home." While walking towards Amma, he felt completely vulnerable, and ready to accept his own death. When he got near Amma, She was quite delighted, smiled brightly at him and then laughed loud telling Carl to sit close by and meditate.

In meditation, Carl had a vision of a door with bright light coming through the cracks at the sides and the bottom. He walked up to the door and opened it. Carl was overwhelmed by the blissful brilliance, and the loud sound of Ohm. The light seemed to be brighter than a thousand suns, though cool and calming. Carl felt that he had come to his real home, the source of his being or the beginning of creation.

One is wonderstruck to see the sudden changes in Amma's face and manner, reflecting the needs of the people who approach Her for blessing. Her face darkens with sadness as She receives sick people or listens to the story of a devotee's relative being seriously ill. In the next moment, She lights up with a bright smile and playfully pokes fun at another devotee.

This reminds me of a story about Paramahansa Yogananda. Once, at his ashram in Los Angeles, he was roaring like a lion, while chastising a nun. A young monk who saw his guru exploding in rage was shocked and distraught, thinking that a true saint could not give in to such anger. Then Yogananda turned around and looked at the monk with a tenderly loving smile. He turned back to the nun and continued scolding her, but ended by facing the monk again with the same sweet smile.

Great Masters like Amma and Yogananda have perfect control over their emotions, and express them externally only for the benefit of the devotees, and never due to a lack of control or owing to their own need. They want nothing from this world for themselves.

When my wife and I saw Amma in 1996 for the first time, we were pleasantly surprised to hear Her talk lovingly with us in Tamil. I had not told anyone around Amma that we were Tamils. We presumed that She came from the part of Kerala where both Malayalam and Tamil are spoken.

Later I went to Her village, and found that nobody spoke Tamil there. Meeting with Her parents, I asked Her father how Amma had learned Tamil. His wise reply was a rhetorical question: "How did Amma learn everything else?"

She had no teachers for Her profound knowledge of the scriptures, medicine, engineering, architecture, nuclear science and so on, as experts in these fields gain new knowledge from Her explanations and illuminative answers to questions. Amma is quick to correct any mistake made by the Swami who translates for Her in English.

A few miles away from Amma's Ashram in Amritapuri, an orphanage housing about five hundred children was in a desperate state. The children had hardly any food and were clothed in rags, in spite of the huge debts incurred to manage the orphanage. The place was polluted due to the lack of toilet facilities.

Amma compassionately assumed the responsibility to care for the children, and repay the debts. As the monks worked hard to renovate the orphanage, the conditions changed around quickly. The children began to receive ample nutritious meals, clean clothing and high quality education.

Their faces blossom with happy smiles when Amma visits the orphanage and pours out Her motherly love, as She hugs, jokes, sings and dances with them. For me, it was an inspiring sight to watch these little children walk cheerfully into the Ashram, and say long prayers before their meals with much concentration and devotion.

Intent on improving the quality of education and inculcating spiritual values to the children in India, Amma has established secondary schools throughout the country. Most of the teachers in these schools are Her devotees, who transform the children more by their example and love than through words.

When an earthquake devastated parts of Gujarat in India a few years ago, and Pakistan last year, Amma felt the pain and anguish of the people. Immediately She sent vehicles with medical personnel and volunteers to treat the wounded and help out the homeless. Three villages in Gujarat were rebuilt by the Ashram.

Thousands in Gujarat became Amma's ardent devotees and were yearning to see Her. Their love drew to them Amma, who insisted on going there in spite of a serious threat of violence along the way, even though the government officials had cancelled their visit.

When the tsunami hit South Asia, and the sea swallowed thousands of people, Amritapuri was also flooded. Amma stood amidst the waters like a valiant general, meticulously directing the operation to rescue the local people and the numerous devotees by Her monastic disciples.

Then She spent long hours consoling the families in mourning due to the death of their loved ones. She acted as their true mother, crying with them, feeling their sorrow completely.

Amma cancelled Her North Indian tour in order to visit the coastal villages of Tamilnad and Sri Lanka, which were ravaged by the tsunami. Her heart went out to all the suffering people in these villages. She embraced them with tears, and listened to their sad stories with great compassion.

With donations from Her devotees and their volunteer labor, Amma has built thousands of houses for destitute families in India, and still continues to build more homes. She has a pension fund to help out the neediest on a monthly basis.

Amma often stresses the importance of cultivating compassion and the habit of selfless service. Her followers from various parts of the world consider it their privilege to volunteer in soup kitchens, prepare tasty vegetarian meals and respectfully serve homeless people.

In one of my early visits with Amma, I told Her that I was unable to go deep in meditation, in spite of trying to meditate for many years. Six months earlier, I had brought this problem to a saintly monk from Self-Realization Fellowship, Brother Bhaktananda. After testing my techniques of meditation, and finding them to be correct, he said: "Don't worry; just continue."

Now I was speaking in Tamil to Amma about my lack of progress in meditation. She switched from Tamil to English to say exactly the same words: "Don't worry; just continue." This convinced me that Amma and the saintly monk were sharing the same Supreme Consciousness, offering me divine counsel.

During the retreats conducted by Amma, there is a question and answer session for all those who attend. A question was raised about abortion. Her reply was insightful and compassionate.

First, She acknowledged that abortion was indeed taking away human life. Then She went on to explain how it can be, for the women concerned, an agonizing experience before, during, and even long after the actual acts of abortion. Hence, these women need to be accepted with understanding, empathy, and love, instead of harsh criticism and condemnation.

Regarding the subject of homosexuality, Amma's attitude is clear from the way She receives homosexual and lesbian couples during dharshan, when people move close to Her for hugs. Amma embraces husband and wife, holding them together with tremendous love, as if to bless their marital union. It is heart-warming to see Amma acting in the same manner with homosexual couples as well. She seems to be glad to honor, bless, and nurture love wherever She may find it.

Not only animals and plants, even so-called inanimate things have consciousness. They too can have a devotional attitude towards Amma. It is manifest from the stories about the Indian Ocean fronting Amma's village in Kerala. Even as a child, Amma loved the ocean, and played on the beach, telling the ocean stories of Lord Krishna, and trying out Her new songs to the Lord.

In the magazine, "Immortal Bliss," Lakshmi, who used to go regularly with Amma to the beach at night and spend many hours with Her there, writes about Amma's special relationship with the sea. Amma asked Lakshmi not to accompany Her thereafter, as She wanted to tell the sea many things, and could not do so freely if someone was with Her.[7]

Earlier, Lakshmi had observed an amazing incident with the sea. Amma was seen gathering jasmine flowers that had fallen from the bush. A devotee asked Her whether She intended to make a garland for the sea. Four or five devotees who were around, told Amma that the same thought had occurred to them too. Amma said it was a message from the sea, and started making a garland with the flowers.

During the night, Amma went with the garland to the beach, telling some monks on the way that the sea has to get it from Her hands. Lakshmi was with Her when She sat on the rocks laid on the beach to protect the land from erosion, and meditated for a while.

Then holding the garland in Her right hand, She said: "Let's see. If the sea really wants this garland, let her come and embrace Me, taking the garland from My hands herself." Lakshmi smiled, thinking it could never happen, as the waters were so many feet below, and the tide never came up that high.

When Mother finished speaking, an enormous wave suddenly burst up from below, soared over Mother's head and crashed over Her with such force, that Mother should have been carried away but She remained still. The wave managed to take the garland from Her grip and returned to the depths below, as Laksmi watched in amazement.

The disciples of Christ, too, were amazed to see the stormy sea listen to their Master's words, and calm down. Christ had been sound asleep in the

7 See Immortal Bliss, 4th Quarter, 1999, M.A. Center, San Ramon, Ca

boat, when the disciples were terrified by the sudden storm and woke Him up. He sadly commented on their lack of faith before telling the sea to be quiet. [Mt.8:23-27]

The apostles had seen the rising waves and the bubbling sea. They didn't know that the sea was not in a rage, but shouting and dancing with joy, because her Lord Creator had come to her lovingly, and was resting in sleep.

That water is conscious, can understand human words in various languages, and respond meaningfully was proved by a Japanese businessman turned scientist. Masaru Emoto was involved in many experiments to prove that water formed beautiful crystals in response to positive words, and the frozen crystals were malformed, when the words were negative. Some people doing a long Buddhist chant with a holy monk near a polluted lake in Japan, observed its waters being visibly purified. One can read more about it in Emoto's book: *The True Power of Water.*[8]

We are carrying old wounds in our hearts due to our pride, greed, lust, and violence. Amma's divine Heart bleeds for us. Selfishness makes us insanely destructive of nature, not caring at all about the consequences. Nature is bound to react with tremendous destruction, unless we open our hearts to God's Love and Compassion, and become peaceful and loving towards each and every human being, and the whole of creation.

This can be the main goal of all the religions, if religious leaders give more emphasis to the inner essence of religion, namely spirituality, rather than to the outer covering of doctrines and rituals. All who are concerned about our present chaotic state of endless conflicts will find the address given by Amma in May 2006 at the Interfaith Center of New York[9] immensely illuminative.

For more information about Amma, go online to www.amma.org or amritapuri.org

8 The True Power of Water by Masaru Emoto, Beyond Words Publishing, Hillsboro, Oregon, 2005

9 Copy available at M.A.Center, PO Box 613, San Ramon, Ca 94583 or at www.amma.org

Amma's Words

Today, vibrations of good thoughts and kind words are more important than ever before.

To console a miserable soul or wipe away the tears of a crying person is far greater than any worldly achievement.

We should always have a positive attitude towards life. Optimism is a powerful factor for eliminating suffering.

Thou Hast Many Names

I say my prayers on beads of love, strung together with everlasting threads of devotion. I hold to no single Name—God, Spirit, Brahma, Allah, Heavenly father, Divine Mother—for All are Thine.

I invoke Thee sometimes as Christ, Krishna, Shankaracharya, Mohammed, Buddha, Moses, and other prophets; for I know Thou hast delighted, and will ever delight, in revealing Thyself in different forms.

In Thy cosmic play on the stage of the centuries, in Thy myriad appearances, Thou didst take many Names; but Thou hast only one Nature: Perennial Joy.[10]

Paramahansa Yogananda

10 Whispers from Eternity, (Self-Realization Fellowship, Loa Angeles) p.88

Paramahansa Yogananda

PARAMAHANSA YOGANANDA

January 5, 1893 is the auspicious day when divine love appeared in the form of a newborn infant at Gorakhpur in the North East of India, close to the Himalayas. His father, Baghabati Gosh, and mother Gyana, were both disciples of the renowned sage Lahiri Mahasaya. They named the child Mukunda, one of the names of Lord Krishna.

The baby was a few months old, when his mother, seated behind many disciples, yearned silently for her Guru's blessing on the child. Lahiri Mahasaya invited her to come up to him; he took the child, and touching his forehead, blessed the child saying that he would take many souls to the Kingdom of God.

Abinash worked under Mukundas's father Bhagabati at Bengal-Nagpur Railway in Calcutta. He told Mukunda the story of how his parents found Lahiri Mahasaya. Abinash asked his superior Bhagabati for one week leave so that he might be with his Guru Lahiri Mahasaya in Benaris. Bhagabati denied the request, saying that he should not be fanatical about religion.

That evening Abinash was walking home, disappointed and depressed, when Bhagabati joined and walked with him, talking about the importance of work and worldly success. But Abinash was silently repeating in his heart that he could not live without seeing Lahiri Mahasaya. As they were admiring the evening sun shining on the tall grass in a field, suddenly, Lahiri Mahasaya appeared there to say that Bhagabati was too hard on his employee, and vanished. Abinash went down on his knees to thank his Guru in tears.

Astounded, Bhagabati was silent for a while. Then he not only gave permission, but also asked if he and his wife could accompany Abinash on the following day to see Lahiri Mahasaya in Benaris, and be initiated by him.

Daily Mukunda and his mother bowed before the photo of Lahiri Mahasaya, offering flowers in worship. As Mukunda meditated before this holy picture, sometimes the image would come out of the frame, change into living form, and sit in front of him. Whenever Mukunda attempted to touch the saint's feet, he reverted back into the image within the frame.

When photos were taken of Lahiri Mahasaya with other people, his image would be missing whereas others appeared on the picture. Kali Kumar Roy was not only an expert photographer but also a devotee of Lahiri Mahasaya. He was certain that the problem could be solved through his expertise. While his Master was sitting in meditation on a wooden bench with a screen behind, Kali Kumar took all the necessary steps to ensure that the Master's image would be reflected on the photographic plates. His pride of being an expert was broken, when he saw only the wooden bench and the screen on the picture; he was in tears.

"I am Spirit. Can your camera reflect the omnipresent Invisible?"[11] asked Lahiri Mahasaya when he came out of silence. As Kali Kumar pleaded with him for a picture of his bodily temple, he agreed to pose for Kali Kumar on the following day. This was the only time that the Master's image appeared clearly on a picture.

At eight years of age, Mukunda was struck with a severe case of cholera. Family feared for his life. Doctors had given up hope. It was his mother's faith in Lahiri Mahasaya that saved him. She motioned Mukunda to look at the picture of Lahiri Mahasaya and mentally bow before him. As he did so, he saw there a brilliant light that enveloped him and the whole room. Immediately, his symptoms disappeared, and he was able to touch his mother's feet, grateful for her faith.

---

1 Autobiography of a Yogi by Paramahansa Yogananda, - Self Realization Fellowship, Los Angeles, 1998, p.11

Mukunda loved his mother immensely. She died when he was only eleven years old, and her death left him utterly inconsolable. The grief of losing his earthly mother made Mukunda yearn for Divine Mother ever more intensely through daily prayers and meditation.

As described in the *Autobiography*, Mukunda had wonderful experiences, visiting various saints. They were naturally fond of him. Most memorable is his contact with Master Mahasaya, a close disciple of Ramakrishna Paramahansa. Mukunda entered the residence of Master Mahasaya at 50 Amherst Street in Calcutta, and stood in awe of the dazzling appearance of the saint. "Little sir, please be seated. I am talking to my Divine Mother."[2]

These words of the saint cut to the core of Mukunda's heart; he intuitively knew that Master Mahasaya was conversing intimately with Divine Mother. He thought that losing his earthly mother brought him the utmost possible sorrow, but now the separation from Divine Mother plunged him into an indescribable torture of the spirit. He clutched the saint's feet, pleading for his intercession to ask Divine Mother whether he, Mukunda, found favor in Her sight. Very reluctantly, Master Mahasaya agreed.

Mukunda was joyful with anticipation and told the saint that he would return on the following morning to learn about Divine Mother's message. Returning home, he walked up to the attic with a light heart, and meditated deeply late into the night, when he had the vision of Divine Mother, beautiful and tender, uttering these words with a smile: "Always have I loved Thee! Ever shall I love Thee!"[3]

Early in the following morning, hiding his inner elation, Mukunda approached Master Mahasaya for the message from Divine Mother. The saint refused to say a word. As Mukunda kept insisting, Master Mahasaya asked whether he could add a single word to the assurance Mukunda had received last night from the beautiful Mother Herself. Mukunda fell at the saint's feet with tears of joy, in contrast to the tears of sorrow of the previous day.

One day Mukunda was walking along Howragh railway station, and stood near a temple watching some men singing a chant with drums and

2 ibid, p.88

3 ibid, p.89

cymbals. He thought how their chanting the divine name lacked devotion altogether. Suddenly he was astonished to see Master Mahasaya who answered his thought, that the Beloved's name sounds sweet from all lips, ignorant or wise.

Mukunda and his younger brother, Sananda, asked Master Mahasaya whether he could call their mother from heaven or the astral world to appear before them. Due to their persistent plea, he agreed to do so on the following Thursday.

They went back eagerly on the appointed Thursday and sat behind Master Mahasaya for two hours while he was deep in meditation. Then, without turning, he asked them to look back. Their mother was standing near the door, smiling at them tenderly. Calling "Mother! Mother!" they wanted to rush to her; the saint told them not to move, but to speak to her. "Mother, do you remember us?" they asked. Sweetly and clearly she replied: "I keep constant watch over all of you. The Divine Mother is protecting you." With these words, she vanished.[4]

After school, Mukunda and his brother Sananda used to run to the Chittagong harbor to watch the ships, and then run back home to be in at six p.m. following their elder brother Ananta's strict order. Along the way, they saw many fruit trees on either side. One day they decided to pick some litchis.

As they picked the luscious fruits, they heard someone call "Mukunda." The twilight was fast fading. They saw a figure in white at a distance, beckoning them. They didn't know who could have known Mukunda. As they went closer, Sananda noted that their visitor was wonderfully luminous. Mukunda bowed before the man who emanated a sense of holiness, and touched his feet.

The saint embraced Mukunda, and kissed him on the head. Sananda too bowed before the saint. After greeting them, he said: "Mukunda, it is God's wish that I come to you today. Remember what I say to you. You have come on earth as God's representative to fulfill His wishes. Your body is His temple, sanctified by prayer and meditation. One day your ideals of yoga will inspire all mankind. Mukunda, march onward!"[5]

4 "Mejda" by Sananda Las Ghosh, SRF, LA, 1980 p.139

5 ibid, p.82

Since Sananda was fidgeting, thinking that they would be beaten at home by Ananta for getting in late, the saint advised him not to be troubled, since no one would notice that they were late. As they turned to go and looked back, the saint blessed them with upraised hands and vanished. On the way home, Sananda tried to talk to Mukunda, but he did not answer, preferring to walk in silence all the way home. Ananta was at a friend's house and father had not yet come back from work. They were saved.

Mukunda had gone straight to the prayer room. So Sananda ran up to give him the good news. Mukunda pointed to the photograph of Lahiri Mahasaya on the wall, and asked whether Sananda recognized him. Sananda was amazed to realize that they had just seen Lahiri Mahasaya, though he had been dead for many years! He felt deeply blessed.

Sananda tells the story of how his brother fought a big bully from school. This robust boy used to beat up small boys, if they were unwilling to serve him. Once, as he was hitting another boy, Mukunda challenged him to a fight.

The surprised bully picked Mukunda up above his head, and threw him down to land on his back with a thud. The bully bent over to pick him up again, when Mukunda grabbed his neck in a strangle-hold, and would not release him, even though Mukunda's head was bruised and bleeding, as the bully kept ramming it on the ground.

The bully's eyes were bulging due to Mukunda's deadly grip; so he admitted defeat and agreed not to pick on small boys thereafter. According to Sananda, later Mukunda was conscience-stricken and hurting more due to his anger at the bully than from the head injury, saying that anger blots out the remembrance of God. We often justify righteous anger. How can it be right, if we are forced to forget God thereby?

While in school, Mukunda, his cousin and a friend ran away from their homes, and boarded a train on route to the foothills of the Himalayas. Mukunda had persuaded his companions that they could reach exalted spiritual states by meeting the saintly yogis roaming the Himalayan Mountain, and meditating in its caves.

Mukunda's brother Ananta sent telegrams to the railway stationmaster of Hardwar and to the police, instructing them to detain the boys until he arrived. When they met, Mukunda was not reconciled to going back home with his brother. Ananta, expecting such a problem, had arranged to take him to Benaris to see a saint, before bringing him home. This saint was supposed to be an incarnation of God.

The saint was resting with eyes closed, half-reclining on a large pillow covered with ochre silk. His disciples refused to let Ananta and Mukunda go near the saint. They said he was resting and would get angry if disturbed.

Ananta hesitated first, but determined to get help for his brother, forced his way through the devotees, gripping Mukunda by the hand. Seated before the saint, he pleaded respectfully that the saint might open his eyes and bless his brother. As Mukunda bowed humbly, the saint opened his eyes and gazed at Mukunda's serene countenance. Then he told Mukunda that his search was over, since he himself was the God Mukunda had been seeking.

Hearing these words, Mukunda's manner manifested shock. The saint reacted with a terrible rage, since he had not been duly recognized as God. He fumed at Mukunda, "You are still blinded by delusion and attraction to family life."[6] His face was dark and distorted with anger. Mukunda took a small mirror from his bag, and held it before his face. "Look at yourself! Is this the face of God? Can the God of love and beauty Whom I have sought day and night, month after month, year after year, have such a face? No! God is not greedy. He does not deceive His devotees to procure a following and the gifts they bring. You are leading your disciples into greater ignorance by flattering your ego and theirs. Everything and everyone belongs to God. He is all. Help your disciples to realize this truth. Or if you cannot rightly guide them, then let them seek their own paths to God. Only he who can impart divine wisdom to others and show them the path to God is a real guru."[7]

Saying this, Mukunda started to leave, followed by Ananta. The saint was thoroughly shaken. His face showed amazement. Running after Mukunda, he humbly thanked him for the words of wisdom that had delivered him from

---

6 ibid, p.102

7 ibid, pp.102-103

his delusion. Mukunda in turn admired the saint for admitting his fault in front of his disciples, and told him that he had a great heart.

Returning home, Mukunda promised his father that he would stay at home until he finished high school. Though he joined Calcutta Hindu High school, most of his time was spent not in studies, but in spiritual practices like meditation and visiting with saints. Hence he was not expected to graduate, yet managed to do so through a minor miracle. A few days before the final exam, a bright student offered to coach him in answers to the exact questions that were set for the examination later.

During his high school years, Mukunda acted like a leader among the youngsters who were spiritually inclined; they found a hut where they gathered to meditate and chant for long hours. To show that Mukunda was enjoying the sweetness of God's Presence in all creation, yet was not averse to boyish mischief, his brother Sananda tells a story in his book "Mejda."

Sananda, Mukunda and a friend, Surendra, were once walking along upper Circular Road in Calcutta, when Sananda and Surendra were overwhelmed suddenly by the putrid smell of rotten rice by the roadside. Not only people, but even a cow avoided that area and changed direction. However, Mukunda was walking along with a sweet smile, as if there was nothing amiss, in spite of his companions' protest.

Surendra demanded that Mukunda move with them to the other side, since even a cow had the sense to move away from the maggoty rice with crawling flies.

"An ignorant animal cannot comprehend that God exists in everything, even in something as offensive as this pile of decaying rice," Mukunda answered. "But I realize that God is in everything; therefore I know I could eat some of that rice and not come to any harm."[8]

Confident that Mukunda could never be that crazy, Surendra jeered at him, and challenged him to do so; saying that if he did, then he too would eat the rotten rice. Surendra went into shock as Mukunda calmly bent down to scoop up a handful, and ate it slowly as if it were a special delicacy. The sudden shock did

8 ibid, pp.146-147

not prevent Surendra from running to the other side of the street. But Mukunda followed him with another handful of the rotten mess to stuff into his mouth.

Surendra vomited and fell to the ground in a faint. Sananda was weeping. With a smile, Mukunda rubbed Surendra's chest. He recovered quickly, admitted defeat and said he would never challenge Mukunda again. Sananda was amazed to find that his brother did not suffer any ill effect from the incident.

After his graduation from high school, Mukunda planned to leave the family in pursuit of his spiritual goal. Consequently the family members were plunged into sorrow. Mukunda was quite attached to the family, especially to his father, younger brothers, and sister. He prayed intensely with tears for two hours, and was given the grace of detachment and determination to leave the home.

Mukunda joined an ashram in Benaris, with a young friend Jitendra. The two aspirants had a hard time adjusting to this ashram, as it did not give much importance to meditation. One morning, Mukunda was praying deeply, crying for hours to Divine Mother for help to achieve his goal, when he was divinely advised about meeting his Guru that day.

His prayer was interrupted by a young priest, Habu, who wanted him as companion for shopping. While returning from the market, Mukunda saw a saintly swami standing at the end of a lane, and felt a strong attraction towards him. Thinking that he was mistaken, he kept on walking with Habu.

After ten minutes he could not proceed further; when he turned around, he could walk again. Throwing the parcels into the hands of astounded Habu, he ran towards the lane and fell at the feet of the Saint, whose face he had seen earlier in many visions as the Guru who would lead him toward God.

Sri Yuketeswar's voice trembled with joy: "O my own, you have come to me! How many years I have waited for You!"[9] Mukunda remembered his past lives with his Guru, and was speechless in ecstatic joy. Communing in the silent eloquence of hearts, they were bathed in eternal, divine love.

Sri Yuketeswar was so sweetly humble as to request the aid of his new disciple: "If you ever find me falling from the state of God-realization, please

9 Autobiography of a Yogi, p.107

promise to put my head on your lap and help to bring me back to the Cosmic Beloved we both worship."[10]

With few words, the Guru made the disciple realize that all the circumstances of his life were an open book to him. He advised Mukunda to get back to his home in Calcutta. But Mukunda could not countenance such a possibility. When he left home, and the family was in tears, his elder brother Ananta had predicted that Mukunda would tire of the high metaphysical skies, and fly back to his family nest. He was not at all inclined to do any such thing. The joyful meeting with his Guru ended in tension due to this reluctance.

Sri Yuketeswar was stern as he predicted that Mukunda would come to him at Serampore, a suburb of Calcutta, in twenty eight days, and go to his family in thirty days. He added that Mukunda would not be accepted as a disciple, unless there was complete surrender and obedience to his strict training.

A few weeks later, planning to go to Serampore, Mukunda and Jitendra left the ashram in Benaris, and visited with Ananta in Agra, where he had been transferred from Calcutta as an accountant.

Though Ananta was a good host, he started lecturing Mukunda that he was wasting his life, and their father should disinherit him. Mukunda was firm. He said he was only seeking the inheritance from the heavenly Father.

On the following day, during breakfast, Ananta countered with a plan to test Mukunda's faith in depending on God alone. He proposed to send Mukunda to Vrindavan, with Jitendra as a witness, just with a one-way ticket but no money whatsoever. They should not ask for money or food or explain their predicament to anyone, and should return before midnight, without missing a single meal.

Mukunda readily accepted the challenge. Ananta brought them to the railway station, checked them carefully to see that they had no money, and gave them the one-way tickets to Vrindavan. He was surprised by Mukunda's firm faith, and promised to accept him as his Guru, if by any chance he passed the test. It was utterly unusual for an elder brother in India to make such a promise.

---

10 ibid, p.108

Seated in the train, Jitendra was in a gloomy mood, feeling victimized by what he considered to be the crazy presumption of Mukunda. Already hungry at just the thought of starvation, he pinched Mukunda severely, saying that he did not see any sign that God was going to provide their next meal. Mukunda, on the contrary, was joyous at the prospect of treading the ground hallowed by the holy feet of Lord Krishna at Vrindavan.

Then two men came into their train compartment. One said that the boys were probably running away from their families, enchanted by the "Stealer of Hearts" (Krishna), and offered to give them meals and shelter in Vrindavan. But Mukunda declined to accept the offer. When they got off the train, the two men linked arms with them, and called for a cab which brought them to a stately hermitage.

They saluted a dignified elderly lady named Gauri Ma, telling her that the invited princes could not come for the banquet prepared for them; so instead, they had brought two devotees of Krishna. Gauri Ma welcomed them with a motherly smile, telling them she was glad that they had come to taste the delicacies prepared for the royal patrons of the hermitage.

When Gauri Ma left them in order to get the food, Mukunda pinched Jitendra in the same soft spot that he had been pinched earlier, saying that the Lord works, and in a hurry too. Gauri Ma re-entered with a *punkha* to fan them in oriental fashion, while the ashram residents served them about thirty courses. They had never tasted such delicacies before.

After thanking Gauri-Ma for the delicious banquet without revealing their situation, they went out and sought shelter from the relentless heat under the shade of a tree. Jitendra again started complaining that the lunch was an accident, and they could not see the sights of Vrindavan or get back to Agra without a cent in their hands.

Mukunda wondered how Jitendra could forget God so quickly, and that the human memory of divine favors was too short indeed. Jitendra retorted that he would not forget coming there with a madcap like Mukunda.

Soon a young man approached them, and bowed before Mukunda, saying that they must be strangers. He offered to be their host and guide. Mukunda politely declined the offer. The stranger seemed alarmed at Mukunda's refusal, and explained that Mukunda was his guru. He had seen his face many times during his meditations. That day, he had a vision of Lord Krishna who showed him their figures under the same tree. His name was Pratap Chatterji.

Mukunda was glad to accept him as a disciple. Pratap invited them to his home, but Mukunda told him that they were already the guests of his brother in Agra. Pratap then offered to take them in a carriage to visit the various Krishna shrines and temples. They readily agreed.

After finishing their tour and worship, it was almost night when they arrived at the railway station. Pratap left, saying that he would be back with some sweetmeats. He came later with the sweetmeats, a bundle of rupee notes, and two train tickets for Agra as offering to his guru Mukunda, who accepted it reverently. Jitendra burst out in tears.

They found a secluded spot at the railway station, where Mukunda initiated Pratap in Kriya Yoga, explaining its immense value for attaining liberation. It is a technique of *pranayama* or a psycho-physical exercise to control the flow of energy in the body, whereby one's consciousness is removed from the externality of sensations and thoughts, and gradually interiorized. Mukunda had learned Kriya yoga from his father who received it from his Guru Lahiri Mahasaya. Pratap was enthused about practicing Kriya Yoga, and bid a tearful farewell to his guru, as they boarded the train.

Ananta was a picture of astonishment, when he saw Mukunda and Jitendra arrive at his home before midnight. Jitendra related to him all the amazing incidents of the day. Ananta insisted that he be initiated immediately into Kriya Yoga by his younger brother, as he understood for the first time why Mukunda did not care about worldly riches. Mukunda had to initiate two unsought disciples in the same night.

It is noteworthy that Mukunda was initially reluctant to accept help from others in both instances. It seems that he wanted to be sure in his heart that he depended on God and God alone.

After bidding good-bye to his elder brother-disciple, Mukunda went with Jitendra to see the Taj Mahal. Though he was enjoying its exquisite beauty, his heart yearned to be with his Guru in Serampore. They boarded the train going South to Calcutta where Jitendra left to see his family and Mukunda took another train to Serampore. He was amazed to find that it was actually the twenty eighth day when he arrived at Sri Yukterswar's hermitage, as predicted by the Guru.

Unlike their first encounter, Sri Yukteswar was cold when he saw Mukunda. The disciple promised the Guru that he would no longer ignore his wishes. Only then was the Master ready to assume full responsibility for his training. The first instruction was to go back to his home in Calcutta and pursue college studies. Though fearful, he agreed to obey the Master in every detail, after getting a promise that the Guru would eventually reveal God to him. He was delighted to find that Sri Yukeswar was also a disciple of Lahiri Mahasaya. Enrolled at Scottish Church College in Calcutta, Mukunda's daily attendance was not at the college lecture halls but in the Serampore hermitage, since Sri Yukteswar did not object to his presence there.

A fundamental transformation was taking place in Mukunda due to his contact with Sri Yukteswar. To quote his words: "I always thrilled at the touch of Sri Yukteswar's holy feet. A disciple is spiritually magnetized by reverent contact with a Master; a subtle current is generated. The devotee's undesirable habit-mechanisms in the brain are often as if cauterized; the grooves of his worldly tendencies are beneficially disturbed. Momentarily at least he may find the secret veil of maya lifting, and glimpse the reality of Bliss. My whole body responded with a liberating glow whenever I knelt in the Indian fashion before my Guru…If I entered the hermitage in a worried or indifferent frame of mind, my attitude imperceptibly changed. A healing calm descended at the mere sight of my Guru. Each day with him was a new experience in joy, peace and wisdom."[11]

The close disciples of great Masters like Ramakrishna Paramahansa, Ramana Maharshi and Ammachi report experiencing similar transformations in their innermost selves due to their reverent contact with the Gurus.

Sri Yuketeswar was a strict disciplinarian. His methods were not merely severe but drastic, pointing out the slightest flaws in the behavior of the disciples publicly. Hence, only very few lasted in the ashram, since most people could not take the blows dealt to their egos, and left quickly. Finding that

---

11 ibid, p.137

the Master's discipline was motivated by pure love, Mukunda learned to accept it gratefully, and found his relationship with the Master to be entirely harmonious.

Though Sri Yukteswar had left school in fifth grade, many learned professors and scientists visited the ashram, surprised to find that his knowledge in their particular fields was very advanced and precise.

He was always affable and courteous with visitors. However, he could be hard on obdurate egotists. Once a famous chemist who was an atheist got into an argument with Sri Yukteswar. He could not admit the existence of God since science had not found a means to detect God, he said. "So you have inexplicably failed to isolate the Supreme Power in your test tubes!" was the Master's stern response. "I recommend a new experiment: examine your thoughts unremittingly for twenty-four hours. Then wonder no longer at God's absence."[12]

When Mukunda stayed overnight at the ashram, he found he could not sleep due to the mosquitoes; he was used to mosquito nets at home. Sri Yukteswar advised him to buy a mosquito net and another for himself as well.

One night, he waited for Master's instruction to arrange the nets before going to sleep. As Master was asleep already, he tried to sleep without the net, but could not do so due to the pain of being stung by several mosquitoes. He tried to get Master's attention by coughing. Seeing that He did not respond, he went near and found that Master was not breathing. He held a mirror near the nose; no vapor appeared. To be sure, he closed Master's mouth and nostrils with his hand; still the body was unmoving. He turned aside in a daze to call for help.

"A budding experimentalist! My poor nose!" said Master shaking with laughter. "Why don't you go to bed? Is the whole world going to change for you? Change yourself; be rid of the mosquito consciousness."[13] Obeying his Master Mukunda went to bed, and found that no mosquito attacked him. He realized that Master was demonstrating yogic trance, and the power of consciousness to be free from external circumstances.

---

12 ibid, p.151

13 ibid, p.129

Six months after his contact with Sri Yukteswar, Mukunda was feeling dissatisfied with his spiritual progress. He thought that his college studies and ashram duties were an obstacle to continuous communion with God. Thinking that going to the Himalayas and meditating in its caves could be more helpful, he asked Master about it. No mountain can give him wisdom, said Sri Yukteswar. As Mukunda repeated the request, Master kept quiet, and he took the silence for permission.

That evening at home, packing few things for the journey, Mukunda was feeling guilty about leaving his Master. To be sure that his trip to the Himalayas was God's will, he decided to seek advice from another illumined Master, Ram Gopal who was also a disciple of Lahiri Mahasaya. Mukunda's Sanskrit professor at college had talked about the sleepless saint, and had given him his address as Ranbajpur near Tarakeswar.

Mukunda reached Tarakeswar by train, and went to the famous shrine of Lord Siva. Entering the sanctuary, he failed to bow before the Lingam (a round stone whose circumference having no end or beginning, has been an apt symbol for God among the Hindus). Thinking that God must be adored only in one's soul, he walked away from the temple, and asked directions for Ranbajpur. One person directed him to take the right when he came to a crossroad. After walking for many hours in the hot sun, he was very weary when he met another person who was rather suspicious at the start.

When Mukunda explained his pathetic plight, the man said that at the crossroad, he should have turned left and not right. He was kind enough to take Mukunda home and provide a simple dinner with a place to sleep for the night.

Mukunda started walking towards Ranbajpur early in the morning on the following day. Again the heat of the sun was unbearable, and the distance seemed endless. He was almost at the point of collapsing, when an ordinary looking, slightly built man with extraordinary eyes, walked towards him and said: "I was planning to leave Ranbajpur, but your purpose was good, so I awaited you. Aren't you clever to think that, unannounced, you could pounce on me? That Professor Behari had no right to give you my address."[14]

---

14 ibid, p.160

There was no need for further introduction to the sleepless saint Ram Gopal. He asked Mukunda where God is, and naturally Mukunda was perplexed; he answered that God is in his soul, and everywhere. "Then why, young sir, did you fail to bow before the Infinite in the stone symbol at Tarakeswar temple yesterday? Your pride caused you the punishment of being misdirected by the passerby who was not bothered by fine distinctions between left and right."[15]

Mukunda agreed fully and was instantly healed by the cooling energy emanating from the saint. Ram Gopal continued, "Yoga through which divinity is found within, is doubtless the highest road, as Lahiri Mahasaya has told us. But, discovering the Lord within, we soon perceive Him without. Holy shrines at Tarakeswar and elsewhere are rightly venerated as nuclear centers of spiritual power."[16]

The omniscient saint compassionately patted Mukundas' shoulder: "Young yogi, I see you are running away from your Master. He has everything you need. You should return to Him. Mountains cannot be your Guru."[17]

Mukunda's lifelong desire for the Himalayas vanished from his heart. Lovingly Ram Gopal took his hand, and led him to a hamlet in the jungle, where they meditated for four hours. After a simple meal, Ram Gopal arranged bedding for Mukunda to sleep on.

The hamlet had a mellow glow. Inspired by the spiritual magnetism of the saint, Mukunda asked him to grant him divine ecstasy or samadhi. Ram Gopal told him that he was not ready for it then, but intimated that he would receive it shortly from his Master.

For forty years, Ram Gopal had been meditating for long hours in secret caves in Bengal. He did not sleep at all, as he could rest his body and mind perfectly through super-conscious meditation. When Mukunda closed his eyes to sleep, he saw flashes of lightning, the vast space within was bright light; opening his eyes, he saw the same dazzling radiance. The saint said he was blessed to be having this experience.

15 ibid

16 ibid

17 ibid, pp.160-161

Next morning Mukunda was reluctant to leave the saint, who looked at him steadily. Vibrations of peace emanating from the saint filled him, healing him instantly from a chronic back pain. He walked back to Tarakesvar, and made a devout pilgrimage to the famous shrine and humbly prostrated before the stone lingam. It enlarged in his inner vision, becoming cosmic spheres, zone after zone filled with divine glory.

Reaching Serampore by train, he appeared before Sri Yukteswar, shame-faced. His Guru invited him casually for dinner. Mukunda was surprised that he was not at all angry. "Wrath springs from thwarted desires. I do not expect anything from others, so their actions cannot be in opposition to wishes of mine. I would not use you for my own ends; I am happy only in your own true happiness," said Sri Yuketswar.[18] They looked into each others' eyes where tears of love were shining.

A few days later Mukunda went to Sri Yukteswar's empty room to meditate, but thoughts gave him no rest. His Guru called him thrice; Mukunda protested saying that he was meditating. Sri Yukteswar told him that he was not really meditating as his mind was disturbed like leaves in a storm. Exposed, Mukunda went sadly to the Master who comforted him, saying that the mountains could not give him what he wanted, but his heart's desire shall be fulfilled. Gently he touched Mukunda's chest. The result was Yogananda's first experience in Cosmic Consciousness, as described in the *Autobiography*:[19]

"My body became immovably rooted; breath was drawn out of my lungs, as if by some huge magnet. Soul and mind instantly lost their physical bondage and streamed out like a fluid piercing light from my every pore. The flesh was as though dead; yet in my intense awareness I knew that never before had I been fully alive. My sense of identity was no longer narrowly confined to a body, but embraced the circumambient atoms. People on distant streets seemed to be moving gently over my own remote periphery. The roots of plants and trees appeared through a dim transparency of the soil; I discerned the inward flow of their sap.

18 ibid, p.165

19 ibid, pp.166-168

"The whole vicinity lay before me. My ordinary frontal vision was now changed to a vast spherical sight, simultaneously all-perceptive…

"An oceanic joy broke upon calm endless shores of my soul. The spirit of God, I realized, is exhaustless Bliss; His body is countless tissues of light. A swelling glory within me began to envelope towns, continents, the earth, solar and stellar systems, tenuous nebulae and floating universes. The entire cosmos, gently luminous, like a city seen afar at night, glimmered within the infinitude of my being…

"I cognized the center of the empyrean as a point of intuitive perception in my heart.... The creative voice of God I heard resounding as *Aum,* the vibration of the Cosmic Motor."

Suddenly, as breath returned to his lungs, Mukunda felt caged in a little body, losing his infinite immensity. He knelt before Sri Yukteswar to thank him for the beatific experience. Master invited him to sweep the balcony and go for a walk with him. Sri Yukteswar explained to Mukunda:

"The Lord has created all men from illimitable joy of His being. Though they are painfully cramped by the body, God nevertheless expects that men made in His image shall ultimately rise above all sense identifications and reunite with Him."[20]

After Mukunda graduated from college, Sri Yukteswar bestowed on him the ochre robe, making him a monk of an ancient order, and allowed him to choose a new name. "Yogananda" was the name selected. It means bliss (ananda) through yoga or divine union.

Following Sri Yukteswar's instruction that renouncing the responsibility of family life can be justified only by serving a much larger family, Yogananda started a yoga school in Ranchi, where boys were instructed not only in the normal academic subjects, but were also taught Yoga in order to live a balanced life. The children were very fond of the staff, especially of Yogananda who was like a loving father-mother to them.

A few years later, Yogananda was immersed in meditation in a storeroom of Ranchi school, when he had a vision of numerous American faces gazing at

20 ibid, p.169

him. Intuitively he knew that they were his future disciples, and felt the call to leave for America soon.

Though he had Sri Yukteswar's blessing to go to America, he prayed deeply to obtain permission from God, and not to get lost in the materialistic West. As his head was reeling under the pressure of his agonized tears, a young man entered his home. Yogananda realized that he had to be deathless Babaji, the Guru of Lahiri Mahasaya.

He acknowledged, "Yes, I am Babaji. Our heavenly Father heard your prayer. He commands me to tell you: Follow the behest of your Guru and go to America. Fear not; you shall be protected."[21]Yogananda was overawed with devotion for Mahavatar Babaji, and his eyes were fixed lovingly on Babaji, who talked with him for a while, then raised his hands in blessing and walked away.

The ship on which Yogananda traveled docked at Boston Harbor in September 1920. He had been invited to address the World Congress of Religions held in Boston. Yogananda gave a brilliant lecture on the philosophy of religion, defining God as the ever-new, endless bliss, sought consciously or unconsciously by all the people.

He stayed in Boston for a few years, giving talks and training some disciples in yoga and meditation. One Christmas Eve, Dr. Lewis, a much loved dentist, went to see Yogananda and asked him for the explanation of a scripture text, a question that he had asked several others earlier and never gotten a satisfactory answer: "If thine eye be single, thy body will be full of light" [Mt.6:22].

Yogananda talked to him about the spiritual eye, and said that when it opens, he would experience his body and all creation as made of light. Then Yogananda gave him this realization by opening his spiritual eye, touching the doctor on the center of his forehead, just above his eyebrows. Dr. Lewis was immediately plunged into a blissful meditation of being immersed in divine light for about five hours.

Due to this experience, Dr. Lewis was a transformed man. As he went home that night, rather late to decorate the Christmas tree, his wife could

---

21 ibid, p.402

not be angry with him, seeing the extraordinary joy on his face. The Lewis family became very close disciples of Yogananda, helping him and his work financially and in many other ways.

In 1925, Yogananda established Self-Realization Fellowship headquarters at Mount Washington in Los Angeles, California. There he trained several monks and nuns in Kriya yoga meditation, even as he continued to go on lecture tours throughout America. He was such a popular speaker that thousands could not be accommodated in the lecture halls.

James Lynn was a brilliant self-made multimillionaire from Kansas. At the pinnacle of worldly success, he was still quite restless until he met Yogananda. Immediately he went into deep ecstatic meditation. Yogananda revered him highly as an ideal disciple who was one hundred percent in tune with him. He was ready to receive s*amadhi* or the experience of cosmic consciousness within six months of starting to meditate.

Even as a little girl, Faye Wright had an extraordinary urge to love God with all her heart. She approached several ministers of churches hoping to find someone who could help her in her spiritual goal. She did not find anyone who seemed to love God as wholeheartedly as she wanted, until she walked with her family into a hall in Salt Lake City, where Yogananda was lecturing on Yoga.

As soon as Faye entered the hall, she was transfixed, looking at Yogananda's face glowing with divine love; she knew that she had found the man who was full of love for God, and would help her in her profound aspiration. She was only seventeen years old when she joined Yogananda's ashram in Los Angeles.

Knowing her high caliber, Yogananda gave her the same drastic training that he had received from Sri Yukteswar, thus producing the precious jewel of a saint, who inspires thousands throughout the world to love God ever more and more. She was at the helm of Self-Realization Fellowship for five decades and peacefully merged into God in 2010 at the age of 96 years.

In 1935 Yogananda got a telepathic message from his Guru to come to India. James Lynn financed his passage by car and ship. On the way, he went first to England and then to Germany where he met with Therese Neumann, a Catholic saint, who had abstained completely from food and drink for many years. In 1926, the sacred wounds of Christ had appeared on her head, breast, hands and feet. She bled from these wounds every week from Thursday midnight until Friday afternoon.

Due to harassment by thousands of visitors, the majority being merely curious, her bishop had ordered that she should not receive visitors without his written permission. Yogananda did not know about this rule when he arrived at her place. Happily, Therese ignored the rule and agreed to receive "the man of God from India." The saints bubbled with joy like two innocent children when they met. "We beamed in silent communion, each knowing the other to be a lover of God," wrote Yogananda.[22]

At this time Therese was staying with her friend Professor Franz Wutz who could translate for her. She said that she took in only the holy Eucharist, and could not swallow the paper thin wafer if it was not consecrated. "One of the reasons I am here on earth today is to prove that man can live by God's invisible light, and not by food only,"[23] she told Yogananda, adding that God does not wish her to teach others how to live without food.

With the permit from the Bishop, Yogananda went back on the following Friday morning to see Therese in her mystic trance of witnessing and participating in the passion of Christ. He saw blood flowing from her lower eye-lids, cloth around her head soaked in blood, as well as the cloth covering her chest.

Yogananda put himself into a yogic trance so that he could see what Therese saw. He saw Lord Jesus carrying the wooden Cross amid a jeering crowd. As Jesus fell down under the weight of the cross, Therese sank back on the bed in sorrow, and Yogananda's vision ceased. Bidding silent farewell to Therese, he left the saint's house.

Yogananda loved Lord Jesus dearly. He reported having many visions of the Galilean Master, especially during Christmas season. He also encouraged his followers to cultivate deeper love for Jesus, and arranged to conduct an eight hour-long meditation at SRF temples and centers to celebrate Christmas spiritually. This custom is still followed devoutly by SRF centers all over the world.

---

22 ibid, p.421

23 ibid, p.422

While Yogananda was in India, James Lynn bought a large property adjoining the sea coast in Encinitas, California, and built a hermitage as a surprise gift for his Master. When Yogananda returned, he was happily and gratefully surprised at Lynn's gesture of love.

It was a thrilling sight for the monks and nuns at the hermitage to see their beloved Master and Lynn walking around the garden, hand in hand like little children, immersed in ecstatic joy, expressing the divine romance between an ideal disciple and a perfect Master.

Years earlier, Paramahansa Yogananda had predicted that he would die talking about India and God. Though he was in perfect health, for weeks before his death he hinted to the disciples about his imminent departure. On March 7 1952, during the banquet for the Indian Ambassador at Los Angeles Biltmore Hotel, Yogananda gave an inspiring talk about love of God, and ended it with his poem about India:

"God made the earth;
Man made confining countries
And their fancy-frozen boundaries.
Where Ganges, woods, Himalayan caves, and men dream God-
I am hallowed; my body touched that sod."[24]

With the last words, he slipped down and was gone. Two hundred participants in the hall were feeling the vibrations of joy and love that exuded from the great lover of God, and could hardly believe that he had left the body.

Yogananda has written many inspirational books. He wrote *Whispers from Eternity* during His early years. It is dedicated to Christians, Moslems, Buddhists, Hebrews, Hindus and all other religionists "in whom the Cosmic Heart is ever throbbing equally."[25]

Yogananda also wrote many poems that have been collected in the book: *Songs of the Soul*. The beautiful poem: "God! God! God!" was written after he saw St Francis of Assisi in a vision and communed with him lovingly. His voluminous commentaries on the *Bhagavad Gita* and the *Bible* are profoundly spiritual, highly scholarly, and deeply appreciated by thoughtful readers.

24 Paramahansa Yogananda In Memoriam, SRF, Los Angeles, 1958, p.69

25 Published by SRF, Los Angeles, 1935

Emphasizing the fundamental unity between the scriptures seems to have been one of the main missions of Paramahansa Yogananda.

For more information about Yogananda, and to learn about his teaching and techniques of meditation, please contact SRF Mother Center, 3880 San Rafael Ave, Los Angeles, CA 90065 tel. 323 225 2471 or www.yogananda-srf.org

Lord, make me an instrument of your peace
Where there is hatred...let me sow love.
Where there is injury. . .pardon.
Where there is discord. . .unity.
Where there is doubt. . .faith.
Where there is error. . .truth.
Where there is despair. . .hope
Where there is sadness. . .joy.
Where there is darkness. . .light
O Divine Master, grant that I may not
So much seek
To be consoled. . .as to console.
To be understood. . .as to understand.
To be loved. . .as to love.
For it is in giving. . .that we receive.
It is in pardoning. . .that we are pardoned.
It is in dying. . .that we are born to eternal life.

St. Francis of Assisi

Francis of Assisi

Francis Of Assisi

Of all the Christian saints, perhaps the most popular is Francis of Assisi. The end of the twelfth century saw the birth of the serene saintly poet and lover of nature in a mountainous and picturesque part of Italy. A successful cloth merchant, Bernadone Moriconi was proud and fond of his rather cultured, French-speaking wife Pica. Hence he called his newborn son Francisco, meaning "Frenchman."

From early childhood, Francis was exuberant, jovial and generous. He gathered friends around him easily; he was their natural leader. His parents provided him with more than enough to entertain his friends. He loved to sing, choosing apt songs for various occasions; he composed them, if none was available to suit the time and the mood.

As a youth, Francis was moved by the spirit of adventure leading to the worldly glory of being a prince one day. Joining the army of Assisi, and dressed as a knight in arms, he fought in the war between Perugia and Assisi. In 1206, Perugia defeated Assisi badly. At twenty years of age, Francis became a prisoner along with many others. Undaunted by the abominable conditions around him, he kept up the spirit of his companions with songs and stories.

He was freed from the prison after a year, but fell ill and was sick for a few months. Then he enrolled in a military expedition again, and was traveling toward Apulia, when his journey was interrupted by another sudden sickness. Lying in bed, he heard a voice telling him that he was serving the vassals instead of the master. He understood it to mean that he had been enamored by mere tinsels, instead of seeking divine glory by serving God. Directed by the voice, he returned to Assisi.

Francis was riding his horse, dressed in rich, stylish attire, when he encountered a begging leper. The sight disgusted him. He was about to leave after throwing some money to the leper, when he remembered the words of Christ: "As often as you did it to one of my least brothers, you did it to me" (Mt 25:40).

The leper was Christ in "a distressing disguise" to use the words of Mother Teresa. Controlling his natural aversion by a heroic act of will, he got down from the horse, and lovingly kissed the leper's hand. His disgust turned into pure joy. From then on, Francis was a transformed man.

Traveling abroad on business, Bernadone was often away from home. Francis never had any aptitude or inkling to follow up on his father's trade. Whenever he sold some clothes, the money was distributed to the poor. Realizing the vanity and emptiness of partying with friends, he visited the hospital for leprosy daily, and cared affectionately for the patients. For days and nights he was in the caves and secluded spots around Assisi, absorbed in fervent prayer. His devout and loving mother, Lady Pica, admired the new values espoused by her son, and was supportive.

Bernadone, on the contrary, was beside himself with wrath, when he came home and heard about the "madness" of his son on whom he had placed so much hope. As Francis refused to change his ways, the father brought him forcibly before the bishop, and disowned him publicly.

Francis was an equal match to his father. Saying that he did not want anything from his father, he removed the clothes he was wearing, laid them before him, and stood there naked. Bishop Guido, a man of faith, aware that divine grace was especially active in the young man before him, covered him with his own cloak.

A little rustic chapel dedicated to St. Damian was located in the outskirts of Assisi. Kneeling before a large crucifix above the main altar at St Damian's Church, Francis poured his heart out in fervent prayers. Then he waited, wrapped in silence, and he heard the Lord's words: "Go, Francis, and rebuild my church, for it is about to fall into ruins."

Francis took the words of Christ to mean the Church of St. Damian and instantly started renovating it, gathering stones from people, and doing the masonry work himself with help from a few others. Love for the crucified figure of Jesus burnt in his heart so brightly that years later he would be blessed with stigmata or the appearance of the real wounds of Lord Jesus in his own body, like in Therese Neumann and several other saints.

He went about renovating more churches, spending time with poor beggars as one of them, sharing their rags and meals, preaching to all and sundry about the love of God and Christ. Most of the people of Assisi were antagonistic to him initially, believing that he was crazy. He accepted their insults humbly as penance for his sins.

Only later history would prove that Christ was referring to the community of Christians, disintegrating due to worldliness, corruption, conflict and scandals, and how the church needed to be saved by the zeal of Francis and his saintly followers. Even the Pope saw in a dream that the Church was about to collapse, and was being held up by the shoulder of a poor beggar whom he recognized to be Francis.

Bernard, a young man from a very wealthy family, had been hearing about and observing Francis for the past two years, being rather intrigued by his attitude. He understood the vanity of worldly life, but wanted to be sure that the saint was truly genuine. One day he invited Francis to his home and arranged for him to sleep in the same dimly lit room with him. Francis went to bed and seemed to be already asleep, when Bernard too lay on the bed and pretended to snore.

Francis, thinking that Bernard was fast asleep, got off the bed, went down on his knees and was praying fervently, repeating the same phrase "My God, My God" throughout the night. As tears poured down his cheeks, the saint seemed to be verily in God's Presence. The day dawned to inaugurate the new order of Franciscans.

Bernard told Francis that he wanted to give away all his wealth and follow him, obeying his guidance. Francis, realizing the momentous significance of Bernard's decision, wanted clear divine approval and grace, before taking on the responsibility of guiding him on the spiritual path. Both went for holy mass and were blessed by the priest.

Afterwards, Francis made a sign of the cross on the missal and opened it at random to read: "If you seek perfection, go, sell your possessions, and give to the poor... Then come back and follow me (Mt19:21). The second reading randomly selected was: "Provide yourselves with neither gold nor silver nor copper in your belts; no traveling bag, no change of shirt, no sandals, no walking staff" (Mt 10: 9-10). Final words were Mt 16:24: "If a man wishes to come after me, he must deny his very self, take up his cross, and follow me."

Immediately Bernard went to the public square, and began to distribute all his wealth to the poor, ably assisted by Francis. A priest named Sylvester who had earlier given Francis some stones to build churches, saw the large amount of money being distributed. He complained to Francis that he had been given only little money for the stones. Francis filled his hands with silver, and was ready to give even more. The priest was ashamed, and went away saying it was enough.

Struck by the contrast between their joyful detachment from wealth and his own miserable attachment to money, Father Sylvester was deeply thoughtful for days. Then he too happily joined Francis, Bernard and their companions in the romantic pursuit of "lady poverty" [a phrase dear to Francis]. For subsistence they helped out in farms or in other trades. They also practiced the trade of begging, to learn humility through humiliation.

The first disciples of Francis were saintly like the twelve apostles of His Master, Lord Jesus. Nineteenth century India produced the magnificent man of God, Ramakrishna Paramahansa who also had twelve close disciples. All of them became enlightened sages with their own disciples later.

Francis and his companions were the first "flower people." Indeed their earliest chronicle was titled "Fioretti," meaning "Little Flowers." Laughing and singing with irrepressible joy, they walked the streets and fields in and around Assisi, and preached the gospel of Jesus to everyone willing to listen.

Most people had by now come to accept Francis as a living saint, an ideal image of Christ on earth. Wherever he went, crowds gathered to listen to his inspiring sermons, and be healed through his powerful prayers.

Bishop Guido recommended the way of life pursued by Francis and his companions to John Cardinal Colona for approval by the Church. When the Cardinal met Francis, he was inspired by the saint's simplicity, humility, burning love for God and loyalty to the Church. Hence he praised him to Pope Innocent the Third who later dreamed about Francis as the one who miraculously saved the Church from collapsing into ruins. The rule laid out by Francis for his community of friars was approved by the Pope.

Franciscan ideals spread like wildfire throughout Europe. This movement was so powerful that within five years, more than five thousand men flocked around the *Poverollo* (little poor man) of Assisi, to catch the fire of his zeal, ready to spread the message of crucified Christ to the farthest ends of the world, and be sacrificed as martyrs, if necessary.

A rich noble family in Assisi had three lovely daughters; worthy suitors came asking for the hand of the eldest, Clare, in marriage. She refused, having already vowed her life to God secretly, which was rather disturbing to her parents. One day, Clare heard Francis preach a stirring sermon at a Church in Assisi. Moved by his ardent love for God, she decided to join him, though he was a man.

Unknown to her parents, she met Francis and revealed her desire to live in poverty like him. Thinking that it was the will of God, he told the Bishop about it. Clare was officially received into the religious life in secret by Francis, who cut her hair and allowed her to change her elegant silk dress into the grey coarse robe of a poor nun. She was sheltered temporarily at a Benedictine convent.

The family was furious when they found what had happened. Her uncle Monaldo went to the convent to remove her forcibly, but desisted when she showed him her cut hair; he realized that she had taken religious vows, and was canonically protected by the Church.

Sixteen days later, Clare's sister Agnes came to the convent, wanting to dedicate herself. Uncle Monaldo was utterly enraged and acted promptly, coming to the convent with twelve armed men, to remove Agnes before she could pronounce her vows. Terrified nuns gave the girl away to the uncle immediately. Agnes was desperate and screamed: "Clare, Clare, help me!" Clare could only summon her Lord Jesus for help.

His help came instantly. The twelve men felt weak, and could not move Agnes at all. Monaldo raised his hand to hit the girl, but it stayed up, as in a paralysis. It was his turn to beg for mercy. As the Lord had shown His will so clearly, the youngest, Beatrice, also joined her elder sisters. After their father's death, mother too entered the first Franciscan Convent, accepting daughter Clare as her superior.

Francis and his companions were going throughout Italy on preaching missions. Near Carnaca, they saw thousands of birds of every species in a field. "Let me preach to our brothers the birds," said Francis and walked into the field. This sermon is taken from Fioretti as given in a modern version:

"My very dear brothers the birds, you are deeply indebted to God, and it is your duty to praise Him and celebrate Him always and everywhere, for He has allowed you to fly freely wherever you please; He has clothed you with double or triple coats and given you elegant, many colored finery.

"And you must also give thanks to the Creator for the food He gives you with no effort on your part. And then there is the beautiful voice He has given you to sing with! You neither sow or reap, my dear little brothers, but God Himself feeds you, and it is He who gives you the brooks to quench your thirst, the mountains, hills, rocks and woods to shelter you, and high trees where you can build your nests.

"And although you cannot spin or weave, He gives you and your little ones all the clothing you need. That's because the Creator loves you very much, as He has proven by so many great favors He has bestowed on you! But you, my dear brothers the birds, take care not to be ungrateful toward Him and always busy yourself praising Him."[1]

And after Francis had spoken these words, all the birds began to open their beaks, flap their wings, stretch their necks and bow their little heads to

1 Saint Francis of Assisi by Leon Cristiani, Translated by Angeline Bouchard, Daughters of St. Paul, Boston, 1970, pp.136-137

the ground in deep respect, and to show by their songs and their movements, that they were truly delighted with what Francis had said to them.

Once, Francis went with Brother Masseo to the principal square of Alviano. He wanted to preach to the crowd that had gathered there, silently waiting for him to begin the sermon. But the silence was disturbed by the raucous noise made by the chattering swallows. Francis spoke to the birds reminding them that they had chatted long enough and should allow him to preach the good news to God's children. The swallows fell silent immediately, and stayed there until the end of the sermon.

Equally dramatic was the way Francis taught Brother Leo about perfect joy. They were returning from Perugia to Portiuncula, and Leo was walking a little ahead of Francis. He called Leo to say that even if they were the best examples of holiness in the world, it would not be perfect joy. After walking a little longer, he told Brother Leo that even if they had the power to make the lame walk, give hearing to the deaf and speech to the mute, restore sight to the blind, and raise the dead, still it would not result in perfect joy. For the third time, he cried out to Brother Leo, that even if they are fluent in all the languages and know all sciences, if they could reveal the future and the secrets of men's hearts, still it cannot amount to perfect joy.

As Francis kept on talking like that, Brother Leo could not contain his puzzled wonder, and asked him eagerly to explain how they could find perfect joy.

Francis replied that they would soon reach Pontiuncula wet with the rain and numb with cold, covered with the mud from the road and exhausted from hunger. If when Brother Porter asks them who they are and they say: "two brothers," and he answers "you are lying, you are nothing but highway robbers!" and he refuses to open the door, leaving them outside shivering in the snow, rain, and cold, and they are patient enough to endure the insults and torments without becoming angry, humbly concluding that it was God who made him speak against them in this way, that would be perfect joy.

Francis said that if, as they knocked again on the door, Brother Porter came out of the house enraged and drove them away with heavy blows, shouting "Go away, you shameless scoundrels," if they could still suffer it patiently, cheerfully and with love, that would indeed be perfect joy.

Francis felt a close affinity to the whole of creation, feeling God's Presence everywhere. One who knows God to be the Father of Creation naturally finds all things to be his brothers and sisters. Composed in this spirit is his famous Canticle of Brother Sun!

Most high, all powerful, all good Lord
All praise is Yours, all glory, honor and blessings
To You alone, Most High do they belong.
No mortal lips are worthy to pronounce Your name.
We praise You Lord for all your creatures,
Especially for Brother Sun
Who brings the day, through whom you give light.
And he is beautiful and radiant with great splendor
Of You Most High, he bears the likeness.
We praise You, Lord, for Sister Moon and the Stars
In the heaven you have made them bright,
Precious and beautiful
We praise you, Lord, for Brothers Wind and Air
Fair and strong, all the weather
By which you sustain all that you have made.
We praise you, Lord, for Sister Water so useful,
precious and pure
We praise You, Lord, for Brother Fire
Through whom you light the night.
He is beautiful, playful, robust and strong
We praise You, Lord for Sister Earth who sustains us
With her fruits, colored flowers and herbs.
We praise You, Lord, for those who pardon
For love of You, bear sickness and trial
Blessed are those who endure in peace,
By You Most High, they will be crowned.

We praise You, Lord for Sister Death
From whom no one living can escape
Woe to those who die in their sins!
Blessed are those she finds doing Your will
No second death can do them harm
We praise and bless You, Lord, and give You thanks and serve You in all humility.

The people of Gubbio were scared to go out of the city. On its outskirts roamed a large voracious wolf that attacked and killed not only other animals, but also human beings. The men went out armed, but a single man even armed, could not defend himself against this wolf.

When Francis came to Gubbio, he saw the panic in which the people lived, and went with his companions to see the wolf. People were scared and warned him about the danger; yet they followed him at a distance. When they saw the wolf, Francis told his companions to stay back. He went alone toward the wolf who opened his mouth wide, staring at him.

Francis made a sign of the cross; the wolf closed his mouth immediately. He addressed the wolf about the serious damage he had caused in Gubbio, and earned the hatred of its people not only by devouring other animals but by killing human beings as well. The saint offered to arrange a peace pact between the people of Gubbio and the wolf. If the wolf agreed not to do any more harm, the people would feed him regularly thereafter.

The people were amazed to see the wolf accepting the peace pact through body language. Then it followed Francis like a gentle lamb, looking mildly at the people gathered there. In the city, the wolf pledged again to be peaceful by lifting up his right paw and placing it in the hands of Francis. From then on, the wolf was affable to the people, visiting their houses and taking food from them on a daily basis. They were very fond of him, as he reminded them of their lovable Saint Francis.

Francis was the first to celebrate Christmas by making a crèche. He instructed his friend, John Vellita in Greccio to make a manger filled with straw, and to place the statue of infant Jesus in it, with an ox and an ass standing nearby. After the midnight mass, Francis went to the manger, and held up the statue towards his face. According to John Vellita, the statue came alive, and the holy infant was caressing the face of Francis.

In his later years, Francis suffered from many bodily ills, his eyes hemorrhaged, and he became nearly blind though he continued to cure the sick who came to him. The religious orders that he had started for the friars, nuns, and laypeople were flourishing and spreading fast everywhere. He was full of joy, as he prepared to meet his Master.

Paramahansa Yoganada was fond of St. Francis, whom he saw in many visions. He was glad to visit the shrines of Saints Francis and Clare at Assisi in Italy, on his way to India in 1935. His saintly disciple, Daya Mata, also spoke about visiting the same shrines later, and being plunged into ecstatic, blissful meditation for several days while there.

Among the many-hued flowers that blossomed in the Franciscan garden, the most beautiful was Anthony of Padua. Born in Lisbon, the capital of Portugal, and living as a young monk at the monastery of St. Augustine in Coimbra, Anthony was passionately fixed on being a martyr for Christ.

Earlier he had hosted five Franciscan friars on their way to Morocco to preach the gospel, and had been deeply inspired by their love and zeal. When their martyred bodies were returned to Portugal, Anthony ardently wanted to follow them. Since his Augustinian superiors did not permit him to leave for foreign lands, the Franciscans accepted him as a friar and sent him to Morocco.

God had other plans for Anthony. In Morocco he fell seriously ill and had to return. The ship in which he sailed was tossed about in a severe storm, and managed, after several days, to find harbor in Sicily. Anthony and his companions were received at the Franciscan monastery at Messina. Then he moved to the hermitage of Monte Paolo, and lived as a recluse given to penance and prayer. One day, some Franciscans had gathered nearby for a ceremony of sacred orders by the bishop; no one was willing to preach before such an august assembly.

The superior of Monte Paolo asked Anthony to deliver the sermon. Being humble, he began to speak shyly at first. Gradually his sermon gained power; delivered in a musical voice, it rose to mystic heights, when he spoke about the immense love of Christ for all mankind. The Church found an extraordinarily gifted preacher in Anthony, and thereafter, he was called to preach everywhere. His words had the power to soften the hearts of hardened criminals, and bring about miraculous conversions.

It was a turbulent time for Europe. The peasants were suffering ruthless oppression by the feudal lords, who also fought among themselves with their private armies. The orthodox believers and heretics were often engaged in rather violent conflicts, with horrendous loss of lives.

In his sermons, Anthony emphasized Christian brotherhood and harmony. Instead of condemning the heretics and sinners, his preaching style was gentle and compassionate. He did not use his profound knowledge of the Sacred Scripture to intimidate anyone, but to humbly persuade his audience to live in a manner that would bring happiness to themselves and to Christ.

The Albigenses were a heretical group that revived Manichaeism; their teaching rejected external worship, and opposed the normal principles of morality; they were violent towards anyone who disagreed with them. Rimini was their headquarters in Italy.

When Anthony went to Rimini, Catholics were scared to come and listen to him. Therefore, he went to the seashore, and called the fish to come and hear him. Immediately, a large group of fish gathered near, raised their heads above the water, and seemed to be listening to the Saint's sermon with rapt attention, until he bid them farewell. After this miracle, people flocked in great numbers to listen to Anthony.

It angered the heretics so much, that they were prepared to kill him; so they underhandedly invited him for a dinner. The saint pointed out that the dish they planned to serve him was poisoned. The hosts quoted the scripture: "If they pick up snakes or drink any poison, they will not be harmed" (Mk. 16:18), saying that a true disciple of Christ will not be affected adversely by poison. Anthony blessed the poisoned food, and ate it without experiencing any harm.

The news about Anthony's power to defeat the heretics with his miracles and sermons spread far and wide. He was welcome in France, where the orthodox were waging a losing battle with the heretics. At Bourges, one heretic named Bonvillo told Anthony that it was not proper for Jesus Christ to appear in the form of bread and wine. Still he agreed to believe if his mule, after fasting for three days, would refuse fresh oats, and go instead to adore the Holy Eucharist [consecrated bread connoting the real Presence of Christ].

Anthony accepted the challenge; he also fasted for three days, and celebrated the Eucharist with great devotion. Then he carried the Blessed Sacrament, with many people following him in a procession, towards Bonvillo's house. Bonvillo brought out the starving mule, which saw a basket of fresh oats, and was ready to pounce on it, when Anthony invited the mule to come and adore Lord Jesus truly present in the Eucharist.

Immediately the mule left the food, turned around, went near Anthony and knelt down in an attitude of adoration, staying there until the saint asked the mule to arise. The orthodox Catholics were thrilled, as Bonvillo was converted to become a devout believer.

Quite numerous were the miracles performed by Anthony, as he moved from city to city through France, Spain and Italy, where he finally settled. He taught at the famous university of Padua, and while there, concentrated on writing his sermons.

In 1231, Anthony, feeling his health decline, retired to the hermitage located in the land belonging to his disciple, Count Tursi. One day he was secluded in a room at the Count's house. The count approached the room, wanting to speak to him, and saw a brilliant light streaming under the closed door. Looking through the keyhole, the Count saw a divinely beautiful child standing before Anthony on a table, and clinging to the saint's neck with both arms, while the saint caressed him lovingly.

The count understood the scene to be Child Jesus playing with the saint. After the Child vanished, Anthony opened the door, and knowing what the Count had seen, charged him solemnly not to reveal it to anyone before his death. Later, the count stirred his audience by describing the incident with tears pouring down his face.

Anthony passed away peacefully on June 13. The body was taken to the Friars of St Mary's at Padua and buried on June 17; since so many miracles occurred there at this time, the funeral turned into a triumphant celebration.

According to the earliest biographers, many sick people were cured, the blind regained sight, deaf their hearing, and the lame the use of their limbs.

St. Anthony is still popular as a wonder-worker among Catholics and non-Catholics. People pray to him for all types of favors. He is said to be quite efficacious in finding lost things.

Anthony was concerned about social issues of his day. He was especially active regarding the many debtors painfully languishing in prisons, and was mainly responsible for getting the first bankruptcy law in history passed. Thus he became the patron saint of social workers.

Peace Pilgrim

PEACE PILGRIM

A modern Francis of Assisi in her utter simplicity, poverty and complete commitment to selfless service, this "religion-less" saint ignored her name and the normal values of the world. She refused to reveal her original name to the public, calling herself "Peace Pilgrim," as she started walking on January 1, 1953 across America from Pasadena, California. Her purpose was to let the people focus on her message of peace, and not on herself. She had vowed to remain a wanderer until mankind learned the way of peace.

In 1952, she was the first woman to hike along the whole Appalachian Trail from Georgia to Maine. Starting her pilgrimage in a spirit of prayer and penance at the Rose Parade in Pasadena, she wore a tunic printed PEACE PILGRIM in front and 25,000 MILES ON FOOT FOR PEACE on the back.

By 1964 she had walked 25,000 miles, and stopped counting the miles; speaking about peace became her priority, though she continued to walk daily. She talked to thousands of people on the streets, in schools, colleges, churches, clubs, and in the media.

At the time of her death in 1981, she was crossing the country for the seventh time. She had walked through all the fifty states, visited ten provinces of Canada and some parts of Mexico. In 1976, a man flew her to Alaska and Hawaii to meet with his children, walk, speak in public places, and give interviews to the media.

Born in New Jersey and lacking any religion as a child, she was brought up with the spiritual values of being truthful and kind. Finding God all by herself through inner seeking, and becoming intimately one with Him through prayer, perfect renunciation, and selfless service, she was always bubbling with love, peace and joy.

Up to the age of twenty nine, she had enjoyed worldly life, wearing fashionable clothes, driving new cars, dancing, and partying with friends. But she did not find much meaning in such a life. The way she changed around and became one of the greatest saints the world has ever produced is beautifully narrated in the book: *Peace Pilgrim*, compiled by five of her loyal followers, using her own words![1]

(The writer is grateful to the Friends of Peace Pilgrim and the board member Bruce Nicols for allowing the following part to be scripted entirely from this book, since the saint's words about herself are quite inspiring.)

"As I looked about the world, so much of it impoverished, I became increasingly uncomfortable about having so much while my brothers and sisters were starving. Finally I had to find another way. The turning point came when, in desperation and out of a very deep seeking for a meaningful way of life, I walked all one night through the woods. I came to a moonlit glade and prayed.

I felt a complete willingness, without any reservations, to give my life – to dedicate my life - to service. "Please use me," I prayed to God. And a great peace came over me.

I tell you it's a point of no return. After that, you can never go back to a completely self-centered living.

And so I went into the second phase of my life. I began to live to give what I could, instead of to get what I could, and I entered a new and wonderful world. My life began to be meaningful. I attained the great blessing of good health; I haven't had an ache or pain, a cold or headache since. From that time on, I have known that my life work would be for peace - that it would cover the whole peace picture: peace among nations, peace among groups, peace among individuals, and the very important inner peace.

---

1 Published by Friends of Peace Pilgrim and distributed freely for donation. It is available at P. O. Box 2207, Shelton, Ct. 06484 tel. no.[203] 926 1581.

If you do not face problems, you just drift through life. It is through solving problems in accordance with the highest light we have, that inner growth is attained. Now, collective problems must be solved by us collectively, and no one finds inner peace who avoids doing his or her share in the solving of collective problems, like world disarmament and world peace. So let us always think about these problems together and talk about them together, and collectively work toward their solutions.

Every morning I thought of God and thought of things I might do that day to be of service to God's children. I looked at every situation I came into to see if there was anything I could do there to be of service. I did as many good things as I could each day, not forgetting the importance of a pleasant word and cheery smile. I prayed about things that seemed too big for me to handle-and right prayer motivates to right action.

Just after I dedicated my life to service, I felt that I could no longer accept more than I need while others in the world have less than they need. This moved me to bring my life down to need level. I thought it would be difficult. I thought it would entail a great many hardships, but I was quite wrong. Instead of hardships, I found a wonderful sense of peace and joy, and a conviction that unnecessary possessions are only unnecessary burdens.

I did not take care of my bodily temple when I was very young; this only happened later in life. Now I eat mostly fruits, nuts, vegetables, whole grains (preferably organically grown) and perhaps a bit of milk and cheese. This is what I live on and walk on.

I began to realize that I was disobeying my rule of life which says: I will not ask anyone to do for me things that I would refuse to do for myself. Now, I wouldn't kill any creature – I wouldn't even kill a chicken or a fish - and therefore I stopped immediately eating all flesh.

The difficulty is we have not learned to stop killing each other yet. That's our present lesson – not to kill each other. To learn the lesson of sharing, and the lesson of non-killing of man by man. The lesson of non-killing of creatures is a little bit into the future, though those of us who know better need to live up to our highest light.

If you realized how powerful your thoughts are, you would never think a negative thought. I don't eat junk foods and I don't think junk thoughts! Let me tell you, junk thoughts are something to be wary of.

You must learn to forgive yourself as easily as you forgive others. And then take a further step and use all that energy that you used in condemning yourself for improving yourself. After that I really started to get somewhere- because there's only one person you can change and that's yourself. After you have changed your self, you might be able to inspire others to look for change.

The motive, if you are to find inner peace, must be an outgoing motive. Service, of course, service. Giving, not getting. Your motive must be good if your work is to have good effect. The secret of life is being of service.

Spiritual growth is not easily attained, but it is well worth the effort. It takes time, just as any growth takes time. One should rejoice at small gains and not be impatient, as impatience hampers growth.

The path of gradual relinquishment of things hindering spiritual progress is a difficult path, for only when relinquishment is complete do the rewards really come. The path of quick relinquishment is an easy path, for it brings immediate blessings. And when God fills your life, God's gifts overflow to bless all you touch.

To me, it was an escape from the artificiality of illusion into the richness of reality. To the world it may seem that I had given up much. I had given up burdensome possessions, spending time meaninglessly, doing things I knew I should not do and not doing things I knew I should do. But to me it seemed that I had gained much – even the priceless treasures of health and happiness.

There were hills and valleys, lots of hills and valleys, in that spiritual growing up period. Then in the midst of the struggle there came a wonderful mountaintop experience – the first glimpse of what the life of inner peace was like.

That came when I was out walking in the early morning. All of a sudden I felt very uplifted, more uplifted than I had ever been. I remember I knew timelessness and spacelessness and lightness. I did not seem to be walking on the earth. There were no people or even animals around, but every flower, every bush, every tree seemed to wear a halo. There was a light emanation around everything and flecks of gold fell like slanted rain through the air. This experience is sometimes called the illumination.

The most important part of it was not the phenomena; the important part of it was the realization of the oneness of all creation. Not only all human beings –I knew before that all human beings are one. But now I knew also oneness with the rest of creation. The creatures that walk the earth and the growing things of the earth. The air, the water, the earth itself. And, most wonderful of all, a oneness with that which permeates all and binds all together and gives life to all. A oneness with that which many would call God.

I have never felt separate since. I could return again and again to this wonderful mountaintop, and then I could stay there for longer and longer periods of time and just slip out occasionally.

The inspiration for the pilgrimage came at this time. I sat high upon a hill overlooking rural New England. The day before I had slipped out of harmony, and the evening before I had thought to God, "It seems to me that if I could always remain in harmony I could be of greater usefulness – for every time I slip out of harmony it impairs my usefulness."

When I awoke at dawn I was back on the spiritual mountaintop with a wonderful feeling. I knew that I would never need to descend again into the valley. I knew that for me the struggle was over, that finally I had succeeded in giving my life or finding inner peace. Again this is a point of no return. You can never go back into the struggle. The struggle is over now because you will to do the right thing and you don't need to be pushed into it.

You are now in control of your life. Your higher nature, which is controlled by God, controls the body, mind, and emotions. The ego is never really in control. The ego is controlled by wishes for comfort and convenience on the part of the body, by demands of the mind, and by outbursts of the emotions.

I can say to my body, "Lie down there on that cement floor and go to sleep," and it obeys. I can say to my mind, "Shut out everything else and concentrate on the job before you," and it is obedient. I can say to my emotions, "Be still, even in the face of this terrible situation," and they are still.

Looking through the eyes of the divine nature you see the essence within the manifestation, the creator within the creation, and it is a wonderful, wonderful world!

I have no money. I do not accept any money on my pilgrimage. I belong to no organization. There is no organization backing me. I own only what I wear and carry. There is nothing to tie me down. I am as free as a bird soaring in the sky.

I walk until given shelter, fast until given food, I don't ask-it's given without asking. Aren't people good! There is a spark of good in everybody, no matter how deeply it may be buried, it is there. It's waiting to govern your life gloriously. I call it the God-centered nature or divine nature. Jesus called it the kingdom of God within.

What I walk on is not the energy of youth, it is a better energy. I walk on the endless energy of inner peace that never runs out! When you become a channel through which God works, there are no more limitations, because God does the work through you; you are merely the instrument –and what God can do is unlimited. When you are working for God you do not find yourself striving and straining. You find yourself calm, serene and unhurried.

My pilgrimage is not a crusade, which connotes violence. There is no attempt to force something on people. A pilgrimage is a gentle journey of prayer and example. My walking is first of all a prayer for peace. If you give your life as a prayer, you intensify the prayer beyond all measure.

I was tested severely in the beginning of my pilgrimage. Life is a series of tests; but if you pass your tests, you look back upon them as good experiences. I'm glad I had these experiences.

If you have a loving and positive attitude toward your fellow human beings, you will not fear them. "Perfect love casteth out all fear."

One test happened in the middle of the night in the middle of the California desert. The traffic had just about stopped, and there wasn't a human habitation within many miles. I saw a car parked at the side of the road. The driver called to me saying, "Come on, get in and get warm." I said, "I don't ride." He said, "I'm not going anywhere, I'm just parked here." I got in. I looked at the man. He was a big, burly man-what most people would call a rough looking individual. After we had talked a while he said: "Say, wouldn't you like to get a few winks of sleep?" And I said, "Oh, yes, I certainly would!" and I curled up and went to sleep. When I awoke I could see the man was very puzzled about something, and after we had talked for quite some time he admitted that when he had asked me to get into the car, he had certainly meant me no good, adding, "When you curled up so trustingly and went to sleep, I just couldn't touch you!"

I thanked him for the shelter and began walking away. As I looked back I saw him gazing at the heavens, and I hoped he had found God that night.

On another occasion I was called upon to defend a frail eight year old girl against a large man who was about to beat her. The girl was terrified. It was my most difficult test. I was staying at a ranch and the family went into town. The little girl did not want to go with them, and they asked, since I was there, would I take care of the child? I was writing a letter by the window when I saw a car arrive. A man got out of the car. The girl saw him and ran and he followed, chasing her into a barn. I went immediately into the barn. The girl was cowering in terror in the corner. He was coming at her slowly and deliberately.

You know the power of thought. You're constantly creating through thought. And you attract to you whatever you fear. So I knew her danger because of her fear. (I fear nothing and expect good, - so good comes!)

I put my body immediately between the man and the girl. I just stood and looked at this poor, psychologically sick man with loving compassion. He came close. He stopped! He looked at me for quite a while. He then turned and walked away and the girl was safe. There was not a word spoken.

Now, what was the alternative? Suppose I had been so foolish as to forget the law of love by hitting back and relying upon the jungle law of tooth and claw? Undoubtedly I would have been beaten – perhaps even to death and possibly the little girl as well. Never underestimate the power of God's love – it transforms! It reaches the spark of good in the other person and the person is disarmed.

During my pilgrimage through Arizona I was arrested by a plainclothes policeman while mailing letters at the local post office in Benson. After a short ride in a patrol car I was booked as a vagrant. When you walk on faith you are technically guilty of vagrancy. Yes, I've been jailed several times for not having any money, but they always release me once they understand.

They put me into a huge inner room surrounded by cell blocks in which they locked the women, four to a cell for the night. As I walked in I said to myself, "Peace Pilgrim, you have dedicated your life to service – behold your wonderful new field of service!"

When I walked in, one of the girls said, "Gee, you're a funny one; you're the only one that came in smiling. Most of them come in crying or cursing."

I said to them, "Suppose you had a day off at home. Wouldn't you do something worthwhile on that day?" They said, "Yes, what will we do?" So I got them to sing songs that lifted the spirit. I gave them a simple exercise which makes you feel tingly all over. Then I talked to them about the steps toward inner peace. I told them they lived in a community and what could be done in an outer community could also be done in their community. They were interested and asked many questions. Oh, it was a beautiful day.

At the end of the day they changed matrons. The girls didn't like the woman who came in. They said she was a horrible person and said not to even speak to her. But I know there's good in everybody and of course I spoke to her. I learned this woman was supporting her children with this job. She felt she had to work and didn't always feel well and that's why she was a bit cross at times. There is a reason for everything.

I asked the matron to visualize only the good in the inmates. And I asked the girls to visualize only the good in the beleaguered matron.

Later on I said to the matron, "I realize you have a full house here and I can sleep comfortably on this wooden bench." Instead she had them bring me a cot with clean bedclothes, and I had a warm shower with a clean towel and all the comforts of home.

If you have a long face and a chip on your shoulder, if you are not radiant with joy and friendliness, if you are not filled to overflowing with love and goodwill for all beings and all creatures and all creation, one thing is certain: you do not know God!

Also life is like a mirror. Smile at it and it smiles back at you. I just put a big smile on my face and everyone smiles back.

If you love people enough, they will respond lovingly. If I offend people, I blame myself, for I know that if my conduct had been correct, they would not have been offended even though they did not agree with me. Before the tongue can speak, it must have lost the power to wound.

During my travels a saloon-keeper called me into his tavern to give me some food, and while I was eating he asked, "How do you feel in a place like this?"

"I know that all human beings are God's children," I replied. "Even when they are not acting that way, I have faith that they could, and I love them for what they could be."

As I rose to leave I noticed a man with a drink in his hand was also on his feet. When he caught my eye he smiled a little, and I smiled at him. "You smile at me," he said in surprise. "I should think you wouldn't even speak to me but you smiled at me." I smiled again. "I'm not here to judge my fellow human beings," I told him. "I am here to love and serve." Suddenly he was kneeling at my feet and saying, "Everyone else judged me, so I defended myself. You didn't judge me, now I judge myself. I'm a no good worthless sinner! I've been squandering my money on liquor. I've been mistreating my family. I've been going from bad to worse!" I put my hand on his shoulder. 'You are God's child", I said, "and you could act that way."

He looked with disgust at the drink in his hand, and then hurled it against the bar, shattering the glass. His eyes met mine. "I swear to you I'll never touch that stuff again," he exclaimed, "Never!" And there was a new light in his eyes as he walked through the door with steady steps.

I even know the happy ending to that story. About a year and a half later I heard from a woman in that town. She said as far as anyone knew the man kept his promise. He never touched liquor again. He now has a good job. He is getting along well with his family and has joined a church.

When you approach others in judgment they will be on the defensive. *When you are able to approach them in a kindly, loving manner without judgment, they will tend to judge themselves and be transformed.*

Some things don't seem so difficult, like going without food. I seldom miss more than three to four meals in a row and I never even think about food until it is offered. The most I have gone without food is three days, and then Mother Nature provided me food – apples that had fallen from a tree. I once fasted as a prayer discipline for 45 days, so I know how long one can go without food! My problem is not how to get enough to eat, it's how to graciously avoid getting too much. Everyone wants to overfeed me!

I sleep equally well in a soft bed or on the grass beside the road. If I am given food and shelter, fine. If not, I'm just as happy. Many times I am given shelter by total strangers. When hospitality is not available there are always bus depots, railroad stations and all night truck stops.

I remember being offered a queen size bed at a fashionable motel one evening and the next evening space on the concrete floor of a twenty-four hour gasoline station. I slept equally well on both. Several times a friendly sheriff would unlock the door of an unoccupied jail cell.

When no shelter is available to me, I sleep in the fields or by the side of the road with God to guard me.

Bridges always offered protection from the elements, as well as dilapidated barns and empty basements of abandoned homes. Culverts and large pipes often served as lodging. But one of my favorite places to sleep is a large haystack piled in an accessible field on a clear night. The stars are my blanket.

People sometimes ask me if I do not feel lonely on holidays. How can I feel lonely when I live in the constant awareness of God's presence? I love and enjoy being with people, but when I am alone I enjoy being alone with God.

Difficulties with material things often come to remind us that our concentration should be on spiritual things instead of material things. Sometimes difficulties of the body come to show that the body is just a transient garment, and that the reality is the indestructible essence which activates the body. But when we can say, "Thank God for problems which are sent for our spiritual growth," they are problems no longer. They then become opportunities.

Let me tell you a story of a woman who had a personal problem. She lived constantly with pain. It was something in her back. I can still see her, arranging the pillows behind her back so it wouldn't hurt quite so much. She was quite bitter about this. I talked to her about the wonderful purpose of problems in our lives, and tried to inspire her to think about God instead of her problems. I must have been successful to some degree, because one night after she had gone to bed she got to thinking about God.

"God regards me, this little grain of dust, as so important that he sends me just the right problems to grow on," she began thinking. And she turned to God and said, "Oh, dear God, thank you for this pain through which I may grow closer to thee." Then the pain was gone and it has never returned. Perhaps that's what it means when it says: 'in *all things be thankful'*. May be more often we should pray the prayer of thankfulness for our problems.

Prayer is a concentration of positive thoughts.

The most important part of prayer is what we feel, not what we say. We spend a great deal of time telling God what we think should be done, and not enough time waiting in the stillness for God to tell us what to do.

Now, besides God's laws, which are the same for all of us, there is also God's guidance and that is unique for every human soul. If you don't know what God's guidance for your life is, you might try seeking in receptive silence. I used to walk receptive and silent amidst the beauties of nature. Wonderful insights would come to me, which I then put into practice in my life.

For those of you who are seeking the spiritual life, I recommend these four daily practices: Spend time alone each day in receptive silence. When angry, or afflicted with any negative emotion, take time to be alone with God. (Do not talk with people who are angry; they are irrational and cannot be reasoned with. If you or they are angry, it is best to leave and pray.) Visualize God's light each day and send it to someone who needs help. Exercise the body, it is the temple of the soul.

One must be very careful when praying for others to pray for the removal of the cause and not the removal of the symptom. A simple healing prayer is this:

> *"Bring this life into harmony with Divine Purpose. May this life come into harmony with God's Will. May you so live that all who meet you will be uplifted, that all who bless you will be blessed, that all who serve you will receive the greatest satisfaction. If any should attempt to harm you, may they contact your thought of God and be healed."*

Eager beaver psychic healers are those who work on the removal of symptoms and not the removal of cause. When you desire phenomena, you possess phenomena; you do not get God. Let's say I am a psychic healer living next door to you, and you have chosen to come into this life to face some kind of physical symptom until you have removed the cause. Well, when the symptom manifests, I remove it. And so the symptom manifests again, and I then remove it again, and I manage to keep that symptom removed.

When you step over to the disembodied side of life, for another reason altogether, instead of blessing me for having removed the symptom you'll say, "That meddler! I came to solve this problem but she kept removing the symptom and therefore I never solved it!"

That's what I mean when I speak about some who are content to deal with removal of symptoms. When one meddles in the life of another it will just cause the symptoms not only to re-manifest, but carry over into another lifetime. Most healers do not know this, and they go on merrily removing symptoms.

If you realized how powerful your thoughts are, you would never think a defeatist or negative thought. Since we create through thought, we need to concentrate very strongly on positive thoughts. If you think you can't do something, you can't. But if you think you can, you may be surprised to discover that you can. It's important that our thoughts be constantly for the best that could happen in a situation – for the good things we would like to see happen.

I have met some 'new age' people who had heard some prediction of disaster, and were actually concentrating on that. What a terrible thing to do! Why, we're creating every moment of our lives through thought. And we're helping to create the conditions around us.

When you hear of any predictions of disaster there's a reason for it. The reason is that you are to throw the entire weight of your positive thought in the opposite direction.

Every good thing you do, every good thing you say, every good thought you think, vibrates on and on and never ceases. The evil remains only until it is overcome by the good, but the good remains forever.

Be a sweet melody in the great orchestration, instead of a discordant note. The medicine this sick world needs is love. Hatred must be replaced by love, and fear by faith that love will prevail.

A song has this phrase: *Love is flowing like a river, flowing out from you and me. Spreading out into the desert, setting all the captives free.*

Yes, the captives are those who don't know who they are, those who don't know they are God's children.

Remember this: Be still and know that I am God. Don't ever forget who you are! **You cannot be where God is not**.

The Change Called Death

I was walking in a very isolated section of the high mountains of Arizona where there was no human habitation for many miles. That afternoon there came a surprising snowstorm, out of season. I have never seen such a storm. If the snow had been rain you would have called it a cloudburst. Never had I seen snow dumped down like that.

All of a sudden I was walking in deep snow and was unable to see through what was falling. Suddenly I realized that the cars had stopped running. I supposed they were getting stuck on the highway and unable to pass. Then it got dark. There must have been a heavy cloud cover. I could not see my hand before my face and the snow was blowing into my face and closing my eyes. It was getting cold. It was the kind of cold that penetrates into the marrow of the bone.

If ever I were to lose faith and feel fear, this would have been the time, because I knew there was no human help at hand. Instead the whole experience of the cold and the snow and the darkness seemed unreal. Only God seemed real... nothing else. I made a complete identification – not with my body, the clay garment which is destructible - but with the reality which activates the body and is indestructible.

I felt so free; I felt that everything would be all right, whether I remained to serve in this earth life or if I went on to serve in another freer life beyond. I felt guided to keep on walking, and did, even though I couldn't tell whether I was walking along the highway or out into some field. I couldn't see anything. My feet in my low canvas shoes were like lumps of ice. They felt so heavy as I plodded along. My body began to turn numb with cold.

After there was more numbness than pain, there came what some would call an hallucination –and what some would call vision. It was as though I became aware, not only of the embodied side of life where everything was black darkness, bitter cold and swirling snow –but also so close it seemed I could step right into it, of the unembodied side of life where everything was warmth and light. There was such great beauty. It began with familiar color, but transcended familiar color. It began with familiar music, but transcended familiar music.

Then I saw beings. They were very far away. One of them moved toward me very quickly. When she came close enough, I recognized her. She looked much younger than she had looked when she passed over.

I believe that at the time of the beginning of the change called death, those nearest and dearest come to welcome us. I have been with dying friends who have stepped over and I remember well how they talked to their loved ones on both sides.. As though they were all right there in the room together.

So I thought my time had come to step over, and I greeted her. I either said or thought, "You have come for me?" But she shook her head! She motioned for me to go back! And just at that exact moment I ran into the railing of a bridge. The vision was gone.

Because I felt guided to do so, I groped my way down that snowy embankment and got under the bridge. There I found a large cardboard packing box with wrapping paper in it. Very slowly and clumsily in my numb condition, I managed to get myself into that packing box, and somehow with my numbed fingers managed to pull the wrapping paper around me. There under the bridge, during the snowstorm, I slept. Even there shelter had been provided – but provided also was this experience.

Had you looked at me in the midst of the snowstorm, you might have said, "What a terrible experience that poor woman is going through." But looking back on it I can only say: What a wonderful experience in which I faced death, feeling not fear, but the constant awareness of the presence of God, which is what you take right over with you.

I believe I had the great privilege of experiencing the beginning of the change called death. So now I can rejoice with my loved ones as they make the glorious transition to a freer living. I can look forward to the change called death as life's last great adventure.

The unembodied side of life is *right here in another dimension.* The worlds intermingle. We are aware of our world but they are aware of both worlds – usually. Some communication is possible; for instance, we can pray for them and they can pray for us.

Death is a beautiful liberation into a freer life. The limiting clay garment, the body, is put aside. The self-centered nature goes with you to learn and grow on the disembodied side of life, and then returns here into a suitable clay garment, and suitable circumstances to learn the lessons we need to learn.

The memorial service should be a joyous farewell party, recalling the good the person has done, reading favorite poems and singing favorite songs. If we did this, the liberated one would be rejoicing with us.

Religion is not an end in itself. One's union with God is the ultimate goal. There are so many religions because immature people tend to emphasize trivial differences instead of important likenesses. Differences between faiths lie in creeds and rituals, rather than religious principles.

How diverse the many paths seem to be at times, but do they not all come together eventually upon the same mountaintop? Are they not all striving for the same thing?

If you are guided toward a faith, use it as a stepping stone to God, not as a barrier between yourself and God's other children or as a tower to hold you aloft from others. If you are not guided toward a faith (or even if you are) seek God in the silence – seek within.

When we attempt to isolate another, we only isolate ourselves. We are all God's children and there are no favorites. God is revealed to all who seek; God speaks to all who will listen. Be still and know God.

It has been truthfully said that the world is equally shocked by one who repudiates Christianity and by one who practices it.

I believe Jesus would accept me because I do what he told people to do. This doesn't mean, though, that all who call themselves Christian would accept me. Of course I love and appreciate Jesus and I wish Christians would learn to obey his commandments. It would be a most wonderful world.

Evil cannot be overcome by more evil. Evil can only be overcome by good. It is the lesson of the way of love. The contest in the world today is between the old way of attempting to overcome evil with evil, which with modern weapons would lead to complete chaos, and the way of overcoming evil with good which would lead to a glorious and mature life.

We need not reach out to tear down that which is evil because nothing which is contrary to God's laws can endure. All not-good things in the world are transient, containing within themselves the seeds of their own destruction. We can help them fade away more quickly, only insofar as we remain in obedience to God's law that evil must be overcome with good. Those who create something which is evil in order to overcome something else which is evil only double the evil.

In order to help usher in the golden age we must see the good in people. We must know it is there, no matter how deeply it may be buried. Yes, apathy is there and selfishness is there-but good is there also. It is not through judgment that the good can be reached, but through love and faith.

Pure love is a willingness to give, without a thought of receiving anything in return. Love can save the world from nuclear destruction. Love God: turn to God with receptiveness and responsiveness. Love your fellow human beings: turn to them with friendliness and giving-ness. Make yourself fit to be called a child of God by living the way of love.

Do you know God? Do you know there is a power greater than ourselves which manifests itself within us, as well as everywhere else in the universe? This I call God. Do you know what it is to know God, to have God's constant guidance, a constant awareness of God's presence? To know God is to reflect love toward all people and all creations. To know God is to feel peace within – a calmness, a serenity, an unshakeableness which enables you to face any situation. To know God is to be so filled with joy that it bubbles over and goes forth to bless the world.

I have only one desire now: to do God's will for me. There is no conflict when God guides me to walk a pilgrimage I do it gladly. When God guides me to do other things I do them just as gladly. If what I do brings criticism upon me I take it with head unbowed. If what I do brings me praise I pass it immediately along to God, for I am only the instrument through which God does the work. When God guides me to do something I am shown the way. I am given the words to speak. Whether the path is easy or hard I walk in the light of God's love and peace and joy, and I turn to God with psalms of thanksgiving and praise. This it is to know God. And knowing God is not reserved for the great ones. It is for little folks like you and me. God is always seeking you – every one of you.

You can find God if you will only seek, by obeying divine laws, by loving people, by relinquishing self-will, attachments, negative thoughts, and feelings. And when you find God it will be in the stillness. You will find God within."

I was pleasantly surprised to hear from the Peace Pilgrim board member Bruce Nichols that we could meet with Peace Pilgrim's 97 year old sister Helene Young at her home in New Jersey. On the phone she sounded younger and gladly agreed to meet me and my wife.

In March 2012, we met Helene at her lovely home in Cologne, New Jersey. The visit was even more pleasant than we expected as Helene exuded sincerity, peace and love like her famous sister. She seemed quite healthy and enjoys riding the bike with friends daily.

Helene told us that Peace Pilgrim was born in the neighboring town Egg Harbor City on July 18, 1908 and named Mildred Lisette by the parents Ernest and Josephine Norman. Their grandfather was the first Mayor of Egg Harbor City which now has a park dedicated to Peace Pilgrim. It has her life-size statue and is well landscaped for peaceful walk and meditation,

Helene said that she and Mildred were employed in a company that produced wine, but they never drank any wine. Her husband Eugene Young was also fond of Mildred and appreciative of her work for peace. He passed away in 2001 after many years of happy marriage. Helene showed us the scrap book that Eugene made with numerous news clippings and photos of Mildred.

Helene now lives alone in the house, but visits with her children and grandchildren. She has many friends who are also like her, dedicated to spreading the message of peace. They meet regularly to plan peace promoting activities.

Cheryl Canfield is one of the five people who compiled the Peace Pilgrim book. Even before she met Peace Pilgrim, she had an experience of illumination described vividly in her book 'Profound Healing'. I found this easily readable book to be a great gift to myself and my friends.

Cheryl remembered Peace Pilgrim as her mentor before coming to this world. In the book she refers to seeing her life before birth in another dimension with a beautiful garden where people gathered to listen to their teacher, preparing them to enter the earth.

The teacher was actually in the physical world teaching others about nonviolence and compassion "before the technological advancement of an as yet immature society render the earth school uninhabitable."[2]

The teacher was aware of her oneness with God and all creation. She could appear in the other dimension at will. The teacher explained to the people preparing to enter the physical world that they would forget their sense of oneness in the material world.

They can choose the lessons they want to learn in the world through various trials and difficulties, but they would have forgotten that they chose their destiny. As they willingly learn the lessons, the veils of forgetfulness may be gradually lifted from them. When Cheryl heard about Peace Pilgrim in Chicago, she immediately recognized Peace Pilgrim as her former mentor.

Cheryl lives with a sense of Peace Pilgrim's ongoing presence, protection and guidance. While moaning deeply the sudden transition of Peace Pilgrim, Cheryl went to Hawaii. Relaxing in the Island of Maui, she walked regularly along a beautiful quiet white sandy beach.

One morning as she walked towards the beach, there were three rough looking young men walking towards her. She could hear them talking about molesting her. Fear entered her stomach like a hard ball.

Then she heard Peace's voice referring to the little girl about to be attacked by a large man." I knew she was in great danger because of her fear."

2 Profound Healing by Cheryl Canfield, Healing Arts Press, Rochester, Vermont (2003) p. 52

Immediately Cheryl used the visualization technique taught by Peace to lift the fear up out of her body and put it in God's hands, while bathing her and the three men in the light of love. She was startled by the ensuing calm.

When she came close enough to the men, she made eye contact and cheerily said: "good morning." The tough men suddenly looked like school boys as they mumbled "good morning" with their eyes cast down. She walked past them without any harm, to hear Peace's voice again: "when you reach for the good in people, they are disarmed."

There are many more like Cheryl Canfield who are guided by Peace Pilgrim in their daily life. She continues to inspire people around the world when they are committed to promoting peace.

For books, DVDs and tapes about Peace Pilgrim, please go on line www.Peacepilgrim.com. Friends of Peace Pilgrim act in her spirit and do not price their products. They depend on donations to continue their work.

Make me *O Silent Laughter of Spirit*
A smile *smile Thou through my soul. Let*
Millionaire *my soul smile through my heart,*
and my heart smile through my eyes. Make me a
smile millionaire that I may freely
scatter to poor hearts the riches of Thy smiles.

Enthrone Thyself in the castle of my countenance, O Prince of Smiles! No rebels of hypocrisy shall enter; Thou wilt be protected by my unassailable sincerity.[3]

3 Paramahansa Yogananda, Whispers from Eternity, p.56

Ramana Maharshi

Ramana Maharshi

People in ancient times were overawed by Lord Buddha's enlightenment and perfect wisdom. He reached that supreme state at age forty, after years of struggle and meditation with utmost determination. Imagine the same state being attained by a sixteen-year-old high school youth, not interested in religion or studies, but mostly in sports, especially swimming and wrestling. No boy dared to challenge him for a fight, as he could easily beat them all. One advantage he had in school was his extraordinary memory. He always remembered whatever was said in class even once.

Venkataraman, later known as Ramana Maharshi, was born to a Tamil Brahmin family in South India on December 29, 1879. His father Sundaram Iyar worked as a pleader at a rural court, and was a prosperous man for Tiruchuzhi, a small town in Tamilnad. Two years senior to Venkataraman was his brother Nagaswami; and six years younger, another brother; the youngest sibling was a sister named Alamelu.

Mother Alagammal cared lovingly for her children and husband, when suddenly it all changed. Sundaram Iyar fell ill and died. The family had to be broken up. Twelve year old Venkataraman and Nagaswami went to live with their paternal uncle Subbier in the city of Madurai. They were enrolled in the middle school first, and later transferred to the American Mission High School.

When Venkataraman was fifteen years old, two incidents happened that foreshadowed his later life. An elderly relative came to their home, saying that he had come from Arunachala. Strangely enough the word 'Arunachala' had fascinated Venkataraman from early childhood, though he didn't know there was a real place named Arunachala. This holy spot was to draw him powerfully after his enlightenment. Hearing about Arunachala, he experienced an unearthly joy.

The second premonition came soon afterwards. His uncle had borrowed a copy of Periapuranam, which contained the stories of sixty three Tamil saints. Reading this book, Venkataraman was overwhelmed that such faith, fervor and love were actually possible for human beings. "Something greater than all dreamlands, greater than all ambitions was here proclaimed real and possible, and the revelation thrilled him with blissful gratitude," wrote Arthur Osborne.[1]

Perhaps the shortest sadhana or striving for self-realization in history, lasting for about half an hour, changed Venkataraman into one of the greatest sages that India has ever produced, according to her famous philosopher Dr. Radhakrishnan. The Sage described it in the following manner.[2]

"It was about six weeks before I left Madurai for good that the great change in my life took place. It was quite sudden. I was sitting alone in a room on the first floor of my uncle's house. I seldom had any sickness, and on that day there was nothing wrong with my health, but a sudden violent fear of death overtook me. There was nothing in my state of health to account for it, and I did not try to account for it or find out whether there was any reason for the fear. I just felt I am going to die and began thinking what to do about it. It did not occur to me to consult a doctor or my elders or friends; I felt that I had to solve the problem myself, there and then.

"The shock of the fear of death drove my mind inwards, and I said to myself mentally, without actually framing the words: 'Now death has come, what does it mean? What is it that is dying? This body dies.' And I at once dramatized the occurrence of death. I lay with my limbs stretched out still, as though rigor mortis had set in, and imitated a corpse so as to give greater reality to the enquiry. I held my breath and kept my lips tightly closed so

1 Ramana Maharshi and The Path of Self-knowledge by Arthur Osborne, Sri Ramanashramam, Tiruvannamalai, South India, 2002, p.6

2 ibid, pp.8-10

that no sound could escape, so that neither the word "I" nor any other word could be uttered. 'Well then,' I said to myself, 'this body is dead. It will be carried stiff to the burning ground and there burnt and reduced to ashes. But with the death of this body am I dead? Is the body "I"? It is silent and inert but I feel the full force of my personality and even the voice of the "I" within me, apart from it. So I am Spirit transcending the body. The body dies but the Spirit that transcends it cannot be touched by death. That means I am the deathless Spirit.' All this was not dull thought; ***it flashed through me vividly as living truth which I perceived directly,*** almost without thought-process. [italics added] 'I' was something very real, the only real thing about my present state, and all the conscious activity connected with my body was centered on that 'I'. From that moment onwards the 'I' or Self focused attention on itself by a powerful fascination. Fear of death had vanished once and for all. Absorption in the Self continued unbroken from that time on. Other thoughts might come and go like various notes of music, but the 'I' continued like the fundamental struti note that underlies and blends with all the other notes.[3]

Whether the body was engaged in talking, reading or anything else, I was still centered on 'I'. Previous to that crisis I had no clear perception of my Self and was not consciously attracted to it. I felt no perceptible or direct interest in it, much less any inclination to dwell permanently in it."

It is quite important for us to remember the ambiguity in the words 'I' or 'self.' The same words may be used for the individual personality as separate from everyone and everything else, and also for the ultimate Reality behind all beings, hence in an almost opposite sense.

Venkataraman was radically changed after the enlightenment experience, although he continued to go to school. Instead of mixing with friends and going out to swim, he preferred solitude and meditation, where he could immerse himself in the bliss of the true Self. He had no likes or dislikes about food, eating whatever was served to him. If other boys teased him and did

3 The monotone persisting through Indian music, like the string on which pearls are hung, represents the Self.

things that would have annoyed him earlier, he now calmly and humbly accepted whatever they did.

Formerly he had gone to the famous Meenakshi Temple in Madurai a few times without feeling much about it. Now, imbued with deep devotion, he started going there almost daily, to stand before the images of Meenakshi, Siva and sixty-three saints, and shed profuse tears.

His uncle and elder bother Nagaswami noticed the change in Venkataraman, and became annoyed that he was not preparing himself properly for worldly pursuits. One afternoon Venkataraman was doing his homework in English grammar, and halfway feeling it was futile, pushed the book away and sat in lotus posture to meditate. Nagaswami, observing his brother, remarked, "What use is all this to such a one?" Venkataraman understood by the question that the school and home life were not relevant to someone who wished to live like a monk. Realizing the truth behind his brother's words, then and there he renounced his home. Immediately Tiruvannamalai, where the holy hill Arunachala was located, beckoned him, and he had no other option but to go there.

Aware that the family would not allow him to go if he spelled out his intention, he told his brother that he had to go to school to attend a special class. His brother asked him to take five rupees and pay his college fees. Venkataraman was always known to be truthful, and never tell a lie. Later he said that this was the only time he lied, with no thought about it. He was led to do whatever he had to do.

Eating his lunch in a hurry and taking only three rupees, he left the two rupees back with a note in Tamil for his brother: "I have set out in quest of my Father in accordance with His command. It is on a virtuous enterprise that this has embarked, therefore let none grieve over this act and let no money be spent in search of this. Your college fees have not been paid. Two rupees are enclosed herewith."[4]

Venkataraman's connection with the ego was so slight, the he started referring to himself as 'this'. From an old atlas, he found Tindivanam to be the station closest to Tiruvannamalai, and walked to the railway station where

4 ibid, p.20

he bought a ticket for Tindivanam, not realizing that the later map showed a connecting train to Tiruvannamalai.

Later in the train, an elderly passenger told him that he could get off at Villupuram, and change there for Tiruvannamalai. Reaching Villupuram at three a.m., he remained at the station until daybreak, and decided to walk to Tiruvannamalai.

He arrived at his destination on the morning of September 1st, 1896, three days after leaving home. Heart throbbing with joy, he hastened straight to the temple of Arunachaleswar (God of Arunachala). The gates of the three compound walls were open; even the door of the inner shrine stood wide open, as if to welcome him. He walked into the inner sanctuary, and stood there overwhelmed with ecstasy, realizing that he had finally come home to his Father.

He remained in various parts of the large temple, day and night absorbed in meditation, completely lost to the world. He never spoke or ate anything. To escape the onlookers who crowded around him, and some mischievous boys who threw stones at him, wondering whether he could be real, he moved to the dark basement of the temple where hardly anyone went, except ants, vermin and mosquitoes.

They preyed upon him and his thighs were covered with sores oozing blood and pus. An itinerant monk and his disciples were informed about the young renunciant seated in *Samadhi* (ecstasy) lost to the world. They carried him out, cleaned and fed him, as he seemed to be unaware of his environment. Later they deposited him before the shrine of Lord Muruga in the outer temple.

At this time, a silent ascetic was inspired to look after the strange young sage. Mainly he had to keep the curious away from him. Other spiritual seekers started coming to him, one by one, and he was persuaded to take shelter outside the temple.

Not wanting to be a burden on others to bring food to him, he went begging from house to house, never going to the same house twice. He continued to remain silent, would clap his hands to notify his presence, and eat whatever was served. An elderly man insisted that he write his name and place of birth; he wrote "Venkataraman, Tiruchzhi" on a piece of paper.

The family had searched and given up the hope of ever finding him. His uncle Subbier from Madurai died in August 1898. During the funeral, a youth told the family that one Tampiran spoke with much reverence about a young sage named Venkataraman from Tiruchzhi being settled now in Tiruvannamalai.

Hearing this news, Subbier's brother Nelliapper went there with a friend, and recognized him, though he was unkempt with matted-hair and long nails. Uncle Nelliapper pleaded eloquently for him to return to the village, where the family would take care of him, while respecting his vow of silence and the need for solitude.

Actually Venkataraman had not taken a vow of silence, and was not doing any spiritual exercise with a purpose, as he was already enlightened, and his state of bliss never changed. He was merely doing what he was meant to do according to God's will.

Venkataraman was indifferent to the pleas of his uncle who left Tiruvannamalai after a few days. During Christmas holidays, his brother Nagaswami, and mother Alagammal, came to see the sage. His mother grieved to see the condition of her son, and tried hard with many tears to persuade him to come with her. He did not respond at all, nor did he even touch the delicacies she made daily and brought to him.

Heartbroken at his stolid indifference, she approached other devotees to plead her cause. One asked the sage to give the mother some reply, even if it was negative. Taking a paper, he wrote an impersonal but relevant message for her.[5]

"The Ordainer controls the fate of souls in accordance with their Karma. Whatever is destined not to happen will not happen, try as you may. Whatever is destined to happen will happen, do what you may to prevent it. This is certain. The best course, therefore, is to remain silent."

The above words merely meant that he was following God's will, and mother's effort to change him would be of no avail. She realized that she had lost a son, but the world had gained a sage, and went home after a few weeks. The words do not mean that man's efforts are futile in following one's

5 ibid, p.40

destiny. First, we do not know our destiny. The sage advocated a proper balance between full surrender to God's will and making strenuous effort to attain liberation.

Some of the spiritual aspirants brought Scriptures and other books in Sanskrit, Tamil, Telugu, and Malayalam to read while they stayed around the sage. He merely glanced through these books, and became erudite and fluent in the respective languages quickly, remembering exactly all that was written. He found that the Scriptures, especially Vedanta, confirmed his experience of non-duality.

Arunachala (sacred red mountain) is said to be one of the holiest places in India. The hill is only 2,682 feet high with an eight mile road going around it. Pilgrims walk around it in silent meditation, chanting or saying mantras. It has several caves, where many saints have dwelt in silence and seclusion. Ramana Maharshi stated that sages still continue to live in the inaccessible parts of the hill.

Lord Siva, conveying wisdom in silence, is said to be Dakshinamurti. Ramana identified Arunachala with Dakshinamurti, hence his ineffable devotion to the holy hill. Two years after his arrival at Tiruvannamalai, he began to live on the hill, staying in one cave or another.

A year later, he started speaking a few words in response to the questions of spiritual seekers. Later he started telling humorous stories, and laughing like an innocent child. His preferred method of teaching was silence, giving his devotees peace and insights through his powerful but loving gaze.

Sometimes he remained in a trance with unmoving, open eyes. Not only adults, even children and animals gathered around him to sit quietly for many hours as the sage sat in silence. They were joyful when they left.

Well known among the devotees of the sage was Ganapati Sastri. He was the one who gave the name Ramana Maharshi, realizing that the young man, whose grace he had received was indeed a Maha Rishi [great sage]. Ganapati Sastri was a genius, having mastered Sanskrit and the Scriptures at a young age; he also had a phenomenal memory like Maharshi. From age eighteen, he traveled around India visiting sacred places, repeating mantras, and performing ascetical practices.

At age twenty nine, doubts started to assail him; he felt he had not gained God or the world. In despair, he went to Arunachala and fell before the sage, pleading for enlightenment. The sage gazed at him for fifteen minutes, and advised him to look for That which is behind the thought "I" and the words uttered in a mantra. More than his words, the grace radiating from the sage filled Ganapati Sastri with joy, and with his usual enthusiasm, he wrote to all his friends about Maharshi.

The first western devotee to see Sri Ramana was E.H. Humphreys. He was only twenty one years old when he went to India in 1911 to work at the Police Office in Vellore. His Telugu tutor was a disciple of Ganapati Sastri. Humphreys was into occultism, and had already seen his tutor, Sastri and Maharshi in astral vision before he met them.

He describes his first meeting with the sage: "On reaching the cave we sat before Him at His feet and said nothing. We sat thus for a long time and I felt lifted out of myself. I began to realize that the body is the Temple of the Holy Ghost. I could feel only that His body was not the man: it was the instrument of God, merely a sitting motionless corpse from which God was radiating terrifically. My own feelings were indescribable."[6]

After being with the sage and doing Self-inquiry according to the instructions of Maharshi, power to perform miracles started to appear in Humphreys; the sage warned him about it. He had the humility not to be tempted by such power, and rejected it.

He wrote a synopsis of his Master's teaching and sent it to a friend in England. It was later published in the International Psychic Gazette. Some excerpts are given here, taken from Arthur Osborne's book:[7]

"A Master is one who has meditated solely on God, has flung his whole personality into the sea of God, and drowned and forgotten it there, till he becomes only the instrument of God, and when his mouth opens it speaks God's words without effort or forethought; and when he raises a hand, God flows again through that, to work a miracle.

"Do not think too much of psychical phenomena and such things. Their number is legion; and once faith in the psychical thing is established in the heart

6 ibid, pp.53-54

7 ibid, pp. 116-121

of a seeker, such phenomena have done their work. Clairvoyance, clairaudience, and such things are not worth having, when greater illumination and peace are possible without them than with them. The Master takes on these powers as a form of self-sacrifice!...

"The phenomena we see are curious and surprising-but the most marvelous of all we do not realize, and that is, that one and only one illimitable force is responsible for

A) All the phenomena we see; and
B) the act of seeing them.

Do not fix your attention on all these changing things of life, death and phenomena. Do not think of even the actual act of seeing or perceiving them, but only of That which sees all these things, - That which is responsible for it all. This will seem nearly impossible at first, but by degrees the result will be felt. It takes years of steady, daily practice, and that is how a Master is made.

"From now onwards, let your whole thought in meditation be not on the act of seeing, nor on what you see, but immovably on That which sees.

"One gets no reward for attainment. Then one understands that one does not want a reward. As Krishna says, 'Ye have the right to work, but not to the fruits thereof.' Perfect attainment is simply worship, and worship is attainment...

"A Master cannot help being perpetually in this state with only this difference, that in some, to us incomprehensible way, he can use the mind, body and intellect too, without falling back into the delusion of having separate consciousness.

"We must take away the world, which causes our doubts, which clouds our mind, and the light of God will shine clearly through. How is the world taken away? When, for example, instead of seeing a man, you see and say. 'This is God animating a body', which body answers, more or less perfectly, to the directions of God, as a ship answers more or less perfectly to her helm."

With the Master's consent, Humphreys gave up his post at the Police Department and went back to England. Since he had been a Catholic, he joined a monastery to be a monk, and continued his spiritual practice.

Paul Brunton, a brilliant English writer, intent on spiritual quest, was keen on finding a Master who could lead him towards enlightenment. In the early 1930's he traveled around India, meeting with many holy men. Sri Sankarachariya of Kumbakonam who impressed him as a great saint, directed him to Ramana Maharshi.

Paul Brunton's meeting with the sage, his first impression and consequent conversations are given in his book: '*A Search in Secret India*.' He wrote: "There is something in this man which holds my attention as steel filings are held by a magnet. One by one, the questions which I have prepared in the train with such meticulous accuracy drop away...

"I know only that a steady river of quietness seems to be flowing near me, that a great peace is penetrating the inner reaches of my being, and my thought tortured brain is beginning to arrive at some rest... I perceive with sudden clarity that the intellect creates its own problems and then makes itself miserable trying to solve them."[8]

Paul Brunton was very concerned about the problems of the world, feeling that God had abandoned it. The sage explained:

"As you are, so is the world. Without understanding yourself, what is the use of trying to understand the world? This is a question that seekers after Truth need not consider. People waste their energies over all such questions. First, find out the truth behind yourself; then you will be in a better position to understand the truth behind the world, of which you are a part."[9]

The writer extended his stay at Ramana Ashram from days to weeks, and had the opportunity to pose several questions to the sage, and receive his wise answers:

"All human beings are ever wanting happiness, untainted with sorrow. They want to grasp a happiness which will not come to an end. The instinct

---

8 A Search in Secret India by Paul Brunton, Samuel Weiser, York Beach, Maine, USA, 1970, p.141

9 ibid, p.146

is a true one. But have you ever been struck by the fact that they love their own selves most?

"Now relate that to the fact that they are ever desirous of attaining happiness through one means or another, through drink or through religion, and you are provided with a clue to the real nature of man.

"Man's real nature is happiness. Happiness is inborn in the true Self. His search for happiness is an unconscious search for his true Self.....

"You ask me to describe this true Self to you. What can be said? It is that out of which the sense of the personal 'I' arises, and into which it shall have to disappear.....

"If you could mentally follow the 'I' thread until it leads you back to its source, you would discover that, just as it is the first thought to appear, so it is the last to disappear. This is a matter which can be experienced.....

"The sense of 'I' pertains to the person, the body and the brain. When a man knows his true Self for the first time, something else arises from the depths of his being, and takes possession of him. That something is behind the mind; it is infinite, divine, eternal. Some people call it the Kingdom of Heaven, others call it the soul, still others name it Nirvana, and we Hindus call it Liberation; you may give it what name you wish. When this happens a man has not really lost himself; rather, he has found himself."[10]

Here Paul Brunton notes the similar note struck by the Galilean Master: "Whoever shall seek to save his life shall lose it; and whoever shall lose his life shall preserve it."

Maharshi continued:

"Know the real self, and then the truth will shine forth within your heart like sunshine. The mind will become untroubled and real happiness will flood it, for happiness and true self are identical. You will have no more doubts once you attain this self-awareness."[11a]

Paul Brunton traveled to other places in India and came back to Ramana Ashram again. One day he left the hall where Maharshi was receiving visitors, and went to his hut to make some tea. As he was about to enter the threshold,

---

10 ibid, pp. 157-159

11a ibid, p. 297

horror faced him in the form of a deadly cobra, its hood raised and venomous eyes fixed on him. Terror rendered him immobile for a while. As he moved back to look for a stick, an advanced disciple of Maharshi, Yogi Ramaiah calmly walked in, both hands stretched out, as if to welcome the snake, which put its head down and waited, as he bent down to caress it. Then it quickly moved out and vanished into the jungle.

Yogi Ramaiah had his own disciples at Vellore; every year, he had been spending two months in silence with Maharshi who seemed to be especially delighted with him. When Paul Brunton asked Yogi Ramaiah later why he was not scared of the cobra, he replied, "What is there to be afraid of? I approached it without hatred and with love for all beings in my heart."[11b]

Paul Brunton's book: '*A Search in Secret India*', which he wrote when he went back to England, was an immediate success in the West. Many westerners came to India after reading this book and were able to receive the grace of the Sage of Arunachala.

One who received an abundance of His grace was Mouni Sadhu who also wrote about his wondrous experiences with the Sage. He had been earnestly seeking spiritual enlightenment for most of his life through theosophy and many other paths.

After reading Paul Brunton's book, he was hooked on Self-inquiry. Looking for a place where he could live in seclusion, he contacted a friendly Catholic priest who invited him to come to their monastery in France for a few months. Though he was established in the habit of meditation through Self-inquiry, the light of illumination touched him only when he went to Arunachala in India and was in the presence of the Sage. Spending week after week near the Master, he felt the shell of the separate personality burst and dissolve, to reveal a sense of inner peace and indescribable happiness.

Mouni Sadhu was very concerned about saving the world. But he abided by the advice of the Master that his own self-realization was the greatest form of service he could render to the world. First and foremost he concentrated on his sadhana or doing the prescribed spiritual exercises.

11b ibid, p. 297

The devotees that came to see the sage were an open book to Him. They felt that He knew them completely, much more than they could ever know.

Many animals like squirrels, peacocks, and even wild monkeys from the neighboring forest came to see Him regularly. They too were individually known to Maharshi. He addressed them as 'he' or 'she' and never as 'it'. Talking about them, he referred to their psycho-social history, and dealt with them showing love or meting out appropriate discipline according to each one's need.

The dog Kamala at the ashram was quite intelligent and very willing to serve others. When guests came to see the Sage and wanted to go around Arunachala, he would tell Kamala to take that person around, and she would guide them to all the temples and sacred tanks, as they went around the hill.

Most remarkable and favored among the animals was the cow Lakshmi. As a calf she used to come from a farm to the ashram; daily she would go straight to see the Sage who had a banana or some other delicacy for her. She had the habit of coming every day at the exact time for lunch to accompany him to the dining hall.

When she fell seriously ill and the end was near, the Sage went to her saying: "Amma (Mother), do you want me to be near you?" He sat beside her and placed her head on his lap. He gazed into her eyes, placing one hand on the head and the other over the heart. Then he caressed her holding his cheek against hers lovingly. Being satisfied that she was now fully liberated, he left for lunch.

After she died, someone asked the Sage whether he referred to the liberation of Lakshmi in a metaphorical sense. He replied that it was a very advanced soul, who took the form of Lakshmi in order to be near him, and attain final liberation. She was given funeral rites and buried at the ashram compound. The Sage also referred to other holy ones coming to him in the form of animals.

Shortly after Mother Alagammal returned from her visit at Tiruvannamalai, her eldest son Nagaswami passed away. On her subsequent visit to the Ramana Ashram, her attitude towards the Sage changed radically. She regarded him as her guru rather than a son. In 1914, on her way back from a pilgrimage, she visited the ashram, but fell sick, severely suffering from typhoid fever for several weeks. The Sage composed a few beautiful verses in Tamil as a prayer for her recovery from the bodily illness, and the disease of ignorance.

Mother recovered from her fever. In 1915, the wife of her youngest son Nagasundaram died leaving a son who was adopted by aunt Alamelu, now married. Alagammal decided to spend her old age at the ashram, and came back to Tiruvannamalai in 1916. She cooked lovingly for all the residents and the Sage, who refused to eat anything that was not served to everyone else.

At the ashram, the animals were fed first. Then the beggars ate. The Sage waited until all the residents were served, to be sure that he was given the same food, which he ate carefully, not leaving a single grain of rice on the leaf-plate.

Nagasundaram was seventeen years of age when he first came to the ashram to see his brother. He burst out crying loudly as he embraced the Sage, who remained quite indifferent. Now that he had no further family responsibility, Alagammal wanted him at Tiruvannamalai.

He resigned his job, moved to Tiruvannamalai, and stayed with a friend in the town. Later, becoming a monk, he donned the ochre rob and went daily to beg for food. The devotees of the Sage convinced him to stay at the ashram, and partake of the food there. He was known as 'Chinnaswami' (little swami), since he was the younger brother of the Sage.

Initially the Sage was strict with Alagamma to wean her from any attachment to his outer form as her son. Sometimes he ignored her questions, while he talked with others. As she sat before him once, his outer form disappeared, and there was a lingam (column) of light instead. Thinking that he had left his body she started crying, but he reappeared as before.

Another time she saw him as Lord Siva, garlanded with serpents. She pleaded with him to be in the human form thereafter. He agreed, as she had learned the lesson that it was as illusory as any other form he could assume.

In 1920 Alagamma's health started to fail. The Sage attended on her, and in silence elevated her understanding. Her last day on earth was May 19, 1922. He sat beside her for the final two hours with his right hand on her heart and left hand on the head. After her death, he asked the ashram residents not to perform purificatory rites since she had attained perfect union with the Self or God.

The Sage did not enjoin Self-inquiry on all his devotees. Some he led through the path of devotion and surrender. He initiated them through silence or by his steady, penetrating gaze so that these devotees felt they belonged to him completely, and he was their Guru.

He said: "God, Guru and Self are the same. The Guru is one who at all times abides in the profound depths of the Self. He never sees any difference between himself and others and he is completely free from false notions of distinction that he himself is the enlightened or liberated, while others around him are in bondage or the darkness of ignorance."[12]

Though miracles happened around Maharshi, he did not give much importance to them, and discouraged others' interest in such phenomena. As he aged and the body became weak, his face shone with even more luster and love. People came to him from far and near. He stopped going around the holy hill so that he may be available to see them all.

For years before his mahasamadhi (great ecstasy), his close devotees noted that the Maharshi was taking a part of the karmic burden of his followers on his own body. He aged quickly and was crippled with rheumatism.

In 1949, a malignant tumor developed on his left arm; doctors from Chennai operated on it; but it grew again, and the medical men suggested amputating the arm. He did not allow it, saying "The body itself is a disease; let it have its natural end. Why mutilate it?"

The devotees were very sad and concerned about the intense pain caused by cancer. He said to one: "They take this body for Bhagavan, and attribute suffering to him. What a pity!" Devotees were used to calling the Sage "Bhagavan" (which means "Lord," a title given to a spiritual Master in India).

As the disease progressed, some of the devotees were inconsolable, but the sage maintained his humor. One woman in grief beat her head against a pillar, he was surprised and said: "Oh, I thought she was trying to break a coconut."

In spite of bodily deterioration, the Sage maintained his correspondence and received visitors until the last moment. Friday April 14, 1950 was his last

12 Ramana Maharshi and the Path of Self-knowledge, pp. 166-167

day on earth. He gave each one a gentle gaze of recognition and parting blessing as they walked past him.

Actually it was not his last day. As he said, he did not go away. "Where could I go? I am here." Anyway he stopped breathing at 8:47 a.m. At that very moment an enormous star trailed slowly across the sky to the peak of Arunachala, and it was seen by people as far as Chennai. Devotees felt a deep peace underneath their sorrow, and knew that his divine Presence was with them internally.

We are very fortunate not only to have the writings of the Sage but also part of his conversations with the devotees, as recorded by Sri Venkataramiah from 1935 to 1939. '*Talks with Sri Ramana Maharshi*' was published in three volumes first, and later as one volume. Following are some excerpts. "D" stands for a devotee and "M" for Maharshi.

D: Thus then, the saint's realization leads to the uplift of society without the latter being aware of it. Is it so?
M: Yes. The help is imperceptible but is still there. A Saint helps the whole of humanity, unknown to the latter.

D: I am a sinner. I do not perform religious sacrifices etc. Shall I have painful rebirths for that reason? Pray, save me!
M: Why do you say that you are a sinner? Your trust in God is sufficient to save you from re-births. Cast all burden on Him.

D: I find concentration difficult.
M: Go on practicing. Your concentration will be as easy as breathing. That will be the crown of your achievements.
D: Is it not possible to get a vision of God?
M: Yes. You see this and that. Why not see God? Only you must know what God is. All are seeking God always. But they do not know it. You find out what God is. People see, yet see not, because they knew not God.

A visitor: "The Supreme Spirit (Brahman) is Real. The world is illusion," is the stock phrase of Sri Sankara, Yet others say, "The world is reality." Which is true?
M: Both statements are true. They refer to different stages of development, and are spoken from different points of view. The aspirant starts with the definition: that which is Real exists always; then he eliminates the world as unreal because it is changing. It cannot be real; "not this, not this." The seeker ultimately reaches the Self, and there finds unity as the prevailing note; then, that which was originally rejected as being unreal is found to be part of the unity. Being absorbed in the Reality, the world also is Real. There is only being in Self-realization, and nothing but being.

D: Are living liberated souls of different kinds?
M: What does it matter if they differ externally? There is no difference in their wisdom.

D: Heaven and hell-what are they?
M: You carry heaven and hell with you. Your lust, anger etc. produce these regions. They are like dreams.

M: If the man mistakes himself for the subject, objects must necessarily appear different from him. They are periodically withdrawn and projected, creating the world and the subjects' enjoyment of the same. If, on the other hand, the man feels himself to be the screen on which the subject and object are projected there can be no confusion, and he can remain watching their appearance and disappearance without any perturbation to the Self.

M: The present difficulty is that the man thinks that he is the doer. But it is a mistake. It is the Higher Power which does everything, and man is only a tool. If he accepts that position he is free from troubles; otherwise he courts them.

M: If anything is to be got anew, it implies its previous absence. What remained once absent might vanish again. So there would be no permanency in salvation. Salvation is permanent because the Self is here and now, and eternal.

M: Does not one find peace while in meditation? That is the sign of progress. That peace will deepen and become more prolonged with continued practice. It will also lead to the goal.

M: Mantra japa leads to elimination of other thoughts, and to concentration on the mantra. The mantra finally merges into the Self, and shines forth as the Self.

D: What is the significance of Christ in the illumination of St. Paul?
M: Illumination is absolute, not associated with forms. After St. Paul became Self-conscious, he identified the illumination with Christ-consciousness. Christ-consciousness and Self-Realization are all the same.

M: The ultimate Truth is so simple. Still, it is a wonder that to teach this simple Truth, there should come into being so many religions, creeds, methods and disputes among them and so on! Oh the pity! Oh the pity!

D: But people will not be content with simplicity; they want complexity.
M: Quite so. For example, an ordinary Christian will not be satisfied unless he is told that God is somewhere in the far-off Heavens, not to be reached by us

unaided. Christ alone knew Him and Christ alone can guide us. Worship Christ and be saved. If told the simple truth- 'The Kingdom of Heaven is within you' - he is not satisfied, and will read complex and far-fetched meanings in such statements. Mature minds alone can grasp the simple Truth in all its nakedness.

D: What is this Self again?
M: The Self is known to everyone, but not clearly. You always exist. The Be-ing is the Self. 'I am' is the name of God. Of all the definitions of God, none is indeed so well put as the Biblical statement: "I am That I am" in Exodus chapter three. There are other statements, such as Bramaivaham, Aham Brahmasmi and Soham. But none is so direct as the name JEHOVAH - I AM. It is the Self. It is God. Knowing the Self, God is known. In fact God is none other than the Self.

D: How to get Bliss?
M: There is nothing new to get. You have, on the other hand, to get rid of your ignorance which makes you think that you are other than Bliss. For whom is this ignorance? It is the ego. Trace the source of the ego. Then the ego is lost, and Bliss remains over. It is eternal. You are That, here and now... That is the master key for solving all doubts. The doubts arise in the mind. The mind is born of the ego. The ego rises from the Self... The universe is only expanded Self. It is not different from the Self.

M: Samadhi transcends the mind and speech and cannot be described. For example, the state of deep slumber cannot be described; Samadhi state can still less be explained...
Samadhi is one's natural state. It is the under-current in all three states... [M is referring to waking, dreaming and deep sleep.]

D: How to get rid of fear?
M: What is fear? It is only a thought. If there is anything besides the Self there is reason to fear. Who sees the second (anything external)? For anything external to oneself implies the seer within. Seeking it, there will arise no doubt, no fear-not only fear, all other thoughts centered round the ego will disappear along with it.
D: The Bible says that the human soul may be lost.
M : The 'I' thought is the ego and that is lost. The real 'I'" is "I am That I am"

D: Is there reincarnation?
M: Reincarnation can be, if you are incarnate now. Even now you are not born.
D: What is the significance of the sea of love?
M: Spirit, Holy Ghost, Realization, Love etc. are all synonymous.

M: Surrender, and all will be well. Throw all the responsibility on God. Do not bear the burden yourself...
D: Surrender is impossible.
M: Yes. Complete surrender is impossible in the beginning. Partial surrender is certainly possible for all. In course of time that will lead to complete surrender. Well, if surrender is impossible, what can be done? There is no peace of mind. You are helpless to bring it about. It can be done only by surrender.
D: Partial surrender-well-can it undo destiny?
M: Oh yes! It can.

D: Is not destiny due to past Karma?
M: If one is surrendered to God, God will look to it.

D: This being God's dispensation, how does God undo it?
M: All are in Him only.
D: How is God to be seen?
M: Within. If the mind is turned inward, God manifests as inner consciousness,
D: How can the mind be made to vanish?

M: No attempt is made to destroy it. To think or wish it is itself a thought. If the thinker is sought, the thoughts will disappear.

D: Will they disappear of themselves? It looks so difficult.
M: They will disappear because they are unreal. The idea of difficulty is itself an obstacle to realization. It must be overcome. To remain as the Self is not difficult.

D: Am I not now born?
M: So long as the body is considered, birth is real. But the body is not "I". The Self is not born nor does it die. There is nothing new. The sages see everything in and of the Self. There is no diversity in it. Therefore there is neither birth nor death.

Your own Self-Realization is the greatest form of a service you can render to the world.

Have faith in God and in yourself; that will cure all. Hope for the best, expect the best, toil for the best, and everything will come right for you in the end."

Prophet Muhammad

Over a billion people in the world look mainly to one man as an inspiring example for their lives. He was illiterate but wise, humble but courageous. People trusted him because he trusted God completely. In spite of severe trials and tests, so surrendered and submissive to divine direction was he that the small community he led expanded quickly to become a great civilization and a new religion.

In the sixth century A.D. Mecca in Saudi Arabia was a flourishing city, an oasis in a desert, a central stop-over for trading caravans moving from Yemen in the South to Syria in the North. It also attracted thousands of pilgrims throughout the year to worship at the Ka'bah, a stone altar erected by Abraham himself, according to local tradition.

The structure surrounding the Ka'bah housed about 360 idols, representing the various gods of all the tribes in Saudi Arabia. Idol worship was a common practice among the people, as Allah the supreme God was thought to be rather remote and removed from the normal concerns of man.

One tribe, namely the Quraishi, made huge profits administering and controlling the services offered to the pilgrims at the shrine. Consequently the tribal leaders became very wealthy. Naturally they could not countenance any significant opposition to the status quo.

Abdel Mutalib, the paternal grandfather of Muhammad was a highly respected leader among the Quraishi. His favorite son Abdullah died, leaving his wife Aminah heart-broken. She was carrying Abdulla's child in her womb. In a dream a voice instructed her that the child would be divinely protected and should be called Muhammad, meaning "highly praised," quite an unusual name at that time.

According to the customary religious ritual, Abdel Mutalib was going around the Ka'bah seven times, when his grandson was born. He heaved with pride as he held the child, calling him Muhammad. God must have been preparing the child for his future mission by allowing him to endure severe pain that seared his tender heart. Young Muhammad lost his mother first, and two years later his grandfather Abdel Mutalib, making him an orphan at age six. He was raised by his uncle Abu Talib, who was kind but the least wealthy of all Abdel Mutalib's sons.

There were no schools in Arabia then, and Abu Talib could not afford a tutor to teach Muhammad how to read and write. So he gave Muhammad chores like caring for the camels and horses, selling and buying things at the market. There Muhammad developed a reputation not only for his industry, but for the extraordinary honesty that earned him the nickname "al Sadiq" (the truthful or reliable).

Abu Talib found his nephew Muhammad to be well-mannered, honest, industrious, and courageous but considered him too poor to marry his own daughter. The youth was pious, spending much time in prayer to Allah, but not given to worshipping the idols like the majority of Arabs. He seemed to have come under the influence of Jews and Christians in religious thinking and practices.

Abu Talib loved his nephew dearly; hence he approached an exceptionally rich woman named Khadijah, and asked if Muhammad could be employed to lead her caravan. Khadijah was glad to favor the son of Abdel Mutalib. Being a shrewd woman, she arranged for one of her trustworthy servants to observe Muhammad, and report to her at the end of the caravan.

Khadijah had received many suitors from noble families earlier. She had refused them, thinking that they were more interested in her money than in her happiness. Admiring the ideal qualities of Muhammad related by her servant, she decided to marry him, if he would be willing.

Muhammad was twenty five years of age when he married the forty year old Khadijah, who had three children from an earlier marriage. It was utterly unheard of in Arabia for a younger man to marry an older woman. The custom was for much older men to marry young virgins. Muhammad and Khadijah were quite attracted to each other, and deeply in love throughout their married life. Khadijah gave birth to two sons and four daughters. The sons died as infants, but the daughters grew to be strong supporters of their father during his troublesome years later in life.

Muhammad and Khadijah prospered due to their managerial skills and honesty. Much of their wealth was spent on the needs of the poor, as they were content to adopt a simple Spartan lifestyle.

Muhammad spent much time in prayer and fasting. For this purpose, he stayed in secluded caves, out in the desert for days and nights. In 610 A.D. he was forty years old, when a momentous event happened that would change history forever. While praying in a cave at Mount Hira during the month of Ramadan, Muhammad saw a bright light in the form of a man who commanded him to recite. Muhammad, trembling with fear, replied that he could not recite.

Then the luminous being embraced him tightly and repeated the command to recite. Muhammad's response was the same again. The being of the light tightened the hold even more as he gave the command to recite for the third time. Now Muhammad asked what he had to recite. Then he heard the melodious tones of the Koran recited for the first time.

"Recite! In the name of your Lord who created, created man from clots of blood.

Recite: Your Lord is the most bountiful One Who by the pen taught man what he did not know.

Indeed, man transgresses in thinking himself his own master; for, to your Lord all things return." (Koran 96:1)

Muhammad repeated these words to himself again and again to fix them firmly in memory. When the vision ceased, the night was darker than before. Muhammad continued to tremble with fear while he ran from the cave. Looking up at the sky, he saw the same figure enlarged like a huge giant, who told him that he was angel Gabriel, and Muhammad was the messenger of God.

Still shivering, he rushed home to Khadijah, who put him to bed and covered him with blankets. Later, when he felt calmer, he told Khadijah what had happened in the cave, and said he wondered whether he was going insane. Khadijah knew her husband to be eminently worthy to receive special favors from God, due to his humble, honest, and kind attitude towards family members and others. She comforted him, saying that God would not allow him to be mad.

In Pre-Islamic Arabia, there was a small group of people called Hanifs. Influenced by Judaism and Christianity, they were monotheists opposed to the worship of idols. They tried to preach their doctrine at the Ka'bah, but were prevented by the Quraishi leadership. Muhammad seems to have been a Hanif from his early youth. One Hanif leader named Waraquah became a Christian, and spent his time in quiet contemplation and reading holy books.

Waraquah was Khadijah's cousin. Letting Muhammad rest in sleep, she hastened to Waraquah to consult with him about Muhammad. After listening intently, Waraquah declared that Muhammad was a true prophet chosen by God; he would be persecuted, but he must be steadfast to the message received from God.

Muhammad did not know who would listen to him, and accept his message as revealed by God. Khadijah declared that she trusted him completely, and would accept him as a true prophet. She was the first to accept Islam, which means surrender and submission to Allah and Allah alone.

The prophet continued to receive revelations from Angel Gabriel, not only at Mount Hira, but everywhere, day and night, giving instructions and guidance for his personal growth, as well as for the material and spiritual welfare of the community of Muslims that gradually gathered around him.

The melodious verses of the Koran were devoutly kept in the memory of the first Muslims. They were written down and codified as a holy book a few years after the death of Muhammad.

There are many passages in the Koran that need to be interpreted symbolically, especially the statements about heaven, hell, and the Day of Judgment. Interpreting them literally would lead to monstrously absurd ideas about God and man. Understood in a symbolic and spiritual sense, the same passages can inspire us to be spiritually mature.

The author of *In the Heart of Koran*, Lex Hixon describes hell as God purifying the soul through the agony of fire so that it may attain the bliss of heaven. He claimed that he was guided by Prophet Muhammad himself in the mystical experience that gave him this insight. The statements in the Bible and the Koran condoning slavery, child and spouse abuse are due to the social conditioning of the scriptural writers by the mores of their time, and cannot be accepted as valid and valuable for all time.

Female infanticide, cruelty to servants and slaves, oppression and exploitation of women, and excessively violent acts of revenge were commonly accepted practices in Arabia of that time. Muhammad, on the contrary, taught that all human beings must be equally respected as the children of one God. Laying much importance on surrender and devotion to God, Muslims were asked to be kind and compassionate towards fellow human beings, while being truthful and courageous at all times.

The Quraishi leadership was disturbed by Muhammad's denunciation of idol worship, and his insistence that worldly wealth and prestige would not count on the Day of Judgment. The leadership put pressure on his clan to change Muhammad; as it failed, they started persecuting the Muslims, drove his clan and the new converts to Islam out of Mecca into the desert, where they suffered intensely from hunger. After two years of such hardship, they were allowed to come back; but the persecution of Muhammad and the Muslims continued.

Muhammad advised his followers to move to Medina. The two dominant tribes of Medina were in continuous conflict. Realizing that Muhammad was wise and courageous, the converts to Islam from Medina invited him to move to their city, where he could be a mediator between the warring tribes and govern them wisely.

Meanwhile the Quraishi plotted to murder Muhammad, by choosing youth from each clan to stab him, in order to avert any retaliation from his clan. Muhammad and his friend Abu Bakr foiled this plan by escaping at night, in disguise, through a roundabout route to Medina. Hijra or this flight from Mecca to Medina occurred in 622 A.D., the starting year for the Muslim calendar.

The Muslim refugees from Mecca to Medina had lost all their property and were destitute. Muhammad did not want them to be a burden on the local people. He organized them to settle in tents outside the city and cultivate the barren land, with the help of Muslim converts from Medina.

In spite of the mounting opposition at the start, through acts of wisdom, courage, and a humane attitude, Muhammad gained the political leadership of Medina. He made alliances with neighboring tribes, Jewish settlements, and the Christian Kingdom in the North.

There were three major battles between the forces from Mecca and the Muslims of Medina. Though the Meccan forces had more equipment and vastly outnumbered the Muslims, they were defeated due to the faith and courage of the Muslims, and the wise leadership of Muhammad who was inspired by Koranic revelations.

Torturing the prisoners of war was a common practice in Arabia at that time. Muhammad abolished it by insisting on a humane treatment of the prisoners. He allowed them to be freed after accepting a ransom payment. He exempted some poor prisoners even from this obligation, and freed them.

For Muhammad, the victory in external battles was less important than the victory in the greater Jihad, namely the battle between the selfish worldly will by which we indulge in desires and aversions, and humbly submitting to the will of God and serving the whole society. He exhorted his followers about engaging daily in this spiritual Jihad.

In 630, Muhammad marched into Mecca with his army accepting a peaceful surrender. He destroyed the idols at Ka'bah and established it as the major Islamic shrine, where Muslim pilgrims from all over the world make a pilgrimage at least once in their life-time. Muhammad taught his close followers to pray often, and practice the Presence of God by saying short prayers numerous times during the day, and at night. His special contribution to spirituality was the emphasis on surrender (Islam). Surrender to God from moment to moment speaks peace and joy.

After the death of Khadijah, Muhammad had many wives. He was always concerned about their welfare, and dealt with them respectfully. The marriages happened not due to any selfish motive of the prophet, but more because he wanted to protect a particular woman or for a political purpose.

Muhammad seemed to have been divinely guided in his daily activities, especially in a matter of such importance as a marriage. His wives and daughters were fond of the Prophet, and were willing to endure many hardships to support him.

Inspired by the example and words of the Prophet, Islamic tradition produced a beautiful tree of heroic sanctity. Its glorious flowers of numerous saints have spread their holy fragrance in several countries for fourteen centuries.

Sufi mysticism is a special branch, where saintly poets like Hafiz, Omar Khayam and Rumi blossomed. Their mystical poems, exuding love and divine wisdom, continue to touch and shape the hearts of spiritual seekers everywhere. A great Sheik defining Sufism as joy meeting disappointment parallels the teaching of St. Francis to Brother Leo about perfect joy. The secret behind it is Islam or surrender.

Perfect devotion and surrender culminates in the devotee's total absorption in God to the exclusion of all thoughts about "I" or "mine." Perhaps the greatest of the mystical poets in Islam is Rumi. He expresses this truth succinctly.

If the Beloved is omnipresent,
The lover is a cover,
But when life itself becomes Love,
Lovers do not appear.

This enigmatic verse of Rumi is pure Vedanta.[1] When life is realized as Love or God, the distinction between the lover and the beloved disappears; the lover's ego that eclipses the divine omnipresence also vanishes in the process. What remains is ecstasy or Being-Consciousness-Bliss (Sat-Chit-Ananda).

1 Refers to the last Vedic scriptures, especially the Upanishads which emphasizes the absolute unity of the ultimate reality or realization.

Paramahansa Yogananda wrote an inspired commentary on the Rubaiyat of Omar Khayam. Published with gorgeous illustrations by Self-Realization Fellowship, the *Wine of the Mystic* is an enchanting work. It shows how the saintly poet constantly calls the reader to taste the intoxicating wine of wisdom, divine love and joy.

Yogananda has a long prayer addressed to Prophet Muhammad in *Whispers from Eternity*, a book of poetic prose, where he extols the Prophet for teaching his people to fast and pray, and stay away from alcohol and opiates that "impair the mind and prevent divine perceptions."

As a young priest I was traveling by train to the North of Sri Lanka. Seated in front was a man with a remarkably intelligent and sensitive face. He was practicing medicine as a psychiatrist in Colombo, and earlier had been a psychiatric consultant in Scotland and England.

When I asked him about the purpose of his visit to the North, he said that he, a Buddhist, was going to see a Muslim saint named Bawa Muhaiyaddeen, "the most phenomenal human being" he had ever met.

According to the psychiatrist, the saint was about 150 years old, hardly ever ate, but liked to cook and feed the many people who came to see him. Full of peace and love, the saint had a great sense of humor, and often made the visitors burst out in laughter. The psychiatrist was amazed to find that Bawa Muhaiyaddeen knew all about him, even before he could talk to the saint. He always felt a healing sense of peace, being in the presence of the saint.

Later, a Catholic youth named Nelson spoke to me about his extraordinary experience with this saint. He told me that he was talking with some friends under a tree, about 200 yards away from the saint's residence, when they invited him to visit the saint. He refused, calling the saint a fraud, and used a curse word in the process. Since his friends kept insisting, he reluctantly agreed to go.

As they entered the hall, Nelson was stunned and ashamed to hear the saint repeat the exact words he used earlier under the tree, with a stern warning about judging others falsely, and the advice to never speak ill of anyone. Inspired by this event, Nelson said that he thereafter visited the saint regularly, and was blessed in many ways.

Bawa Muhaiyaddeen lived in Philadelphia from 1973 to 1986, exuding extraordinary love to the many American devotees who visited him regularly and were transformed by the saint's grace and wisdom. My niece Mathy and I visited the saint in Philadelphia for two days and were blessed by his loving attention and wise guidance. Islamic tradition has produced numerous such saints from the time of Muhammad, inspired by his holy example and words.

George Washington Carver

George Washington Carver

Glenn Clark was a professor of English literature, and enthused about campus ministry as a lay preacher. He saw an ordained minister of the gospel, Jim Hardwick, capturing the hearts of young men and women for Christ everywhere he went. When Glenn wondered about the source of Jim's hidden power, the reply was clear and definite: "From an old negro in Alabama."

Hearing the famous black scientist George Washington Carver speak about his discoveries in agriculture was an amazing experience for Rev. Jim Hardwick. He had learned about prayer while studying theology, but he learned much more about the power of prayer while listening to George Carver lecture on his scientific discoveries. Thrilled by his experience, he stood transfixed when Carver left the hall and walked by. Carver turned to Jim and said: "I want you to be one of my boys."

That was a turn-off for Jim, whose family had been wealthy slave-holders in the South. He wanted to forget the old gentleman. A few days later, faced with a serious problem, he found himself mentally turning to the simple scientist for help.

Instantly he felt the black scientist's spirit, with unearthly brilliance, filling the room; peace entered his heart, and the problem was solved. "Since then I have found that merely turning in thought to that dear old gentleman creates an atmosphere about me in which God can come very, very near to me. That is why God is as close to me as He is now," said Rev. Jim Hardwick.[1]

Year after year, Glenn Clark met more and more of Dr. Carver's "boys" whose sweet, gracious quality impressed and influenced him. Finally feeling a deep desire to meet their spiritual master, but unable to go there, he wrote a letter instead, and received a reply by return mail from George Carver, stating that he was praying for Glenn to write to him when his letter came. From that moment Glenn knew that he, too, was one of Carver's "boys."

Carver had an unusual childhood. The Civil War was raging in the South when armies raced back and forth past the Moses Carver plantation near Diamond Grove, Missouri. Once, some soldiers raided the plantation, and carried off a black woman, her little son and an infant daughter.

Mr. Carver gathered a rescue party and gave chase up to Arkansas and found the raiders. The black woman and her daughter were already sold and gone. Carver negotiated with the captors to release the little boy in exchange for an old race horse worth $300.

He was a frail and sickly little boy; as he grew up he was not given heavy tasks; so he was free to roam the fields giving vent to his extraordinary curiosity about plants, flowers, trees, and insects.

The boy had another special quality. He could never tell a lie. Hence he was named George Washington Carver. The Carvers were fond of their slaves, treated them like their own family and had freed them. George's mother had preferred to live with Moses and Sue Carver rather than go away. Her sons George and his elder brother Jim knew that uncle Moses and aunt Sue Carver genuinely cared for them.

George was six years old when another boy taught him how to pray. That night he asked God for something that he wanted very much, namely a pocket knife. In a dream, he saw in a field where the rows of corn were separated from the rows of tobacco, a water melon cut into two halves, and a little knife stuck in one. In the morning he walked straight to that exact spot in the field, and found the knife delivered to him by God.

---

1 The Man Who Talks with the Flowers by Glenn Clark, Macalester Park Publishing Co., Minneapolis, 1999, p.7

Feeling grateful, his trust and intimate connection with God grew ever deeper through the years, as George sought and received His help in all that he wanted to know and do. Every early morning was reserved for communing with God manifesting as nature. George went for long solitary walks lovingly conversing with nature and the God in nature.

Wandering around the woods, he gathered various types of plants, and started a botanical garden of his own, where he cared for the plants with much love. He developed a knack to heal the plants that seemed to be ill. People got to know about his special skill with plants, and asked the help of the young 'plant doctor' when their plants caught any disease. They were amazed to see how quickly the plants became healthy and strong again with his touch.

He yearned to know as much as possible about plants and the earth, hence learning to read and write was a passion with George. There was no school at Diamond Grove. In Neosho, the town nearby, he discovered a school for black children. Uncle Moses knew that the boy had to go there.

In 1875 at about eleven years of age (George never knew exactly his year of birth), he moved to Neosho, finding shelter next to the school with a black family. Aunt Mariah was pious and proud, being an experienced midwife for blacks and whites alike. She was also a laundress, in which task George was a willing and efficient help.

In Neosho George had to behave differently with the whites, unlike in Diamond Grove where he had been treated like a family member. His teacher, Stephen Frost, taught him not to look white folks in the eye, to call only the whites, "Mister, Miss or Missus," and to walk along the edge of the road, leaving the main path for them.

The new behavior code disturbed his heart, but he accepted it, wanting to practice the virtue of meekness. From Lord Jesus, he learned to live without resentment, anger or hatred, though it was not always easy. Uncle Moses was a Mason, and had not taken George to church. Aunt Mariah and Uncle Andy insisted that George accompany them to the Church on Sundays, and read the Bible on other days.

George was able to read many books within a year, as he had memorized the dictionary itself. Since he could not learn more at Neosho, he moved to Fort

Scott in Kansas. Earning the money for board, lodging and books by working at homes or in hotels, George excelled in whatever work he set out to do.

One day, while he was walking along a road with his books, two white men accused him of stealing the books, and beat him up severely. His schooling at Fort Scott was thus ended, and he started to work with a colored blacksmith.

Some whites in the town hated the blacks intensely. George hid in a barn, and watched in horror, as they stormed the town jail to drag out a black man accused of molesting a little girl. Though he was screaming about his innocence, they hanged him, and then burnt the body. George was shaken to the core by witnessing such cruelty.

He walked out of Fort Scott, doing odd jobs along the way, and never forgetting his goal of higher education. He was glad that his application to Highland College in Kansas was accepted, only to be sorrowfully disappointed later, when the dean was surprised to see that the new student was black, and refused to admit him.

His pain due to racist bigotry was assuaged by the friendliness of white families, who admired the moral fiber and the extraordinary talents of George Carver. A few years later, George found himself studying at Simpson College in Iowa. He was an extremely gifted painter, and his art teacher Miss Etta Budd was quite fond of her black student.

She was also aware of his passionate interest in plants, and the lifelong desire to help his race. With the aid of her father, Dr. J. L. Budd, Professor of Horticulture, George was admitted to the Department of Agriculture at Iowa State College.

He was the only black student at the College. Initially he met with much prejudice and hatred from the white students. But quickly he won the hearts of the student body and the professors, due to his brilliant mind, innate humor and courage.

Iowa State College was well known for its experimental agricultural station, headed by Professor James Wilson, who later became the Secretary of Agriculture under Presidents McKinley, Theodore Roosevelt, and Taft.

James Wilson was a deeply devout Christian. His Bible classes and prayer groups were so popular that he needed someone to lead more groups. Naturally he called on his favorite student, George Carver, whose Bible classes started attracting even more students.

When George graduated with a Master's degree, Iowa State was intent on keeping him there as a teacher, but he preferred to dedicate his talents to serve the poor farmers in the South. Booker Washington wanted him to start an agricultural experimental station at his all-black college in Alabama.

At the Tuskegee Institute in Alabama, the scientific genius of George Carver blossomed with numerous discoveries and inventions. Cotton was the main and the only crop cultivated by the Southern farmer. It was impoverishing both the soil and the farmer.

To enrich the soil, George Carver taught the farmers to cultivate alternately sweet potato and peanuts. He solved the problem of overproduction of these new crops, by making hundreds of other by-products like face powder, axle grease, ink, milk, shampoo, vinegar, coffee, soaps, wood stains, oil dyes etc. from them.

George Carver was always aware of being an instrument in the hands of God. He attributed all his inventions and creativity to the Creator. Similarly his friend, Thomas Edison too lived with the awareness that his scientific genius was entirely due to divine inspiration. Carver also corresponded with Mahatma Gandhi, considering him to be a great saint who was guided by God in all his activities.

Carver loved all of nature, but his love for flowers was especially intense and joyful. Flowers talked to him about things divine. He communed with them as a genuine lover with the beloved. Hence he was fond of these famous lines of Tennyson:

> "Flower in the crannied wall
> I pluck you out of the crannies;
> I hold you here, root and all, in my hand,
> Little flower-but if I could understand
> What you are, root and all, all in all.
> I should know what God and man is"

Like flowers, Carver was modest and humble. Most of them start to bloom in the early hours of the morning. From a young age, Carver had the habit of waking up daily at 4.00 a.m., and going out for a quiet walk to commune with nature and God. During these sacred moments, he gathered the inspiration and the energy for the activities of the day.

Being an artist, he loved the beauty of colors. By digging in the hills, he discovered permanent dyes, in layers of clay, some known to the ancient Egyptians, and then lost to humanity for thousands of years. He knew exactly which color and how much beneath the soil he would find it, as he had been divinely inspired earlier about the specifics of his discoveries. A New York Times editorial ridiculed the scientist for attributing his discoveries to divine inspiration. The presumption and prejudice of unbelief!

From flowers, Carver learned that there would be a great revival of Christianity, not as an institution, but as a living force, through which people would experience the presence of God and the power of prayer, so that wars would become impossible. He was sure of this outcome, as flowers always told him the truth.[2]

A harrowing sense of insecurity, with consequent greed and arrogance is the main reason for the rampant destruction of nature and human life in the modern era. When man becomes more spiritual and psychologically mature, we can organize ourselves in such a way, that there will be no more wars in the world.

Both active engagement in wars, and passive participation through the media, evoke much excitement in most people. That is the reason why they are easily manipulated into wars. A genuine appreciation of all forms of life and compassion for the suffering of others will enable us to grow out of such psychological immaturity.

Man must mature quickly. Unless our psychology changes radically, the progress in technology is placing the survival of humanity as a whole at stake. The psychology of scarcity by which some people are deprived of necessities does not suit our present era.

---

2 ibid, p.37

Instead of selfish, irresponsible profiteering, violence and deception, a sincere co-operation of countries using modern technology can bring about a well-planned, rational economy. No one on earth has to starve or be homeless. Medical care, education and employment with a living wage should be available to everyone.

Not merely nuclear bombs, but all the bombs need to be banned. Bombing a place terrifies the people there. It destroys innocent lives, and makes the rest live in fear. **Making, selling, buying, and using bombs are clearly acts of terrorism.** Invading another country, under any guise, has to be a thing of the past. All the military forces in the world must be disbanded and bombs banned, allowing an army and navy for the UN alone. They should be capable of intervening quickly in conflict situations anywhere in the world, to restore order with justice and peace.

If the UN were reorganized as a powerful, democratic and governing institution, it could foster open and honest communication between peoples, in order to create global economic prosperity without wasteful production or consumption, clean environment, and an increasing respect for nature and science. Then the prayerful expectations of the saintly scientist George Washington Carver and the predictions of his lovely flowers shall find fulfillment sooner rather than later.

> *"Every gun that is made, every warship launched, every rocket fired, signifies, in the final sense, a theft from those who hunger and are not fed, those who are cold and are not clothed."*
>
> President Dwight Eisenhower

Poems by Peace Pilgrim

WAR FEVER

The terrible blindness—
Which makes your foe appear like a fiend
And makes you appear like a fiend to him—
War fever!

That awful insanity—
Which makes the same act brilliant strategy for you
And foul treachery for the enemy—
War fever!

That frightful drunkenness—
Which muddles the mind until wrong seems like right,
Hate appears good, and murder a virtue—
War fever!

That horrible sickness—
For which no cure is sought, but instead
Ways are sought to spread the disease—
War fever!

FOUNTAIN OF LOVE

Fountain of Love
My source is in Thee—
Loving Thy will
My spirit is free—
Beautiful day
When all of us see
The hope of the world
Is Love

Yogaswami

YOGASWAMI

A devotee of Yogaswami was collecting information about his Master, and told him that he intended to write his biography. After the devotee left, the sage said "No one can ever write about me". Can anyone plumb the depths and scale the heights of an enlightened sage's life?

For that matter, we hardly understand ourselves. Yet we presume to judge and condemn others easily. When we are tempted to indulge in such a pretentious play, let us remember that actually WE DO NOT KNOW. It is one of the four great aphorisms learnt by Yogaswami from his guru Sellappa, that he repeated often to his followers.

Prominent politicians and the Sri Lankan social elite frequented Yogaswami's little hut in the north of Sri Lanka. One young man asked the sage why he mixed more with the rich and the famous, and went about in cars unlike other ascetics. Yogaswami laughed to say that the poor are already devoted to God and can hardly harm others, whereas the powerful can do much harm to society, hence needed his help even more.

Yogaswami was born on 29th of May, 1872 at Maviddapuram, a small village in the Northern Province of Sri Lanka. His parents Ambalavanar and Sinnachipillai called him Sathasivam. Even in early childhood, Sathasivam was fearless and energetic. He was often seen on the top branches of tall mango trees reading books. Before the child reached the age of ten years, his mother passed away. Thereafter he was brought up by his uncle and aunt living in a suburb of Jaffna called Colombogam.

Here the child attended a primary school managed by Christian Missionaries. For high school, he went to St. Patricks in Jaffna to learn English and Tamil. In Colombogam, the young boy received the name Yoganathan due to his yogic habits.

After graduating from high school, Yoganathan went to Maskeliya in Central Sri Lanka to work with his father at his shop. The father--seeing that his son was wandering around the hills, valleys, and rivers in Maskeliya, communing with nature in solitude, and did not have the heart for commerce--sent him back to Colombogam to try some other profession.

At age eighteen, he joined the Irrigation Department and worked as a store-keeper under an Englishman named Brown. In the morning he opened the store to distribute the tools for the workers, and in the evening put them back. This work gave him ample free time for prayer and spiritual reading. He spent most of the night in meditation.

Yoganathan won the hearts of his co-workers and the supervisor Mr. Brown due to his exemplary work habit and respectful manner towards everyone. Five years later the time arrived for Yoganathan to meet his Guru and Master.

Sellappa was known as a mad-man to most of the people in and around Jaffna. Looking unkempt and wearing some rags, he begged for his food. Night and day he stayed around Nallur temple dedicated to Lord Murugan. He was often muttering some apparently meaningless words.

Those who approached him out of curiosity were chased away with stones or shouts of obscene words. Hence only a handful of people from Colombogam recognized Sellappa as a spiritual giant. These fortunate individuals received valuable guidance from the Master, and were advancing steadily on the spiritual path.

Sellappa's disciples, seeing that Yoganathan was deeply religious and spiritual–minded, decided to bring him to their Master. As soon as Sellappa saw Yoganathan, he roared like a lion to ask again and again "who are you?" Immediately Yoganathan plunged into deep meditation, taking the question as a divine mantra leading him beyond body consciousness to the silent depths of his being.

The elderly gentlemen who brought Yoganathan were perturbed by the severe reception given to the young man by Sellappa. The Master waited till Yoganathan came out of his meditation, and received his most apt disciple lovingly with endearing words. Yoganathan was completely captured by the divine madness of Sellappa; worldliness disappeared from his heart and he was radically transformed.

Yoganathan returned to his store-keeping job in Kilinochchi, but was continuously immersed in the image of Sellappa. Mr. Brown rather reluctantly accepted his resignation after Yoganathan brought his cousin to take his place as the store-keeper.

Sellappa chased Yoganathan away few times, but his beloved disciple kept going back. The sage relented and allowed him to stay around and absorb his wisdom given in pithy sayings uttered amidst crazy muttering. Sellappa slept on the bare ground, using his hand as a pillow. The disciple gladly followed his guru's example and learnt to survive with the minimum.

They were often without food. Once, after fasting for three days they bought rice and eggplant from the market and cooked a tasty meal in clay pots. Yoganathan was rather hungry and ready to eat when Sellappa asked himself: "Do you want tasty food?" and kicked the pots and broke them.

Then he went to the usual spot neat the temple chariot and sat to meditate. Yoganathan too plunged into silence, and found that the joy and wisdom gained in deep meditation seemed to satisfy his body as well.

While reading the sacred scriptures extensively, Yoganathan had found certain points difficult to grasp. His questions were adequately answered by his guru Sellappa in silence, as it happened to the close disciples of Ramana Maharishi.

Sellappa directed Yoganathan to sit in meditation near Nallur temple chariot day and night for forty days without any food. The guru served the disciple only water or tea. At the end of forty days Yoganathan was luminous with a spiritual luster, having gained the ultimate experience of oneness or enlightenment. The guru did not allow him to stay around any longer, since "two large elephants should not be tied to the same post."

Following inner guidance Yoganathan went on a pilgrimage to the famous shrine of Lord Murugan at Kadirgamam about 300 miles away. He walked in silence often fasting or begging for food along the way. After a month, Yoganathan's family, not seeing him around, asked Sellappa what had happened. Sellappa told them that Yoganathan was dead. The family returned home sadly and performed the funeral rites for him.

A few months later the family was surprised to see him again and complained to Sellappa for announcing the death of Yoganathan. The saint replied that he never says any untruth, and Yoganathan was indeed dead. In the Master's view Yoganathan had lost his personal identity or ego as separate from God and others, thus dead as Yoganathan, but alive as Yogaswami, one with God and all creation.

Yogawswmi went to Colombogam and sat in ecstatic meditation or samadhi under an Iluppai tree, day and night for a few years, unmindful of the weather, whether rain or shine. He ate rarely some of the food brought to him by a pious lady from the neighboring house.

The young sage chased away curiosity seekers with stones and harsh words. Initially he did not allow even genuine devotees to be around him. Afterwards he changed to spend most of his time taking care of sincere seekers. They prevailed on him to occupy a hut not far from the tree.

Many years earlier in 1889, Swami Vivekananda visited Jaffna and was taken in procession along Colombogam Road. When they neared the compound with Iluppai tree, Vivekananda alighted from his carriage and walked slowly, noting that it was "a holy place like an oasis in a desert."

The future is present to a sage who sees the world with the eyes of God. Vivekananda experienced the holy vibrations of the ground that would be sanctified years later by the meditation and austerities of Yogaswami.

On the following day Vivekananda gave a public speech in Jaffna starting with the words "the time is short, but the subject is vast." Yoganathan was 17 years of age when he heard Vivekananda, and was immensely impressed by the powerful presence of the sage on the stage, passionately pleading with the audience to realize their true Self or God. The fire lit by Vivekananda in the heart of the youth burnt brightly to make him into a sage who transformed the lives of thousands

The last Governor General of Sri Lanka or Ceylon as a British colony was Lord Soulbury. His son James Ramsbotham, knowing that the Canadian High commissioner Dr. James George was spiritually inclined, advised him to visit Yogaswami. When Dr. George went north and knocked on the door of Yogaswami's hut in Colombogam, there was a roaring response from inside: "Is that the Canadian High Commissioner?" Dr. George replied that it was his work, and not truly he. The sage received him with a loud laughter and made him sit by his side.

Dr. George had been a spiritual apprentice for many years doing Gurdjieff Work with one of his chief disciples Madame de Salzmann. Hence he bonded easily with Yogaswami whom he visited often. The sage advised him to spend more time in meditation, instead of wasting his energy attending too many official functions.

Once the saint asked him to go within with the question: "Who am I?" Yogaswami kept repeating the question louder and louder until he screamed out loud and fell silent. It was such a powerful silence that Dr. George went deep within himself to realize the purity of his being. He understood that "I am" is enough, and "Who?" is not needed.

Later Dr. George came out of the experience of Self-realization due to thinking and doing. Yet he managed to go back into it through meditation. Being established in a state of Self-realization takes much effort and time. Dr. George seemed to be well on his way due to the grace of the Master.

Yogaswami went on a pilgrimage to India and visited Ramana Maharshi at Annamalai for a whole afternoon in silence. No word passed between them. Later Yogaswami commented: "We said all that had to be said."

Lord Soulbury's son James Ramsbotham was one of the few monk-disciples of Yogaswami. They were later enlightened due to their utmost devotion and dedication to their Master. The most influential disciple of Yogaswami was an American by birth.

Robert Hansen from California, inspired by the books of Vivekananda, mastered yoga postures and the art of dance to join San Francisco Ballet Company at nineteen years of age. After a year he went on a pilgrimage visiting holy places and persons in India and Sri Lanka. Three years later he met Yogaswami, and was eager to stay around the great Master.

The guru initiated him with a new name, Sivaya Subramuniya, and started him on a worldwide mission. With a loud slap on his back, the sage said: "This sound will be heard in America. Now go round the world and roar like a lion. You will build palaces (temples) and feed thousands."

Subramuniyaswami did indeed build beautiful Hindu temples in America and all over the world. He started a large monastery in Hawaii to train young monks. His lectures and inspiring books seemed like a lion's roar reaching far and wide.

Chunnakam is a village about five miles north of Jaffna. It is well known for its market and a great woman saint called Sellachi Ammaiyar or Mother Sellachi. Poets, pundits and many others visited this saint regularly. Yogaswami was very fond of Sellachi Ammaiyar, went to her place often and served her humbly. Sellachi Ammaiyar also showed much affection to the young sage and spoke of him so highly that her followers became his devotees after her passing.

Once a devotee was getting ready to visit the sage after a bath. His body was clean, but he was concerned that the mind was not as clean, since it was prey to some ugly thoughts. He was ashamed to go before the sage with such a mind, and hoped that the sage would be talking to the devotees and not see deep into his mind.

As he approached the hut he was glad to hear the Master laughing and talking with the devotees. When he went in and prostrated, the sage looked at him with a smile to say: "Remember that I know you from head to toe. I see all your thoughts. Not only yours. I see the thoughts of everyone, since I am one with everyone."

Even one's past thoughts were present to him, as noted in the following incident. Master directed a devotee to touch his forehand and asked him whether it felt like a stone. When the devotee admitted that it was so, the master said: "The celibacy here is the same both inside and outside." Then the devotee remembered that few years ago, a suspicious thought about Master's celibacy had been in his mind, and regretted it.

When young men came to Yogaswami with enthusiasm, and wanted to take the vow of celibacy, more often he did not permit it. He accepted only a few as monks. They took up celibacy naturally, without any vow.

Markkandu Swami was one of them. As a young man he worked for the government in different parts of Sri Lanka. Yogaswami visited him in all these places, staying at his house for weeks to give him spiritual direction. Later he presented Markkandu Swami to other devotees as a model on the spiritual path.

Hundreds of Yogaswami's disciples experienced miraculous help from their Master in times of sickness or financial stress, even without their asking for it. He visited them in different parts of Sri Lanka, often as they were about to start a celebration at home, blessed them and left soon afterwards.

There were times when Yogaswami took on himself the symptoms of sickness suffered by his devotees or their children. At times, he prepared a medicinal concoction to give to the sick, and then consumed it himself, declaring that they were healed, and it was indeed true. Thus he proved his sense of identity with the devotees and all creation.

People from various races and religions approached the sage for his blessing. He received them all equally, and encouraged them to continue with their respective religious practices.

Besides the external rituals, Yogaswami emphasized the importance of realizing the Truth within ourselves, by cultivating the habit of being still—not to do anything in particular but merely witness or be aware of whatever happens within us.

He would say with much power in Tamil: "Summa Iru" or in English: "Just be, do nothing." Hearing his words some devotees were able to plunge into inner silence, and experience unearthly peace and bliss.

Professor A.S. G. Sampanthar from Chennai, India came to Jaffna and Colombo often to deliver lectures on Tamil literature and spirituality. He was friendly with many Tamil leaders in Sri Lanka. One of them brought him to see Yogaswami in 1950 for the first time.

He had heard about a crowd of people waiting outside the hut of the sage. The hut could accommodate only about fifteen persons. They prostrated at the feet of the saint seated on a mat or a chair, and stood around in silence, knowing that the Master understood their problems, and would bless them even without their asking. After few minutes they left with the Saint's permission, thus giving room to the people waiting outside to go in.

After Sampanthar prostrated, laid the offering of fruits near the saint's feet and was standing respectfully with the others, the sage said in Tamil "Let the little boy come here," pointing his hand to the right. It took some time for Sampanthar to realize that the sage was referring to him. He was quite scared. Then the saint gently coaxed him saying "come son, come here and sit" indicating the exact spot to sit.

Sampanthar visited the sage later about twenty times and was asked to sit at the same spot each time. Thus he became an ardent devotee of Yogaswami and a friend of other close disciples including Sri Kantha, the government agent of Jaffna.

Sampanthar seemed to be in awe as he wrote in Tamil about his contact with the sage. Sri Kantha used to celebrate the main festival of Lord Murugan every year at Kadirgamam. One year he was sad that he could not do so due to a special instruction from the government and told Sampanthar about it.

Yogaswami was also in the habit of being at Kadirgamam for the festival every year. Sri Kantha, his wife, and Sampanthar decided to visit the sage's hut in Colombogam, feel his vibrations and be blessed by Lord Murugan while the sage was away.

As they entered the compound, they were pleasantly surprised to hear the voice of the sage from the hut, lovingly calling them to come inside. They went in and prostrated at his feet. Yogaswami asked Sri Kantha why he had not gone to Kadirgamam. Sri Kantha burst out sobbing as he told the sage the reason.

Yogaswami said, "Son, do not worry. Do we have any vehicle? The fool has the peacock as his vehicle. Let him come to us. Where can we go?" With these words he laughed and started to sing; it went on for an hour. As the three devotees were returning home, Sri Kantha commented that he felt as if he had been at Kadirgamam.

Why did Yogaswami refer to God or Lord Murugan as "the fool?" Only a perfect lover can dare to call his beloved a fool. People in love are often known to act like fools. The sage was alluding to the foolishness of God's love.

Lord Murugan mounting his vehicle, the peacock, means overcoming the vanity of the devotee who thereby begins to see the splendor and majesty of God. Vehicle of God stands for His grace. Hence the words of Yogaswami that only Lord Murugan has his vehicle, and must come to us.

Yogaswami's close disciples sensed the presence of Lord Murugan in their Master, as Yogaswami himself had seen the Lord in his Guru Sellappa. In the same vein Sri Kantha felt that he had been at Kadirgamam after seeing his Master at the hut.

Two days later Sampanthar was in Colombo lecturing. After the lecture, he saw a film of the recent Kadirgamam festival where Yogaswami was seen giving a talk. He could not believe his eyes but heard from several others that Yogaswami was indeed at Kadirgamam, about 300 miles away from Colmbogam when he, Sri Kantha and his spouse visited the sage at the hut in Colombogam.

Later Sampanthar saw Yogaswami and started to raise the question of his bilocation (being in two separate places at the same time), but the Master shut him up quickly, and was talking lovingly about other things.

Many devotees while sharing experiences of meeting the sage found to their amazement that he had appeared at distant places at the same time. They were prudently silent about it, since they knew that the Master would be displeased if they gave importance to such phenomena.

In 1955, Sampanthar was scheduled to give a series of lectures for ten days in the evening at a suburb of Jaffna. He was staying at the house of Murugappa and had a car at his disposal. After the first lecture, he drove to Colombogam to spend few minutes in the holy presence of Yogaswami. On the following morning, Murugappa asked as usual whether Sampanthar had slept well. He opened his mouth to reply, but no sound came, though he tried many times.

He was deeply distressed by his condition, and drove the car to the house of a retired ENT specialist who had practiced medicine in Colombo for more than forty years. He gave a note saying "paralysis of the vocal cord" to the physician who confirmed the patient's diagnosis after several tests.

The doctor had not heard of a cure for this very rare condition in medical history. As Sampanthar seemed to be overwhelmed and about to start his car, the doctor suggested that he should go immediately to see Yogaswami..

Sampanthar knew that no one went to see Yogaswami before 6pm since he was out during the day visiting various devotees. Yet Sampanthar drove with tears to the hut in Colombogam. Yogaswami called him to come inside and scolded him severely for going to see the doctor as if he were Lord Murugan.

Sampanthar was perplexed to hear the sage say that he should continue lecturing in the evening. Realizing that the healing power of the sage had penetrated his vocal cord, he replied "I will do as you wish," the first words spoken with great relief.

Instead of going home, he went back to the physician's house, calling out: "Doctor! Doctor!" The old gentleman came rushing out to the road and prostrated before Sampanthar who protested about it. The physician held Sampanthar's hands as one worthy of the sage's grace, brought him inside the house and insisted on his taking lunch there.

Many other devotees of Yogaswami were also wonderstruck by the miracles that did abound around their Master. Besides the external wondrous events, the most amazing and significant miracle was the profound transformation that he wrought in the hearts of his followers.

They gratefully realized that even his apparently irrational, harsh, and cruel acts were motivated by his love, as he never shirked on his responsibility to purify and bring them closer to God.

Many melodious songs that he composed and sang often were collected by his devotees and compiled as a book called "Natchintanai." It is verily a beacon light to take the seekers out of the darkness of delusion into the eternal light of Love and Truth.

Yogaswami started a bimonthly magazine 'Sivathondan' (Servant of Siva) with informative and inspiring articles written by his close disciples. It flourished with the deeply devotional and philosophical poems of Sellathurai Swami. It continues to be published even now.

Sellathurai had been a total success as a teacher and a principal in various schools, being always the first to enter the school, and the last to leave it. He spent all his holidays and vacations visiting holy shrines in Sri Lanka and India. Every year he sat in silence before Ramana Maharishi for a few weeks, having deep spiritual experiences. After Maharishi passed away, Sellathurai travelled through India to find a Master and live with him. He was in a room near the Himalayas when Yogaswami appeared to him in a vision with the words "come home immediately."

Sellathurai instantly recognized Yogaswami as his Guru, and came back to Sri Lanka. He found that he had been transferred to a school not far from Colombogam, accepted his new post, and in the evening went to see the Master.

Yogaswami installed Sellathurai at Sivathondan Ashram in Jaffna, as the one most suited to take care of it while continuing to be a teacher. The Master carefully nurtured his spiritual development in the meantime.

Sellathurai washed his feet like the other devotees before entering the hut of the sage. Once he heard the sage tell a devotee that the teacher does not know how to wash his feet properly. Sellathurai could not figure out what he could do to improve.

A few months later he observed another devotee washing his feet devoutly and carefully, cleaning between the toes like a mother lovingly washing her infant. Sellathurai asked him how he had learnt to wash so well. The devotee explained that the Master advised him to regard his feet as holy and to wash them as if he were washing the Guru's feet.

Veneration and worship of Guru's feet, his sandals or shoes is an ancient Hindu tradition. They are not only symbols of God's grace but are understood to be actually the means of expressing humble love for God and receiving all His blessings.

Yogaswami had yearned for a disciple with perfect renunciation, and was content when Sellathurai came to him. Sellathurai absorbed the Guru's lessons so well and quickly, that he appeared to shine like a new copy of Yogaswami to other devotees. He blossomed out with beautiful devotional poems, reflecting his Master's poems that he had internalized and digested fully.

Yogaswami was nearing ninety years of age, still quite active, sweeping his hut as well as the compound, and caring for his cow Valli fondly, when one day Valli knocked him to the ground, and he had to be hospitalized for treatment.

He stayed in the hospital for three months, and had to use a wheelchair thereafter to move around. The number of devotees wanting to see him kept increasing. He continued to bless them lovingly until his mahasamdhi (great ecstasy or conscious final exit) in March 1964 at age 92.

Sellathurai Swami receiving the ochre robes happened a year after the death of his Guru. He had gone on a pilgrimage to India, dipped into the holy river Ganges after leaving his clothes on the shore. When he came back to the shore, he found there ochre robes instead of his clothes, and was internally directed to wear them.

Actually Yogaswami has not departed from this world. Where can he go when he is everywhere, being one with God? Those who are in tune with him can feel his holy Presence at any time.

Sivathondan Ashram in Jaffna is a very peaceful place where devotees and spiritual seekers go to meditate, worship the sandals of Yogaswami and be blessed by the sage. I enjoyed my visit there, as I was lovingly received and allowed to take the back copies of Sivathondan magazine without even a suggestion of a donation.

Both Sellappa and Yogaswami were known for many aphorisms that they repeated often to impress spiritual principles in the minds and hearts of their followers. These aphorisms can be comprised into four "great sayings" (Maha Vakyam) in Tamil.

1. Oru pollappum illai

THERE IS NOTHING WRONG OR HARMFUL

We can realize the truth of this saying when we take a long view of things. Every evil is turned into good and wrong righted due to the wisdom, power and love of God. Repeating this saying often enables us to surrender ourselves to God's holy will more easily and find peace.

2. Nam Ariyom

WE DO NOT KNOW

Though we do learn from our own experience and the experience of others to have some knowledge for practical life, we actually do not know the real or essential nature of anything or anyone. Unless and until we acknowledge our fundamental ignorance, wisdom will be a closed book to us.

3. Eppavo Mudintha Kariyam

A THING THAT FINISHED LONG AGO

There is no past or future in God. Since we are bound by time, it is hard for us to understand how the future can be in the past, as both are in the here and now of God. Faith means acknowledging that whatever happens now, finished long ago in God's consciousness.

4. Muluthum Unmai

ALL IS TRUTH

God is unchanging, eternal truth. He is the heart of everything, including evil and falsehood. Whatever changes does not remain real. Therefore there is nothing but truth. God is all in all.

Pearls Of Wisdom From Yogaswami [1]

Wander about in the jungle of the world with the assurance of a lion roaming the forest. Do not be discouraged on any account. There is nothing strange here. All is truth. There is not even one thing that is wrong.

1 From Natchinthanai published by Thiruvadi Trust of Sivayogaraswami, Sri Lanka, 2004 with the kind permission of Sivathondan Society

O man! Even if heaven and earth be offered to you, do not seek to rule or possess them. Be a witness. Greatness is your birthright.

By what does the eye see? By what does the ear hear? By what does the nose smell? By what does the mouth speak? That is the Atma or God. What an easy path!

Ponder on this and see. Everything is in your grasp. Think deeply just for one instant and you will know clearly that you are That. Realize the Divine Nature within yourself. You are your own master. It is you who directs yourself. You are the sole emperor of the universe! If you forget this pure thought you will continue to suffocate in the ocean of birth and death.

Arise! Awake! Henceforth nothing can overcome you! To light a lamp, the wick and the oil are both necessary. If you want to succeed in this, you must repeat Om Tat Sat (Om is That, the Reality) incessantly and with feeling - that is, you must rouse your soul.

Have faith in God. Believe in Him with all your heart. Think that in the world He is for you the sweetest of all sweet things. Think that there is nothing other than God. Sitting or standing, walking or lying down, think of Him. Let the thought of Him permeate your nerves, flesh and blood. Think that you are non-existent and that He alone exists. Let the aim of your life be to worship Him.

What one thinks, that one becomes. Have God in your heart and bring Him up there. Let all actions be His action. Finally all will be seen as He.

We are bringing up God in our hearts. We are His mother. There is nothing lacking either for us or for Him, He cannot separate Himself from us. All is truth.

O man! You are Truth. You are indestructible. No one can cause you harm. You are present here, there and everywhere. You are eternal.

Do not put on any outward show. Become strong within yourself. True religion is a solitary state that conforms to no pattern. Body, soul, possessions -surrender all three to God. Thereafter, give up everything that concerns yourself and see that all is He and He alone.

Each class proclaims that its habits and ways of life alone are good. The various religions also do the same. But all these are nothing but the distinctive characteristics of the world. All these different conflicts were also prevalent in times of old. There is nothing strange about them. They are simply the phenomena of Nature. The sage, who knows that they are one thing and that he is quite another, will live with them and yet remain unaffected by them.

Though great incarnations of the highest level have come at different times and performed many mighty works, yet even so the world remains the same. This is a great mystery.

Moving Beyond Doubts

In this chapter we will examine some common doubts and questions in order to help the reader to move beyond them, and not to waste time and energy being caught up in a play of the mind. Inner peace is found when we leave behind the games of our mind, and live in our heart.

1. *If God created the universe, who created God?*

This question arises due to imagining God as a particular entity, located somewhere up there. Then it is meaningful to ask how God came to be, or what or who created God. But God cannot be an object of imagination or knowledge. As human beings, we cannot help but imagine God, yet we must realize that He is far, far beyond any imagination or thought.

Curvature of space cannot be an object of imagination, yet physicists following Einstein accept it as real to explain gravitational forces. Similarly God cannot be imagined or even thought of properly, since images and thoughts are naturally limited. Saints say that we must leave words and thoughts behind, in order to find God.

God is not a particular entity, or a being among many beings. He is the essence of all beings. Every being derives its reality from God, Who is the absolute reality or pure Existence itself. He is the Supreme Consciousness giving reality and meaning to our thoughts, sustaining everything, the Life behind all lives, the unmoved Mover, the Ultimate Truth whom we glimpse very slightly through all the amazing truths that are revealed to our little minds.

Past and future are not, for God. He is ever present or eternal. Time and space are being created by God. It is more correct to say that God is presently creating the universe than that He created it. The concept of God implies that He has no beginning or end, since He is absolute or pure existence.

If we imagine God to be a being among other beings, though first and supreme, other beings will limit the first being by their very existence. But God is <u>not</u> a being among other beings, an entity that comes first, and is limited by entities that follow later. For God to be first, there should be a second or third thing that is separate from God. Creator and the created are not separate, but one; creation is a manifestation of the Creator. Nothing can be real, if separated from God.

God is infinite and eternal, has no beginning or end, no past or future; He is ever now. Therefore God cannot be created. With a proper concept of God, the question "who created God?" becomes meaningless.

2. *God is impersonal, intelligent universal energy. Belief in a personal God seems to be a superstition.*

Joseph Campbell is well known for his joyful discovery of spiritual themes in world mythology. Albert Einstein was in a state of wonder, as he explored the universe and delved deep into physics and mathematics, to formulate the theory of relativity and other laws that fundamentally shifted the outlook of modern science.

Campbell, Einstein and many other thoughtful people accept God as an impersonal, intelligent, universal force or energy, but are definite in their opposition to belief in a personal God. Most religious people on the other hand, are firm believers in a personal God, and are opposed to thinking or speaking about God in impersonal terms.

Both sides are right in their affirmation, but wrong in the negation. God is actually impersonal as well as personal. Mystics and Masters testify to this fact from their experience. It is not difficult to see a personal and impersonal aspect in our own being, as we introspect deeply.

The great Indian philosopher and saintly sage, Sankara affirmed that Absolute Reality or pure Self is impersonal, transcending the distinctions of knower, knowing and known. He also experienced, wrote and spoke about God as personal, praising and thanking Him or Her in deeply devotional poems.

Since we are personal beings, most of us have to relate to God in a personal way, and God will respond to us in a personal manner. This has been the experience of man throughout history, and will continue to be so.

3. *If God knows the future of man, then man's future is determined, and he cannot have free-will. But we are conscious of having a free-will. Then how can you affirm the existence of an omniscient or all knowing God?*

The famous American spiritual teacher, Ram Das, was taking about forty young men and women by bus, on a tour in North India. He had not seen his guru Neem Karoli Baba for more than a month, and didn't know where he could be. When the bus came to a fork in the road, the driver asked whether to turn left or right. Ram Das thought for a while and decided to turn left.

As it was noon, they stopped the bus in a small town to try to get lunch. When they alighted from the bus, they were received by Neem Karoli Baba, who told them that lunch was ready for forty people, and they could wash up beforehand. The saint manifested clear foreknowledge of an event that depended on many free decisions of Ram Das and forty others.

To cite another example, Sri Yukteswar told Yogananda many years earlier in India, that one day, he would be served strawberries by a lady in America and he would find them bitter. Then she would mash them, adding heavy cream and sugar. He would taste them and say: "How delicious these strawberries are!" and remember the Guru foretelling him about it. It happened exactly as predicted by Sri Yukteswar, according to the *Autobiography of a Yogi*.

The foreknowledge of saints is a well-known fact, as they share in the omniscience of God to a greater extent. Freedom of man and God's foreknowledge are facts that cannot be reconciled, given our present understanding.

Light should be either a wave or a particle; logically it cannot be both at the same. But modern physicists accept as a fact that light is both wave and particle. In the same manner, we accept omniscient God and man's freedom. Man's will is participation in God's will. Human freedom is relative, and depends on God's freedom. If there is much mystery in matter, should we not expect even more mystery in spirit?

4. *If there is a loving and omnipotent God, why does He allow so much suffering in the world? Holocaust, child-abuse, rape, torture, murder, economic and social oppression and exploitation, war, famine, AIDS, cancer, earthquakes, tsunami and floods are proof that there is no God. If there is a God, He is cruel or weak.*

Only the saints understand this problem properly. They do not close their eyes to evil and suffering in the world. Instead of intellectual talk, their hearts weep for the victims and the criminals as well. Identifying with the people in pain through Her compassionate tears, Ammachi brings light into the lives of suffering masses by Her affectionate attitude, while offering them also practical help to improve their condition.

She does not fear death even slightly, and is willing to undergo any amount of pain for the sake of others. Why? Because She lives in the awareness of God, as present within Herself and in others. She says that She sees only God everywhere and in everyone.

God allows evil and suffering in the world, that we may be healed or purified through temporary pain, and find Him who is eternal bliss. Those who have found God do not suffer, even if they are in intense pain. Their heart is full of joy and love.

Ramana Maharshi was suffering from a most painful form of cancer, according to a doctor attending on Him. A devotee wondered aloud how Maharshi could show no sign of pain externally. He responded: "Now that you tell me, there is some pain!" The Sage was so much immersed in divine bliss that He was hardly aware of His painful body.

Ordinarily God allows man's free-will and the law of *karma* to operate in the world. It is a mathematically precise and wise law. Both good and evil acts have proportionately good or bad consequences, taking place sooner or later, over many births.

We cannot remember our past acts in this life, let alone past births. Therefore we do not understand our own *karma*, or the *karma* of other people, individuals and groups. This we know, suffering is never in vain. We are truly purified thereby, more so if we accept it willingly.

When a mother gives a bitter medicine to her sick child, only gross ignorance can accuse her of being cruel or weak. Yogananda often complained to God about the evil in the world. He said that when one sees the end of the drama of creation, as he had seen already in God, one can understand and appreciate fully the wisdom of God that allows all the evil and suffering. Now we have to accept it on trust.

God's love for every individual is infinite. He is guiding each soul according to its particular needs. There is tremendous wisdom involved in this process. Let us not be too hasty in jumping to false conclusions in an area where so much is unknown.

5. *(a) If God knows everything and loves everyone infinitely, why do we have to pray?*

God does not need our prayer, but we need to pray in order to find God. God is a mere word or a concept, and He becomes real to us, only when we pray with ever deepening concentration and devotion. Praying for our needs and the needs of others is a way of cultivating faith in God. When our prayers are answered, our faith naturally increases.

Daya Mata says that she talks to God constantly as her beloved Friend, without being concerned about His response. You can tell Him anything and everything. We have only a slight understanding about ourselves, whereas His knowledge about us is complete and limitless. When we communicate to God fully and freely our desires, disappointments, hurts, anxieties and hopes, we move into His understanding and acceptance; we find peace. When this communication or prayer becomes unceasing, peace expands and deepens to turn into joy.

(b) Is God not ready to give us what we need, even before we ask Him?

God gives us our life, and all that we need before we ask Him. Hence we need to be grateful always. We must tell Him again and again that we love Him or Her (God is our Father and Mother). Our life itself is His unconditional love for us. There is no need to feel anything before we express our love for God sincerely. Wanting to love God is the beginning of love. Do not wait for the feeling of love to arise before you express your love for God or to anyone else for that matter. The feeling is bound to come later.

(c) Does God wait for our prayers before He heals the sick, feeds the starving millions, and brings about peace in a violent situation?

God does not wait, but wants our prayers here and now for our sake, and for the sake of others. Sickness, starvation and violence are due to the law of *karma*. They have value as means of purification for souls.

It does not follow that we can be complacent, and not act out of a compassionate and caring heart. We are instruments of God's love and compassion when we pray and act effectively to eradicate disease, poverty, injustice and violence in the world. God is not bound by *karma*; and as His children, we too can overcome *karma* through strong personal determination and action.

6. *Honest to God, I cannot believe in God. Where do I stand?*

When some people came to Ammachi saying that they could not believe in God, She responded that She would not ask them to believe in God or in Amma; it would be enough if they cultivated faith in themselves. Faith in oneself is necessary to live a fruitful, contented life.

Cultivating faith in oneself means being completely truthful, without exaggeration, understatement, or any distortion. In Shakespeare's *Hamlet*,

Polonius advises his son Laertes about leading a noble, virtuous life ending with the words:

> "This above all – to thine own self be true;
> And it must follow, as the night the day
> Thou canst not then be false to any man."

Being totally truthful is not at all easy in the modern world, as we are bombarded by falsehoods from all sides by the media and society. When we are genuinely sincere and yearn for Truth with all our hearts, we will be invisibly guided towards Truth in all that we do. We will not be too concerned about our past failures or others' negative opinions about us. Instead, we can walk steadily with heads held high, relying on the strength and wisdom provided continually by our true Self.

Profound respect and love for one's true Self naturally results in love and caring for others. As Shakespeare declared, being true to ourselves, we cannot help but be true to others as well. When we are true to ourselves, we discover our original innocence instead of the original sin, and are joyful in our own being. Love is nothing but living in Truth.

Sages live in Truth. When we think about their lives, they become a mirror to see our own true Self. They reveal our inner beauty and glory, reflecting the deepest part of our being. They belong to us more closely than our closest relatives. That is the reason why the lives of saints inspire us with greater self-confidence and faith.

Ramana Maharshi's normal response to people who came to Him with doubts and questions was to tell them to find out who was behind those doubts and questions. Persistent Self-inquiry removes all doubts and leads to liberation.

According to Pramahamsa Yogananda nobody on earth can ever leave the spiritual path. Even the materialists and atheists are on the spiritual path, since it is man's nature to seek happiness. God is nothing else but perfect happiness.

One may feel the absence of God intensely, as the saints themselves experience when they go through what is called "the dark night of the soul." During her last years, St. Therese of Lisieux doubted the existence of God, and had to make acts of faith numerous times.

The anguish of the "dark night" is so acute that the most severe physical suffering imaginable is nothing compared to it, says St. Teresa of Avila. It is the process of final purification. Thereby the ego with its sense of duality disappears and the soul experiences oneness or constant communion with God.

7. *Christ alone was pure and sinless. Other human beings are all sinners.*

Original sin or man being born in sin due to the sin of Adam and Eve is a myth that needs to be understood symbolically. Many people carry certain sinful tendencies from birth due to their wrongful acts of past lives. Yet it is wrong to identify oneself with sin or evil habits.

Paramahansa Yogananda, often advised people against thinking or calling themselves sinners, as we are essentially children of God. Our radical reality is purity or perfection. We are pure gold, covered by the mud of maya, delusion or ignorance.

We might have sinned even grievously in the past. Once we are consciously anchored in the Divine, we must let those errors stay in the past, and not disturb our present memory with them, being happy here and now in the love of God.

Most of the saints from all the religions seem to have been quite innocent from early childhood. Great Masters came from God merely to help mankind. They were saints in former births and had attained final liberation or perfect union with God. Hence their life on this earth is pure and sinless like Christ.

8. *Christ suffered and died for our sins, and thereby has redeemed mankind. Being the only Son of God, He alone can expiate and atone for our sins. Before God, there can be no other acceptable sacrifice to redeem man.*

For two thousand years, Christians have meditated on the passion and death of Christ in order to avoid sin and grow in love for God and neighbor, thereby becoming truly holy. Centuries have produced many hundreds of great saints following the same tradition. However some of the concepts explicit and implied in the statement above need to be clarified.

Does God require a bloody sacrifice as expiation for the forgiveness of sins? The practice of placating God to avert His anger through the sacrifice of animals and even human beings came into the traditions of various peoples around the world at a certain period in history. Implying a defective concept of God and sin, this tradition was never universal.

God is not a revengeful tyrant who demands blood as expiation for sins. The beauty of life is never lost on Him, as He is the giver of life, and cannot ask for its unnecessary destruction. Christ said: "Go and find out what is meant by the Scripture that says 'It is kindness that I want, not animal sacrifices.'" [Mt.9:13]

When certain acts of man thwart his own welfare and that of others, we assume that God would be offended and angry. Though God is eternal, unchanging love, and cannot be offended, He wants our repentance. To repent from such acts and become whole again, the type of expiation needed would be determined by the nature of each case.

God's love for us is unconditional. His forgiveness of our sins is instantaneous with our repentance. Depending on our latent sinful tendencies, further suffering may be needed for purification. Moreover man has to suffer the consequences of sin, though the suffering may be mitigated by masters assuming part of the burden of karma of their disciples upon themselves.

Masters enduring much pain for the sake of their disciples, manifests the beauty of their immense love for them. The followers of Christ have always felt the glory of His great love which motivates them, and still moves them to be selfless servants of mankind.

The statement that Lord Jesus is the only son of God must be understood in its context, as explained earlier in the first chapter. He was fully conscious of being one with the Heavenly Father. All the great Masters have the same supreme divine consciousness, and are aware of being one with God.

Though belonging to various religious organizations, we must move quickly to realize the fundamental importance of unity in spirituality. When I worship Ammachi, I am worshipping thereby Christ, Yogananda and all the Masters, because I am bowing to the Supreme Consciousness or the One God manifest in Her and in all the Sages. Masters cannot be separated from each other.

Swami Ramananda was feeling quite sad about parting from his Guru AnandaMoiMa. Joyfully She assured him of Her inseparability from him, as one can separate matter from matter, but never spirit from spirit, since in Spirit we are always one.

Dividing and comparing Masters is a materialistic attitude. God is our only Reality. Ammachi tells reporters that She sees all the people that come to Her as God. In our innermost being, we are not different from Christ. That is why He demands us to be "perfect as the Heavenly Father is perfect." (Mt.5:48) Children must behave like the Father.

Christians say that Christ is the only Son of God, and they are merely God's adopted children. As far as the disciples of Christ understood, He was the only one who knew the Heavenly Father intimately. Hence they could focus on Christ calling Him the only Son of God. Such focus develops genuine devotion.

It is important to stay on one path, and focus on one Divine Form in order to deepen one's devotion and concentration. If we concentrate on Christ, and go deeper into His consciousness, we will realize God's glorious Presence within us and everywhere. The distinction between being a natural Son of God and divine adoption will become pointless then.

Christians can and should think of Christ alone as their sole Savior. However they must desist from passing negative comments about other Masters, as it would be tantamount to despising the divine sanctity of Christ Himself.

The divine consciousness that was and is in Christ is found in all the Masters. Lord Krishna came with the same consciousness. Hence His devotees adore Him as the supreme Lord God and the Savior of all creation.

To know many Masters, and think of each one as the sole savior of the world is paradoxical; but it is true based on a practical imperative that we can focus only on one divine form in order to deepen our concentration, expand our consciousness, and attain liberation, when we will realize the one God as the All in all.

9. *There are several passages in the Bible that speak about Lord Jesus coming again in glory to judge the living and the dead, bringing some to heaven and sending others to eternal hell. Some feel that His second coming and the end of the world are imminent.*

During the early Christian era, the political persecution of the Jews by Romans intensified. To put down their rebellion, in 70 A.D. Roman legions under Titus marched on Judea from all sides, and laid siege to Jerusalem, camping outside its walls and cutting the food and water supply.

Though the Jewish zealots fought the Romans valiantly, the Romans were able to set the walls surrounding Jerusalem on fire which eventually destroyed the magnificent temple. About 110,000 Jews were killed and 97,000 taken as captives to work in the mines, according to the historian Flavius Josephus. It sent shock waves to the Jews and Jewish Christians in Diaspora.

Their despair was transformed into a hope for the imminent coming of the Messiah who will bring freedom and prosperity to the Jews as their king, while destroying injustice and unrighteousness everywhere, so that there would be no more wars or famine in the world. Messiah comes from Hebrew, meaning "anointed"-which is translated into Greek as Christos. Christ means one who was anointed as king.

For the followers of Jesus, He was the true Messiah or Christ. Therefore to believe in an imminent arrival of the Messiah would be, to proclaim the second coming of Christ. Being under tremendous stress, they expected the world to end within their own generation, when Christ would come again in glory to judge the living and the dead, bringing the righteous with Him to Heaven and sending the wicked to eternal hell under Satan.

The concept of eternal hell is derived from Persian and Babylonian myths that were based on a philosophy of dualism. Reality is not ultimately one but two, good is equally opposed to evil and cannot triumph over evil according to this teaching. It is a pessimistic philosophy, based on false concepts of God and life.

Though the idea of everlasting punishment impinged on Judaism late in its history (see Daniel 12:2), it was never accepted by the majority of the Jewish rabbis. They taught that Gehenna (hell) would be temporary, (not more than twelve months) to purify the souls and prepare them for paradise.

Everlasting punishment means: evil begets evil; there will be no end to evil and consequent misery, unless the chain of evil is broken by God's grace and man's effort. It is possible that Christ may have spoken about everlasting punishment in this limited sense. His words must be understood in their context. The statement of Christ: "It is impossible for the rich to enter the kingdom of God" must be balanced by the words: "Nothing is impossible for God" (Mt. 19:23-25).

Being one with God, Jesus emphasized His amazing grace and mercy. His parables of the good shepherd who leaves the ninety-nine and goes after the one lost sheep, and the joy of the father who celebrates the return of his prodigal son, stress the ever abiding love and mercy of God. It is not possible for God to stop being merciful at any moment, nor can the human spirit ever lose its innate capacity to decide freely to be purified and be united with God.

Paramahansa Yogananda interprets the second coming of Christ as Christ coming into the hearts of His devotees. Yogananda himself had many visions of Lord Jesus in ecstatic meditation and communed with Him deeply. .

Christ coming at the end of the world may be understood in a spiritual sense. It means that the world has to end in our heart before Christ can come there. We need to be fully detached from the world in order to feel the loving Presence of Lord Jesus in our heart.

As opposed to Christian fundamentalism, a true Christian would not care about the end of the world that may happen soon or after many millions of years. Nor would he be interested in life after death, a future heaven or hell. His task is to get out of the hell of egoism here and now, love Christ with his whole heart, and love others as himself. Then he will experience the joy of heaven in this world itself.

The purifying power of God as manifested by Mother Kali or Lord Siva may be symbolized by the eternal fire of hell. Eternity is an attribute of God. Fire stands for His Love that burns the dross of sin, purifies and enlightens the heart of man. Then eternal fire could be awesome, but must be welcome as redemptive, divine Presence. We should be willing to go to the depths of hell and conquer all the demons there for the sake of His Love.

"Judge not, lest you be judged" (Mt 7:1) are words of Jesus, central to spirituality. Judgment here does not refer to legal affairs but to morality. When I point a finger at another person in judgment and condemnation, three fingers are pointing towards me. I cannot judge others without condemning myself in the process.

Non-judgmental attitude is based on a simple truth, namely that I don't know my own heart properly and depend on God's love and mercy for my salvation. Then how can I presume to know others and judge them? Humility is merely a matter of being truthful.

Fanatical fundamentalism ignores the fundamentals of religion such as humility, truthfulness, trust in God, love and compassion. Fanaticism implies a gnawing sense of insecurity, wanting to dominate and control others, whereas genuine faith bespeaks serene self-confidence, expressed in selfless service and a profound respect for all human beings.

Fundamentalism is found in almost all religions. It is a sad commentary on human nature. Hopefully it will pass away soon, seeing itself mirrored in opposing religious fundamentalist systems, as an insane phenomenon.

10. *I am very much bored by spiritual teachers. Why do they keep repeating the same stories and thoughts again and again?*

Your boredom is a clear sign that you are in dire need of such teachings. You need to listen to them more attentively and more often.

Boredom, cold indifference, sense of emptiness and loneliness are symptoms of spiritual sickness. Trying to cover them up with worldly pleasures and entertainment or superficial camaraderie are no help. They are a sure road to despair.

Medicine is the means to cure sickness. We do not take medicine to please ourselves, but to heal. Spiritual teachers and teachings may cause us boredom, pain and hardship, as we struggle to wake up from the stupor of worldliness and ignorance. Yet we must take the medicine of fellowship with saints, and listen to their teachings to heal ourselves from ignorance, which is the cause of all evil. We are not likely to overdose on such medicine.

Boredom, hardship and discouragement are experienced more during the initial stages of the spiritual journey. As we progress spiritually, life becomes more peaceful and joyful.

Brother Bhaktananda, who passed away a few years ago in California was a direct disciple of Paramahansa Yogananda. After living at the ashram for a few years, he, bored and discouraged, approached Yogananda, to say: "I don't find saintly models or inspiring examples here." He was unaware that he was speaking to the greatest example on earth. His Master looked at him steadily, and said: "You, you become that example!"

Precious are the gaze and words of a Master. They are truly divine grace to a receptive disciple. Bhaktananda started practicing the Presence of God intensely, mentally saying "I love you God" or "I love you Guru". Yogananda responded to his mental act once by looking at him lovingly and saying: "I love you, too, Michael". Bhaktananda was known by that name then. He was overwhelmed with bliss for days afterwards.

Several years ago I said to Bro. Bhaktananda: "Brother, we have heard you saying that your life with Yogananda was often joyful. He passed away forty years ago. How do you feel now?" In his simple and humble way, he answered: "From the time I wake up until I fall asleep at night, I am in a state of bliss. It never changes by whatever I do." Amazed, I asked: "Brother, what about when you are fast asleep? Don't you feel joy then?" "That will happen when I am enlightened like Master. I will be consciously blissful even during sleep then," he replied, as if his enlightenment was a matter of course, just around the corner.

A simple way to be rid of boredom is to be more aware. All the spiritual Masters advise cultivation of total awareness here and now. Instead of taking things for granted, awareness enables us to appreciate nature, people and the things around us much more. There is a certain innocence and freshness in full awareness, as it tends to be free from prejudices and judgments.

11. *Did divine revelation end with the Bible as believed by the Christians, or finish with the Koran as claimed by the Muslims?*

Divine revelations of the past have value only to the extent that they can inspire us to yearn for Gods' revelation to us personally here and now. In the seventeenth century a seventeen-year-old Catholic youth saw a barren tree during winter, and thought how it will have fresh leaves in spring, and that God was in the tree giving it life. God revealed Himself with such power and grace to the youth at this moment that the sense of His Presence never left him thereafter.

Later he became a monk and worked in the monastery kitchen. Brother Lawrence said that the sense of God's Presence remained the same, without increase or decrease, whether he was receiving the holy Eucharist or washing dishes in the kitchen amidst much noise.

Peace Pilgrim had not read or heard any Scripture before receiving her personal divine revelation through a determined effort to find God. Crying for God is fundamental. Divine revelation has no end. God reveals Himself through everything. His beauty is manifest when we see a splendid sunset or the amazing colors and designs of flowers. His joy is revealed in the heart-warming smiles of children.

The great Masters of modern times are the magnificent manifestations of God for us here and now. Their lives and words are truly Sacred Scripture. These modern Scriptures are often easier to read with understanding and inspiration.

There have been some books written in recent times by ordinary people who felt that they were receiving direct messages from God, like *A Course in Miracles* or *Conversations with God* by Donald Weltsch. The authors initially resisted the inspirations thinking they were hallucinating or unworthy, not unlike the prophets of old. There are outstanding writers like Marianne

Williamson and Dr. Gerald Jampolsky who are inspired by *A Course in Miracles*. They help thousands of people to walk steadily on the spiritual path through their books and workshops.

12. *Is there a distinction between divine revelation and enlightenment?*

There is a vast difference. The distinctions between the knowing subject, act of knowing and the object of knowledge are transcended in enlightenment. It is not conditioned by an individual's knowledge and experience, whereas divine revelation is conditioned by the consciousness and unconscious expectations of the subject of divine revelation.

A father talking to a child who believes in Santa Claus can address the child referring to Santa Claus as real, whereas he may talk differently with a child who does not have such belief. Similarly God can reveal Himself differently according to people's different beliefs and expectations.

Thus the visions and revelations of a Hindu devotee differ widely from a Christian's experience both in the forms seen and the doctrines received. Hence they should not be taken as the last word on what is true objectively for everyone, though they may be helpful in moving towards Truth.

Revelation happens through forms, words and thoughts, whereas enlightenment is plunging into infinite consciousness in total silence, beyond thoughts and words. A prophet who transmits messages received from God may be close to God, yet need not be an enlightened Master who is fully aware of being one with God like Lord Jesus Christ and other great Masters.

13. *Are there practical, spiritual principles and methods to resolve conflicts?*

Spiritual principles are always practical. Amma says: "Spirituality is the art of living." It is the way to be wonderfully successful in life.

Conflicts arise due to fear. It is said that there is nothing to fear but fear itself. This statement is doubly false. There are many things people are scared of, and fearing fear itself is not at all helpful. One has to understand and accept fear and the object of fear in order to be freed from fear.

Violence is more often based on fear. To condemn violence indiscriminately is itself a violent and fearful act. Instead, one needs to inquire why and how violence originated, and find ways to resolve the underlying problems that created, and are still creating fear in the hearts of people.

A conflict cannot be resolved unless one or both parties to the conflict move beyond the conflict level. In conflicts among individuals where personalities or egos clash, thinking and acting creatively beyond the confines of the ego can and will help to resolve the problem.

This principle is true in ever widening contexts. In tribal, ethnic and national conflicts, there is the fear of losing the group identity. Continuing to act out of fear will eventuate in such a loss. Fear is focus on the bad. Increased concentration on the negative gives it more energy, and brings about the result that one fears.

Unless a conflict is resolved creatively on a higher level, both sides to the conflict lose. Wanting and willing what is good for both sides is the way out of conflict. In other words, love is the only method to resolve a conflict.

Love is not weak sentimentality but a powerful force that "casts out fear." Not denial or suppression of fear, but accepting fear fully and letting it go, while acting out of trust in oneself and in the other, wanting the best for all, is the way towards positive peace.

No one with proper understanding or awareness can be evil. Evil is certainly not overcome by evil; instead, it increases and multiplies. To believe that violent hatred can be eliminated by more violence seems to be rather absurd. As Lord Buddha said, "Hatred is not overcome by hatred; hatred is overcome only by love." (Dhammapada 1:5)

It may appear that military might and cleverness of political leadership can establish peace in conflict situations. How can those who have no peace within, bring about peace outside? Peace proceeds from the core of love. Whether in the past, present or future, it is love and love alone that brings peace to the world.

Love has certain qualities that are required to resolve a conflict.

- being open and truthful
- listening with empathy
- flexibility: fixed positions preclude creativity and moving towards greater good for everyone concerned.
- trust
- wanting everyone to be happy

The memory of past hurts and consequent labeling of opponents as terrorists or racists is a severe obstacle to peace. The wise words of Lord Buddha are pertinent in this context: "'He abused me, he beat me, he defeated me, he robbed me;' in those who harbor such thoughts, hatred is not appeased." (Dhammapada 1:3). One who is happy and full of love for oneself easily forgets the past acts of others, and is able to approach them with love and respect.

Visualization of both sides prospering and being fulfilled in their aspirations must underscore the process of conflict resolution. Prayer and meditation are necessary means to establish a state of peace within and without.

14. *Does God have favorites? Are some people specially chosen by God? Does it mean they are better than others?*

God can select an individual or a group for a special task in the world. Actually everyone has a special function on earth. We are happy when we find what it is, and perform it with love.

God has no favorites. Everyone is infinitely precious to Him. Hence any comparison between persons or peoples is altogether meaningless before God. All human beings are one body, each part having a unique function for the welfare of the whole.

Whatever we do including our every thought affects the whole of creation, as the slight movement of a butterfly wing in Russia has a direct bearing on the speed of wind in America, according to scientists. Hence the importance of improving the quality of all our acts, in order to bring about peace and harmony in the world.

According to the Bible, Israelites were specially selected by God to be His people. Some Christians think that, with the New Testament, they replace the Israelites as the chosen people of God. Can the true God choose a people and set them apart from others, implying that others are not special to Him? Can He encourage a people to destroy another nation, not even sparing a single woman, child, or an animal, and occupy their land? Only a false concept of God can come to such beliefs.

It is all right to think that you are very special to God as long as you do not conclude that others are not special to Him. God chooses everyone and everything, as He creates only out of love and joy. Even a snowflake is specially chosen by God and given a unique beauty. Then all are the chosen people of God.

Passages in the Bible, Koran and other Scriptures that instigate violence and aggression must be understood in their historical context, and need to be interpreted symbolically. Enemies stand for the evil habits within oneself. Waging war signifies the internal struggle needed until the bad habits are routed totally.

Human life in our fragile little planet is on the verge of extinction due to man's sense of insecurity that is compensated by his aggressive over-consumption and acts of devastation. Giving up fear, we need to co-operate lovingly with all the people, as specially chosen by God to preserve His beautiful earth for His future children.

15. *Some people believe that the caste system comes from their sacred tradition, and must be honored in practice.*

The caste system was functional when it started as the economy then was primarily agricultural. Children learned the trades from their parents, and the society was rigidly stratified. Genuine practice of religion resulted in people respecting and caring for each other.

With the modern economy that promotes high mobility, the caste system has no practical value. Moreover it has been severely abused by individuals and groups to oppress and exploit others. Due to its inhumanity, Mahatma Gandhi strove hard to eradicate the caste system from Indian society.

Ramdas, well known as the smiling saint, gathered many disciples in India and abroad due to his contagious joy. At his ashram in South India, spiritual seekers of different castes came to see him often, staying at the ashram for days and months. He inculcated equal vision, advising them to worship everyone as Ram (the name of God that he constantly repeated to attain liberation).

He had advised an orthodox Brahmin who visited the ashram regularly in the same manner. One day this gentleman was laying out a cloth, and setting the idols on it for worship at the ashram compound. A so-called low caste youth walked into the ashram, greeted the saint with much devotion, went near the Brahmin, and bent down respectfully to touch his feet.

The Brahmin withdrew violently, furious at the youth for daring to 'pollute' him. The youth moved aside with a sad face, and the Brahmin started chanting the mantras for worship. Saint Ramdas had observed this scene from afar. His smiling countenance appeared severely stern as he took long, firm strides towards the Brahmin, made a bundle with the cloth and all the idols in it, and threw it away with such force, it landed quite far away. He said to the Brahmin, "first worship the God who came to you and wanted to touch your feet with love; then you will be fit to do idol worship."

The saint's grace transformed the Brahmin who humbly touched the youth's feet, and befriended him later. Brahman is the essence of all human beings and animals as well. Then we must think of all as Brahmins, without any distinction. Our future will be bright and wonderful if we get into the habit of considering all races as specially chosen by Yahweh, and all human beings and animals as Brahmins.

16. *Throughout history religion has been connected with much violence. Religious leaders are known to advocate wars and ruthless elimination of "enemies".*

It is a strange and curious fact that "holy" men in all religions, including Hinduism and Buddhism, have been involved in killing other people who had a different religious viewpoint.

Spirituality embraces unity of creation and the primacy of selfless love at all times, whereas religion may sometimes ignore such imperatives in favor of other interests.

The destruction of idols and idolaters in the past had political and economic interests besides a religious motive. Pure love for Yahweh or Allah would have seen His Presence in the idols and idolaters as well. Such purity is very rare. More often our love is mixed with self-serving intentions that may be conscious or unconscious.

Religious people must become honest enough to accept that we are mere beginners on the spiritual path, stuck with images and hardly able to go beyond. God remains an image or a word for us, (we may get glimpses of His Presence now and then), until He is felt as the All in all, the ever shining Truth, endless ever new Bliss, the only Reality beyond the subject and object of knowledge. Then there would be no room for the desire to destroy others; there will be no "others" to destroy. Masters see only their Self everywhere.

17. *Does Near Death Experience have any spiritual value or is it mere hallucination?*

Millions of people all over the world have had what is called NDE or Near Death Experiences. There are many books written on this subject. To claim that these experiences are mere hallucinations is to forget that hallucinations are often accompanied by mental disturbance and anxiety. Moreover in hallucination the subjects are aware later that they were hallucinating.

People who undergo near death experiences are in quite the opposite camp. They are convinced that their experiences were real and authentic. They say that their NDE seemed to be more real than the ordinary experiences of their waking consciousness.

Subsequently, not only are they much happier, they are also no longer afraid of death; and their lives are changed positively to express more love to their family members and friends, as well as compassion and caring towards people in general.

Philip L. Berman, in his highly inspiring book: *The Journey Home* shows a close connection between NDE and mystical experience, expounding the main theme with illustrations from various religious traditions throughout history. The subjects of such experiences are convinced of their essentially spiritual nature, and do not give any importance to the doubts of materialistic scientists.

A phenomenal account of Near Death Experience is narrated in a recently published, powerful book 'Dying to be Me' by Anita Moorjani, with a touching foreword by Dr. Wayne Dyer. Anita Moorjani's body was completely consumed by cancer to end in a coma, when she experienced another dimension that bathed her in unlimited, unconditional love and fed her much wisdom.

She came back to body consciousness with the conviction that she will heal quickly, though it was altogether impossible according to the physicians attending on her. She did heal and showed no sign of cancer in four days. Now Anita is on a mission to teach others about the importance of being true to themselves without any fear realizing that they are truly magnificent, and loving everyone and everything unconditionally.

18. *How do we know that what you say is true? It may be the devil's trick to persuade us into false beliefs about idolatry, polytheism, reincarnation, incarnation, hell and so on.*

A sincere and humble prayer from the heart is one sure way to find whether what you hear or read is true or not. Sincerity and humility make us non-pretentious and realize that we truly know nothing. Then we will approach any question as a beginner, innocent as a child, with an open mind and a receptive heart.

What we can know through words and thoughts is a mere drop compared to the vast ocean of knowledge available to human beings who experience their union with God. St. Thomas Aquinas, the prince among Christian theologians underwent a profound mystical experience during the last months of his life on earth. He refused to complete his famous *Summa Theologiae*, saying that all what he had written was a mere straw, compared to the Truth he experienced.

When we live with saints and sages, we abide in the Heart of God, covered by His eternal and unconditional love. Love casts out fear including the fear of the devil. A fearless or courageous yearning for Truth will expand our minds and hearts. Then we will begin to live in the peace and simplicity of God, beyond the usual doubts and complex questions that arise from restlessness.

19. *Is it necessary to be committed to a particular spiritual path or a Master in order to find God and be Self-realized?*

This is a significant question for those who are serious about the spiritual search and desire to progress steadily towards their goal. The saints, as a rule, emphasize that it is practically impossible to advance spiritually without the grace and guidance of an enlightened Master.

There are many paths that lead to salvation and full liberation. It is good to explore various paths initially. When one finds a suitable path that he or she can follow in all sincerity, then it is time to be committed and follow it to the end.

To keep changing the spiritual paths often can be even harmful. There may be many boats to cross a river, but if one continues to jump from boat to boat, instead of crossing the river, one may easily fall into it.

In the beginning I was quite committed to the Catholic Church which I quit later for reasons given earlier. This does not deny the fact that many sincere and holy people still belong to the Church and other religions including the fundamentalist groups. Personally being burnt once, I was rather wary of joining any religious organization again.

The turning point came in 1981 while meeting a holy monk from Self-Realization Fellowship, Brother Turiyananda. He was so warm-hearted, friendly and humorous. He kept me enthralled for hours, relating inspiring stories from his own life.

Born and educated in Switzerland, he started exploring many spiritual paths in his teen years. Then he met Saint Ramdas on the saint's first tour of Europe, and spent a year at his ashram in India.

A few years later he saw Saint Ramdas again in Switzerland. Now he was ready for initiation and approached the saint, wanting to be his disciple. Though Ramdas had many Indian and Western disciples, he declined to accept him, saying "no, I am not your guru. You have a guru already. Yogananda is your guru. Go to him."

This happened in 1953, a year after Paramahansa Yogananda had left his body. Taken by surprise the eager seeker replied, "I do not want a dead guru. I need a living guru. I have known you for many years and have followed your teachings. Please accept me as your disciple."

The usual smile from the saint's face vanished. He looked at the young man before him with piercing eyes and said sternly: "Never, never call an enlightened Master 'dead'. Not Yogananda, you are dead. If you want to live, go to him. He is waiting for you."

Two weeks later Turiyananda was in California to be accepted as an apprentice and later as a monk by Self-Realization Fellowship. This moving interview with the saintly monk was the decisive moment that enabled me to accept Paramahansa Yogananda as my guru and commit myself to Self-Realization Fellowship.

Few Masters have been an exception to this rule. Some were born enlightened like AnandaMoiMa and Ammachi. Others like Ramana Maharshi and Peace Pilgrim were later enlightened without any external guidance. However it does not seem to be the will of God for most people. Therefore to advance spiritually, it is necessary to select a particular spiritual path, and be totally committed and loyal.

20. *What can we do to eliminate wars and starvation in the world?*

Wars and world hunger are closely connected. Wars and preparation for wars are a big business. It depends on the psychological manipulation of the vast majority of people, political corruption and economic exploitation of man and nature.

The root cause for this perennial problem of man is fear. Fear of extinction drives man to perpetuate himself in others' memory through fame and name. It makes some people amass wealth at the expense of others and nature itself.

Mahatma Gandhi was astutely perceptive when he said that fear, violence and deception are essentially related, since fear leads one to violence and deception. If the root cause is fear, then rooting out fear is the solution. It is easier said than done.

From early childhood, man is socialized through fear. Parents fear for their children, and frighten them in the process of teaching them personal and social skills. Thus fear is deeply embedded in society. The fearful can be easily manipulated.

Due to the progress in technology and modern weaponry, the survival of mankind is at stake now, unless our psychology is radically transformed, warned Einstein. Man cannot go on with greed and personal profit as the main motive for economic progress.

It is imperative that the welfare of all mankind and nature itself become the primary motive for economic, political and social activities including education and scientific research. Such a fundamental change can happen, only when man realizes that he is essentially immortal or spiritual.

Then fear naturally disappears from his heart to be replaced by love and loving acts that will make the world more harmonious and beautiful. We need to become conscious of the basic truth that we are one, and responsible for every individual on earth.

We can and do contribute to the elimination of wars and starvation at the causal level, when we work to remove fear from our own hearts and from the hearts of others, especially children. Our contribution increases as we exude peace and love towards all creation, and educate others to do the same.

Imagination is more important than knowledge, said Einstein. It is the internal cause of external manifestation. As we persist in acts of vivid imagination with appropriate feeling, we are ensuring the eventual outcome of our goals in life.

We can usher in a peaceful world without wars, wasteful production and consumption leading to starvation sooner than later, if we consistently visualize a different scenario as already accomplished.

We must imagine a world where economic activities are imbued with honesty and transparency, as everyone is concerned with everyone else. Conflicts are resolved amicably due to open, honest communication. Production and distribution are locally, regionally and globally planned with proper feedback from the base.

America consuming most of the world's resources must come to an end. We can willingly give up unnecessary luxuries and wasteful consumption in order to respond to the necessary needs of others. Thereby we will find genuine fulfillment and peace.

Thus only the needed goods are efficiently produced and distributed to everyone in need, while respecting nature and all creation. Continuous imagination of such a world will contribute significantly towards its eventual fulfillment.

PRACTICES FOR LOVE AND JOY

CHOOSE TO BE HAPPY AND LOVING NOW

Many people believe that happiness depends on their outer circumstances. Unfortunately this is a wrong belief, designed to perpetuate man's misery. As Wayne Dyer says, a belief is merely a habitual thought. If false, it must be changed. Whatever the circumstances, we can choose to be happy and loving now.

Barry Kaufman and his wife Samharia believed that love and happiness is their choice at any moment. When we are genuinely happy and loving, we follow our inner guidance relentlessly.

They demonstrated it by raising at home their two-year-old child, who was diagnosed as autistic and severely retarded. Following their inner guidance, they used original and innovative techniques to treat him, against all professional advice. The child became a brilliant student later, so as to graduate *cum laude* from an Ivy League college.

They adopted three so-called "problematic" children from foreign countries who flourished in their new home, due to the love and happiness they experienced there. Barry who is fondly called Bears and Samharia opted not to select a child from the agencies but to love and adopt any child sent to them.

Happiness is our primary duty; all the other virtues flow from it, said the Jewish philosopher Benedict Spinoza. That means, we always choose to be happy or unhappy. Happiness is linked to goodness and diffuses by itself. Hence we enjoy the company of happy people. On the other hand, evil avoids happiness, and seeks out misery. Only the miserable turn out to be wicked.

There are two ways to get rid of misery. First, since unhappiness is a sign that our mind is engaged in negative thoughts, we can challenge them, and change to positive thoughts, with resultant happiness.

The second way is through surrender. Resistance to unhappiness gives it more strength. Instead, a relaxed and calm acceptance of unhappiness or surrender surprisingly leads to happiness. Surrender may not be easy at the start, but true surrender leads to genuine freedom. That allows us to realize happiness within unhappiness, in the same manner as by looking deeper into falsehood, one can find truth.

Some modern sages seem to have found perennial joy in this manner. Victor Frankl's parents, brother and wife perished in prison camps and gas-ovens during the holocaust. As a psychiatrist, he had seen mental suffering close at hand, but the brutal conditions in the concentration camp at Auschwitz brought him to the depths of despair.

It was his total surrender to the suffering in and around him that enabled Victor Frankl to find inner peace and help out his fellow prisoners. Even the SS guards sought his company and wisdom to solve their personal problems.

Brother Bhaktananda was able to hide his inner bliss, but in some others, it shines brightly on their faces and draws people to them. Luther McKinney, an elderly black gentleman, belonged to this category. During the SRF annual convocation in Los Angeles, a crowd gathered around Luther, as if to drink the wine of divine joy from him.

After the crowd left, he told me how for many years, he had enjoyed sweeping the Times Square subway station in New York City, to keep it clean for the children of God who came there. Walking through the same subway station a few months later, I felt that it was a holy place since Luther McKinney had worked there joyfully as a custodian. It does not matter what you do; the "why" makes all the difference. Living for others willingly is genuine happiness.

Judge Not

"Judge not lest you be judged," said Christ. It means that we are actually condemning ourselves when we condemn others. Negative judgments underlie negative moods like holding on to past grievances, fear, anger, and hatred. The survival of the ego or the false self depends on such moods. Due to the ego, one may feel superior while judging others negatively. But it is closely related to a sense of insecurity and inferiority.

From moment to moment we have the choice to side with the ego or the soul. The soul is ever-forgiving, innately peaceful, loving and joyous. Those who have complete control over their egos are truly the greatest conquerors, much more than Alexander the Great or Genghis Khan. Saints are the heroes of heroes, because they succeeded in the battle of life - the struggle between the soul and the ego. Their hearts shine with the light of love.

When Yogi Ramaiah saw the cobra with its raised hood, ready to shoot out its deadly poison, there was no fear in the saint's heart. Instead, it was filled with pure love for all creatures. Hence he bent down and tenderly caressed the snake which was content and moved away quickly. Ammachi expressed divine love when She touched the flicking tongue of the cobra with Her own tongue.

A hefty man was walking intently to beat up a little girl cowering in a corner with fear. Most of us would have condemned him on the spot. Peace Pilgrim responded differently. She looked at him with love and compassion, and was thus able to save the girl.

When you become aware of being disturbed or angry at others due to negative judgments, pray sincerely for their peace and happiness. Visualize them as covered by white or golden light shining with joy and limitless love, (their essential nature is ever perfect and joyous) again and again, until you feel peaceful. Repeat this exercise as often as needed in order for you to feel consistently peaceful.

Many people think that they can be happy by being better than others. The habit of comparison comes out of ignorance and delusion. The truth of our being is oneness. What one needs is not to be better, but just be one with others. Oneness is love, peace and joy. It is the Presence of God within us, or our conscious presence within God.

Practicing the Presence

God and His saints know all our thoughts and feelings. The habit of talking to God constantly, offering Him both the good and the bad, knowing that His energy is behind all that we do and experience, will surprise us with peace and joy. God loves us unconditionally. To feel His love, say: "I love you, God" again and again, with more and more feeling.

Thinking of God as formless, visualize a bright light in the heart or the spiritual eye (center of the forehead, slightly above the eye-brows), and say: "I love you, Lord," or anything that comes to your heart and mind: "Where are you, Lord? When will you come to me? You are present now, within me. Make me realize it. Reveal Yourself. Why are You hiding?"

God is your Mother. You should be free to scold Her. "Lord God, my Mother, you are so mean and cruel. How can we love you? Why do you allow so much suffering and evil in the world? I am very angry with you, Lord, for all the victims of torture and rape, for the sick and the starving. Are you suffering through them? You are in their hearts. They cannot feel any pain without your energy. You are the heart of suffering. Please help them Lord. Give us the grace to be compassionate and helpful to others."

The Masters stress the importance of crying for God. The yearning for God must be intense. Being alone with God alone, and shedding tears, especially at night, brings us closer to Him.

Those who believe that God comes in forms like Christ, Krishna or Amma, can visualize such divine forms in their hearts, and pray in the same manner. Short prayers are called 'Mantra' in Sanskrit. Receiving a mantra from an enlightened Master, and repeating it constantly so that it becomes automatic, is a powerful way to purify ourselves, and feel the Presence of God.

When you greet anyone with the words "good morning," become aware that you are practicing the Presence of God. For, as Lord Jesus said; "No one is good but One, that is, God" (Lk. 18:19). All goodness flows from God. With the words "good morning" or "good night," we can affirm the good God's holy Presence within the other person and in us.

Conversations with the saints are important on the spiritual path. They are always with us, to help us even in small details, if we turn to them for guidance. George Carver will help you in studies, science, gardening and appreciating flowers. Yogananda was a poet, powerful orator, great cook and host. But the saints need not exhibit any talent. They are able and willing to help us in every area of life, if we approach them with trust.

Reading more about the lives of saints, telling the stories of saints to children at home, and talking about them in schools, without imposing any viewpoint, can bring much blessing to families, society, and the world itself.

Meditation

In our normal living, we are bound by desires and aversions, because creation itself is a state of delusion that makes us forget our true Self, our eternal nature of joy and wisdom. Creation is like a hypnosis, wherein we forget our real identity. The hypnotized subjects cannot come out of their hypnosis without the help of the hypnotist.

God has hypnotized us through His act of creation, into believing that we are separate, limited, finite beings. Therefore only God the Divine Hypnotist or Mayadevi (the Goddess of Delusion) can bring us out of our delusion or maya. There can be no salvation without the grace of God, and the Masters are God's loving grace, calling us to be free from the bondage of delusion.

For salvation or liberation, it is important to find an enlightened Master, and be guided by him or her in everyday living, especially in meditation. There are many false gurus pretending to be enlightened Masters, and Christ Himself warned us against them. Selecting a true Guru is not easy. However, a sincere search has to draw a genuine Master toward the spiritual seeker.

Kabir, the medieval saint, venerated by Muslims and Hindus alike, praised HAMSA Meditation, as a valuable way to find God. Ham (I am) Sa

(He) meditation means eventually going within and being still, in order to forget the little ego of body and mind, and feel the Presence of God.

Prepare for meditation with a short vigorous exercise, then tense and relax all the different parts of the body from the feet to the head. Say a short prayer, asking for the Masters' help to meditate well. Breathe in slowly and deeply, and breathe out slowly and completely. Do such deep breathing four or five times. Then allow your breath to be natural, without controlling it in any way.

While breathing in, say "Ham" mentally. Breathing out, mentally say: "Sa." Keep the eyes closed and gently raised to the spiritual eye, in the center of the forehead, slightly above the eye-brows. If the eyes drop down, bring the focus back gently to the spiritual eye. There should be no strain or tension in meditation. The most important habit to cultivate is observing the breath calmly, without looking for results. Anxiety for results creates tension, and defeats the purpose of meditation.

Distractions are bound to come; ignore them without being upset about them. Remember that meditation is an attempt to be still, the results are in God's hands, and every sincere effort brings us closer to God, though we may not feel it at all. Meditate for about ten minutes at the start. Increase the duration very gradually. End the meditation, by being still, feeling the peace, and then talking to God lovingly.

Those who wish to meditate on Christ, can start in the same manner, while breathing in, mentally say "Jesus" or "Jesu;" breathing out, mentally say: "Amen" or "OM." Amen stands for Christ, the word of God [Rev. 3:14]. OM is the primary vibration of Divine Consciousness leading to creation. Thus OM is another name for God. Amen and OM have the same connotation.

Always remember that meditation is the art of relaxation and concentration. While learning this art, utmost patience is needed. It is an ascetical practice which definitely purifies you, unlike the severe acts of penance from the past ages, such as hair shirts, flagellation and so on.

Even children can be taught to meditate by observing their breath, since it enhances their attention span and memory. Some companies found increase in productivity and less absenteeism, after introducing the practice of meditation to their workers. In general, a significant consequence of meditation is the improvement of emotional intelligence in people.

Meditation at times leads to certain spiritual experiences. Take care not to talk about them indiscriminately. Such talk increases vanity and egoism, thereby hiding God even more. Our personal relationship with God is sacred and secret, like genuine lovers being unable to reveal their acts of intimacy. The purpose of spiritual practices is not passing experiences, however pleasant they may be, but abiding lovingly in God's Holy Presence, the peace and joy of Silence.

Concentration and Will Power

Success in any field depends on the amount or degree of concentration and will power that one brings to the task at hand. This is especially true about spirituality. The great saints are known to have extraordinary concentration and tremendous will power.

There is unlimited power within us to develop in both areas. While distracted during meditation, when we keep bringing back the mind's focus to the spiritual eye, breath and the mantra as often as needed, each effort increases our concentration and will power. A monk asked Yogananda to remove sexual temptations from his mind. Master responded: "How can you grow in love for God without struggling against such temptations again and again?"

Temptations, distractions and an unremitting struggle against them are essential for spiritual growth. The more attention we bring to whatever we do augments the power of concentration. Hence the importance of being alert and aware in the present moment while we perform our routine activities.

Will power increases in small increments when we don't do what we feel like doing, for example not scratching while it itches, not interrupting a person talking, delaying to overtake a car that goes slowly in front, not taking another bite of a tasty food and so on.

Thus going against likes and dislikes increases our will power, as long as our acts are balanced with common sense. It means avoiding tension and rigidity, being always relaxed and light-hearted with a gentle smile.

Accepting telephone calls from telemarketers with respect while being firm about our not wanting their products, helps our spiritual progress. Being patiently respectful and listening attentively to a person talking apparent nonsense increases the power of concentration and will.

Brother Bhaktananda was in charge of SRF Hollywood Temple, ministering to its large congregation, while being responsible for the formation of young monks. Brother directed the monks not to screen his telephone calls. He took all the calls even interrupting his meals to answer the phone.

A young woman, an SRF member from Hollywood was in New York City. She seemed to be mentally disturbed. I saw her calling Brother Bahaktananda by phone about four or five times a day, talking at length each time. Brother's patience and compassion was heroic, naturally resulting in the young lady gaining a great measure of peace.

We too can follow this saint's example to go beyond likes and dislikes, and humbly accept those who reach out to us as special manifestations of God. Our concentration and will power are thereby greatly enhanced. Eventually they take us to a place of one-pointedness where thoughts disappear in ecstasy or samadhi.

Never Give Up

The importance of utmost patience, persistence, and perseverance cannot be over-emphasized. The only difference between a saint and a sinner is this: the saint is a sinner who never gave up, said St. Teresa. Be so determined that you will never give up. There is unlimited strength within you, as you are a soul.

Thinking that you are weak or giving in to discouragement and despair is to side with the ego against the soul. God's grace is always with you. Make His will your will. Follow your Master's will, since the will of a true Master is identical with God's will. The more in tune we are with a genuine Master, the more grace and power will manifest in our life. There will be no room for discouragement.

It does not matter how many times we have failed. Thomas Edison made thousands of attempts before he succeeded in inventing the electric bulb. Keep making a sincere effort again and again, remembering that failures make us humble, and motivate us to love God even more.

Give us a true conception of brotherhood

Divine Mother, give us a new, true conception of brotherhood. May we forsake wars and heal the wounds of all nations with the salve of Christ-love and the lasting balm of sympathetic understanding. Cosmic Mother, awaken in us Thine impartial love for all; bless us that we be free from the sway of greed and delusion. Inspire us to build a new world - one in which famine, disease, and ignorance will be only memories of a dismal past…

O Mother of All, teach us to call each man by his rightful name of brother.[1]

Wisdom From …

A human being is a part of the whole that we call the universe, a part limited in time and space. He experiences himself, his thoughts and feelings, as something separated from the rest - a kind of optical illusion of his consciousness. This illusion is a prison for us, restricting us to our personal desires and to affection for only the few people nearest us. Our task must be to free ourselves from this prison by widening our circle of compassion to embrace all living beings and all of nature.

Try not to become a man of success, but rather to become a man of value. He is considered successful in our day who gets more out of life than he puts in. But a man of value will give more than he receives.

Albert Einstein

All man's miseries derive from not being able to sit quietly in a room alone.

---

1 Paramahansa Yogananda, Whispers from Eternity, p.40

We are naught but lies, duplicity, contradiction, and we hide and disguise ourselves from ourselves.

Blaise Pascal

I hate war as only a soldier who has lived in it can, only as one who has seen its brutality, its futility, its stupidity.

General Eisenhower

Hatred ever kills, love never dies. Such is the vast difference between the two. What is obtained by love is retained for all time. What is obtained by hatred proves a burden in reality, for it increases hatred. The duty of a human being is to diminish hatred and to promote love.

Gandhi

Man's unhappiness comes of his greatness; it is because there is Infinite in him, which with all his cunning he cannot quite bury under the finite.

Under all speech that is good for anything there lies a silence. Silence is deep as Eternity; speech is shallow as Time.

Carlyle

Only Love Speaks the Truth

Only love speaks the truth
Everything else is a lie.
Lost in the silly games we play
As lies and pretense
Words and thoughts escape,
Truth hides deeper within.
Ideas, opinions
Hardened positions
Viewpoints stagnate,
Destruction cause.
Yearning for the light
In darkness dwell.
In confusion serene,
Waiting, open,
No words to distract.
Plunge into pain,
Deep despair
Twist and turn
Searing sadness
Sharp beyond endure.
Trust,

Silent Witness,
Gentle Surrender.
Great Courage
Facing directly chaos and suffering.
Sorrow conscious of itself heals
Confusion to meaning leads
Embraced by the dark light of love,
Feel the pain
In the mind of plants
Animals
Human beings.
Moans, cries and tears fossilized,
No one, nothing excluded.
Soul stealing flute of Krishna
Buddha's infinite compassion
The saving cross of Jesus
All in the heart of God.
Transcendent One
In the depths of everything
God, God everywhere
Eternity in the flash of a moment
Unity in diversity
Harmony
Aware and calmly happy.
Shining smile,
Sparkling laughter,
Peace, joy
Flow forever from silent love
That alone speaks the truth
Everything else is a lie.

EPILOGUE

"You all are saints," said St. Augustine addressing his congregation. Ammachi worships all the people who come to Her, bowing down with the words: "I prostrate before you as the embodiments of pure love and supreme consciousness."

We are all holy since the very essence of our being is God. We are everywhere and in everything. Everything is a miracle. We can love everything. That means aches and pains as well. Let them fulfill their purpose. Everyone is holy as God alone is everywhere. People are supremely precious beyond all imagination, and need to be deeply respected and loved dearly.

God alone is ultimately responsible for all our acts. Our very breath is His. All the movements of the body are His. All our words and thoughts are His. Hence the praise we receive belongs to Him, and we can lay it at His feet.

When we accept blame and insult as necessary for our purification, we are grateful for them. Besides gratitude, there may be some pain and anger. They are offered to God. He is responsible for the good and the bad of creation, though He is far beyond them, and is ever pure. Humiliation and failure peacefully accepted is the path leading to humility, a virtue very pleasing to God.

The purpose of 'Limitless Love' is to realize that we are saints here and now. God is utterly happy with us, as much as He is with the greatest saints. He does not discriminate between His children. We are in God, and God is in us. That can never change. Om Tat Sat. Amen. That is Reality.

Let us lay all our fears and anxieties at His holy feet. Witnessing the fears, we are ever free, and observe the fears slowly vanishing from the mind and body. We feel deeply peaceful, and are swimming in a sea of joy and love.

The most important time of the day is the few minutes before you fall asleep, as we are then in a hypnotic state and are easily influenced by thoughts. Agitating the mind with negative thoughts at that time is bound to strengthen the negativity considerably, since the subconscious mind continues to pursue these thoughts during sleep. Therefore it is important to throw out all negativity, and feel calm before you fall asleep.

If you are anxious about fulfilling certain goals, happily visualize them as already accomplished and thank God for it. Affirm a few times: "I am perfectly healthy, wealthy, and peaceful. I love everyone," while feeling the truth of these affirmations more and more. We become what we think.

Fall asleep saying again and again: "Lord God! I love you." Repeating the mantra given by a Master just before falling asleep is very valuable, since it will go on automatically in the subconscious mind to bless the spiritual aspirant abundantly.

The author has had this dream for a long time. We can envision libraries everywhere dedicating a special section for the collection of books about saints and sages with their pictures and statues displayed around the area. Looking at the images of saints and sages is itself a blessing and an inspiration. Such a place will vibrate with peace, love and joy, attracting adults and children to rest there for a while.

A Note of Thanks

Sincere thanks to all my teachers and the wonderful writers who have educated and inspired me. I feel truly grateful to the large family of Paramahansa Yogananda, especially from New York City Center and the Meditation Center of Northampton, PA and to the devotees of Ammachi for the holy fellowship of chanting, meditation, selfless service, loving and inspiring communication. I owe special gratitude to the Catholic clergy and laity of Sri Lanka, family members and friends for their kind prayers and supportive understanding. I acknowledge with many thanks the authors and publishers referenced in the footnotes for graciously allowing me to use their material.

May I express my heartfelt gratitude to all the lovely people who labor cheerfully to produce and distribute this book. My special thanks to Dr. Quincy Howe for kindly reviewing the manuscript to write such a glowing foreword. Thanks to Mark Ihle for the beautiful cover design, and to Renate Brosky for the careful editing. Peace, Love and Joy to you all.

www.ingramcontent.com/pod-product-compliance
Lightning Source LLC
Chambersburg PA
CBHW051818090426
42736CB00011B/1540

9780997607444